KS3 Maths Progress

Confidence • Fluency • Problem-solving • Progression

π THREE

Series editors:

Dr Naomi Norman • Katherine Pate

ALWAYS LEARNING

PEARSON

Published by Pearson Education Limited, Edinburgh Gate, Harlow, Essex, CM20 2JE.

www.pearsonschoolsandfecolleges.co.uk

Text © Pearson Education Limited 2015
Typeset by Tech-Set Ltd, Gateshead
Original illustrations © Pearson Education Limited 2015
Cover illustration by Robert Samuel Hanson
Index by Wendy Simpson

The rights of Nick Asker, Sharon Bolger, Andrew Edmondson, Bobbie Johns, Catherine Murphy and Mary Pardoe to be identified as authors of this work have been asserted by them in accordance with the Copyright, Designs and Patents Act 1988.

First published 2015

18 17 16 15
10 9 8 7 6 5 4 3 2 1

British Library Cataloguing in Publication Data
A catalogue record for this book is available from the British Library
ISBN 978 1 447 96236 6

Printed in Italy by Lego S.p.A

Acknowledgements
The publisher would like to thank the following for their kind permission to reproduce their photographs:

(Key: b-bottom; c-centre; l-left; r-right; t-top)

123RF.com: Boris Rabtsevich 11, niyazz 5, orangeline 157, Thawatchai Tumwapee 236, viewstock 162, Wilawan Khasawong 159, zhudifeng 91; **Alamy Images:** Andy Guest 188, Cultura Creative 108, 130, 132, Dario Sabljak 112, Dennis Hallinan 233, Matt Kenyon 63; **Pearson Education Ltd:** Jules Selmes 179; **Shutterstock.com:** amenic181 205, Anna Frajtova 53, Cristi Matei 115, Dmitrij Skorobogatov 81, EpicStockMedia 230, Galyna Andrushko. 138, iko 207, Jerome Scholler 182, Joggie Botma 9, Lipik 210, Lisa F.Young 87, MarcelClemens 14, Mark III Photonics 60, Mike Flippo 3, Monkey Business Images 57, Moolkum 185, Morgan Lane Photography 65, Nataliia Melnychuk 212, Ng Yin Chern 135, nikoniano 79, Nomad_Soul 7, Pavel L Photo and Video 191, Photo Africa 83, Sergey Nivens 1, somchai rakin 85, Stefan Schurr 55, Stephen VanHorn 89, Zoltan Major 140; **Veer / Corbis:** Alexey Stiop 34, Ambient Ideas 110, Corepics 105, dosecreative 36, GoodOlga 51, Henryk Sadura 165, Igor Korionov 31, lightpoet 238, veerguy 227

All other images © Pearson Education

We are grateful for the following for permission to reproduce copyright material:
Number of cars in the UK for the past 10 years (p145) from 'Vehicle Statistics: 2013', Department for Transport licensed under the Open Government License v.2.0.

Every effort has been made to trace the copyright holders and we apologise in advance for any unintentional omissions. We would be pleased to insert the appropriate acknowledgement in any subsequent edition of this publication.

CONTENTS

Unit 4 Fractions, decimals and percentages

Unit 5 Geometry in 2D and 3D

Unit 6 Algebraic and real-life graphs

Unit 7 Multiplicative reasoning

Unit 8 Algebraic and geometric formulae

Unit 9 Probability

Unit 10 Polygons and transformations

KS3 Maths Progress

Confidence • Fluency • Problem-solving • Progression

Pedagogy at the heart – This new course is built around a unique pedagogy that's been created by leading mathematics educational researchers and Key Stage 3 teachers. The result is an innovative learning structure based around 10 key principles designed to nurture confidence and raise achievement.

Pedagogy – our 10 key principles

- Fluency
- Mathematical Reasoning
- Multiplicative Reasoning
- Problem Solving
- Progression
- Concrete-Pictorial - Abstract (CPA)
- Relevance
- Modelling
- Reflection (metacognition)
- Linking

Progression to Key Stage 4 – In line with the 2014 National Curriculum, there is a strong focus on fluency, problem-solving and progression to help prepare your students' progress through their studies.

Stretch, challenge and support – Catering for students of all abilities, these Student Books are structured to deliver engaging and accessible content across three differentiated tiers, each offering a wealth of worked examples and questions, supported by key points, literacy and strategy hints, and clearly defined objectives.

Within each unit:

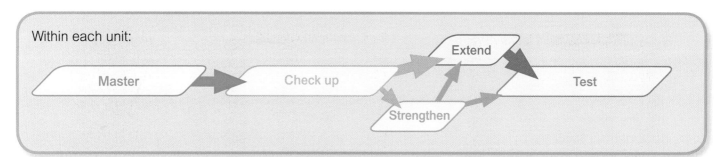

Master → Check up → Strengthen → Extend → Test

Differentiated for students of all abilities:

Student Books

Pi	Theta	Delta
1, 2, 3	1, 2, 3	1, 2, 3

Progress with confidence!

This innovative Key Stage 3 Maths course embeds a modern pedagogical approach around our trusted suite of digital and print resources, to create confident and numerate students ready to progress further.

Help at the front-of-class – **ActiveTeach Presentation** is our tried and tested service that makes all of the Student Books available for display on a whiteboard. The books are supplemented with a range of videos and animations that present mathematical concepts along a concrete - pictorial - abstract pathway, allowing your class to progress their conceptual understanding at the right speed.

Learning beyond the classroom – Focussing on online homework, **ActiveCourse** offers students unprecedented extra practice (with automarking) and a chance to reflect on their learning with the confidence-checker. Powerful reporting tools can be used to track student progression and confidence levels.

Easy to plan, teach and assess – Downloadable **Teacher Guides** provide assistance with planning through the Schemes of Work. Lesson plans link both front-of-class **ActiveTeach Presentation** and **ActiveCourse** and provide help with reporting, functionality and progression. Both **Teacher Guides** and **ActiveTeach Presentation** contain the **answers** to the Student Book exercises.

Teacher Guides include **Class Progression Charts** and **Student Progression Charts** to support formative and summative assessment through the course.

Practice to progress – KS3 Maths Progress has an extensive range of practice across a range of topics and abilities. From the **Student Books** to write-in **Progression Workbooks** through to **ActiveCourse**, there is plenty of practice available in a variety of formats whether for in the classroom or for learning at home independently.

> For more information, visit
> **www.pearsonschools.co.uk/ks3mathsprogress**

Welcome to KS3 Maths Progress student books!

Confidence · Fluency · Problem-solving · Progression

Starting a new course is exciting! We believe you will have fun with maths, at the same time nurturing your confidence and raising your achievement.

Here's how:

At the end of the *Master* lessons, take a *Check up* test to help you decide to *Strengthen*, or *Extend* your learning. You may be able to mark this test yourself.

Choose only the topics in *Strengthen* that you need a bit more practice with. You'll find more hints here to lead you through specific questions. Then move on to *Extend*.

Extend helps you to apply the maths you know to some different situations. *Strengthen* and *Extend* both include *Enrichment* or *Investigations*.

When you have finished the whole unit, a *Unit test* helps you see how much progress you are making.

Clear *Objectives,* showing what you will cover in each lesson, are followed by a *Confidence* panel to boost your understanding and engage your interest.

Have a look at *Why Learn This?* This shows you how maths is useful in everyday life.

Improve your *Fluency* – practise answering questions using maths you already know.

The first questions are *Warm up*. Here you can show what you already know about this topic or related ones...

...before moving on to further questions, with *Worked examples* and *Hints* for help when you need it.

Your teacher has access to Answers in either ActiveTeach Presentation or the Teacher Guides.

Topic links show you how the maths in a lesson is connected to other mathematical topics. Use the *Subject links* to find out where you might use the maths you have learned here in your other lessons, such as science, geography and computing .

Explore a real-life problem by discussing and having a go. By the end of the lesson you'll have gained the skills you need to start finding a solution to the question using maths.

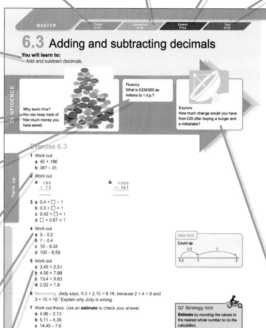

STEM and Finance lessons

Context lessons expand on *Real, STEM* and *Finance* maths. Finance questions are related to money. STEM stands for Science, Technology, Engineering and Maths. You can find out how charities use maths in their fundraising, how engineers monitor water flow in rivers, and why diamonds sparkle (among other things!)

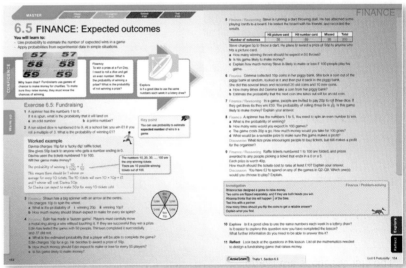

Some questions are tagged as *Finance* or *STEM*. These questions show how the real world relies on maths. Follow these up with whole lessons that focus on how maths is used in the fields of finance, science and technology.

As well as hints that help you with specific questions, you'll find *Literacy hints* (to explain some unfamiliar terms) and *Strategy hints* (to help with working out).

You can improve your ability to use maths in everyday situations by tackling *Modelling, Reasoning, Problem-solving* and *Real* questions. *Discussions* prompt you to explain your reasoning or explore new ideas with a partner.

At the end of each lesson, you get a chance to *Reflect* on how confident you feel about the topic.

Your teacher may give you a Student Progression Chart to help you see your progression through the units.

Further support

You can easily access extra resources that tie in to each lesson – look for the ActiveLearn icon on the lesson pages for ActiveCourse online homework links. These are clearly mapped to lessons and provide fun, interactive exercises linked to helpful worked examples and videos.

The Progression Workbooks, full of extra practice for key questions will help you reinforce your learning and track your own progress.

Enjoy!

1.1 Adding and subtracting

You will learn to:
- Solve problems by adding and subtracting
- Add and subtract decimal numbers.

CONFIDENCE

Why learn this?
You use adding and subtracting when making a budget – whether it is what you do with your pocket money or for a multi-million pound business.

Fluency
What do you add to each number to make 1000?
- 375
- 629
- 406
- 909
- 101

Explore
How are large numbers written in newspaper reports?

Exercise 1.1

Warm up

1 Round each number to the nearest 100.
  a 3583   **b** 7167
  c 4543   **d** 2199

2 Work out
  a 4275 + 3656   **b** 6000 − 2856
  c 3756 + 350 + 99   **d** 8500 − 3651 − 472

3 Work out
  a 3.4 + 5.7   **b** 6.3 − 3.6
  c 12.56 − 9.27   **d** 16.45 − 4.05

4 **Real** The table shows the population of some Welsh towns.
  a Round each one to the nearest 1000.
  b Estimate the total population of all three towns using your rounded numbers.
  c Work out the actual total.
  d Find the difference between the actual total and the rounded total.

Cardiff	335 145
Aberystwyth	18 093
Lampeter	2970

> **Q4 hint**
> Line up digits with the same place value.

5 Corbin flies 2508 km from London to Moscow. He takes the train for 633 km to St Petersburg, then flies 2094 km back home to London.
  a What is the total distance he has travelled?
  b How much further is London from Moscow than London from St Petersburg?

> **Key point**
> When adding and subtracting decimal numbers, use the same method you use for integers, and line up the decimal points.

6 Work out the sum of
  a 7.45, 3.49 and 5.62   **b** 11.4, 7.38 and 12.91
  c 21.67, 45.9 and 56.78   **b** 10.23, 3.1 and 6.08

Topic links: Perimeter, Distance, Money, Length   **Subject links:** Geography (Q4, Q5, Q16)

7 a Work out the total of this bill.
  b Gary pays with a £20 note.
    How much change does he get?

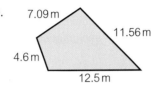
```
0.65
£2.75
£3.05
0.99
£2.99
```

8 Work out
  a 12.35 − 7.82 + 3.5
  c 43.65 − 19.4 − 7.05
  e 150 − 48.39 − 50.2
  b 49.8 + 34.75 − 12.08
  d 265.99 − 62.7 + 12.84

9 Lucie buys some items for £34.99, £4.05 and £29. She pays with four £20 notes. How much change should she receive?

10 Work out the perimeter of this shape.

7.09 m
11.56 m
4.6 m
12.5 m

11 Real In a triathlon Lai swims 500 m, cycles 8 km and runs 2.5 km. How far does she travel in total?

Q11 hint

What fraction of a kilometre is 500 m?

12 Problem-solving The perimeter of a rectangle is 62.8 cm. One of its sides is 12.46 cm. What is the length of its other side?

13 1 000 000 = 1 million. Use this fact to copy and complete
  a 3 000 000 = ☐ million
  c 4 500 000 = ☐ million
  b 7 000 000 = ☐ million
  d 3 500 000 = ☐ million

Q13c hint

500 000 is half a million.

14 Write each number as a decimal number of millions.
  a 5 600 000 = ☐.☐ million
  c 5 090 000
  e 250 000
  b 2 305 000
  d 400 000 = 0.☐ million
  f 345 000

Key point

To find how many millions there are in a number, divide by 1 million (1 000 000).
1 567 000 = 1.567 million

15 Write each number using only digits.
  a 1.4 million
  c 3.05 million
  e 6.205 million
  g 0.456 million
  b 7.48 million
  d 3.176 million
  f 0.7 million
  h 2.811 million

16 Real a Write the populations of these capital cities as a decimal number of millions.
  Paris   2 145 000
  Madrid   2 941 000
  Zagreb   790 000
  Lisbon   475 000
  Berlin   3 470 000
  London   8 300 000
  b What is the total population of Paris, Madrid and Zagreb?
  c What is the total population of Lisbon, Berlin and London?

17 Explore How are large numbers written in newspaper reports? Look back at the maths you have learned in this lesson. How can you use it to answer this question? What other information do you need?

18 Reflect Look back at Q16. Did you add the decimal numbers of millions or the numbers using only digits? Why?

Explore

Reflect

1.2 Multiplying

You will learn to:
- Multiply numbers including decimals
- Use multiplicative reasoning to multiply numbers.

CONFIDENCE

Why learn this?
Decimal numbers are used in lots of places, including banking and the Stock Exchange.

Fluency
What is half of each number? What is double each number?
- 450
- 224
- 340
- 156
- 3008

Explore
Does multiplying one number by another always make it bigger?

Warm up

Exercise 1.2

1 Work out
- **a** 7×0.4
- **b** 4×2.1
- **c** 6×2.5
- **d** 4.25×9
- **e** 6×8.09
- **f** 30×1.01

2 Work out
- **a** 46×24
- **b** 35×13
- **c** 72×14
- **d** 56×38
- **e** 1.2×35
- **f** 15×3.4
- **g** 0.5×0.5
- **h** 0.5×100

> **Q2a hint**
>
> $\begin{array}{r} 46 \\ \times\ 24 \\ \hline \end{array}$

3 Copy and complete

a
$$\times 2 \left(\begin{array}{c} 25 \times 48 \\ 50 \times 24 \end{array} \right) \div 2$$
$$\times 2 \left(\begin{array}{c} 50 \times 24 \\ 100 \times 12 \end{array} \right) \div 2 = \boxed{}$$

b
$$\div 2 \left(\begin{array}{c} 12 \times 25 \\ \boxed{} \times 50 \end{array} \right) \times 2$$
$$\div 2 \left(\begin{array}{c} \boxed{} \times 50 \\ \boxed{} \times \boxed{} \end{array} \right) \times 2 = \boxed{}$$

- **c** 36×25
- **d** 44×25
- **e** 25×28
- **f** 32×25

> **Q3 hint**
>
> You can multiply and divide the numbers in a calculation to make them easier to multiply.
> When you multiply one of the numbers you need to divide another number, to keep the calculation the same.

4 a A game at a fair costs 25p. In the first hour 24 people play the game. How much money is collected?
b Badges cost 50p each. How much will 16 badges cost?

5 Work out
- **a** 2835×4
- **b** 4196×8
- **c** 6×5273
- **d** 5×37.56
- **e** 18.96×7
- **f** 9×34.17

> **Q5a hint**
>
> Multiply the single digit by each digit in the other number.
> $2835 \times 4 =$
> $4 \times 2000 + 4 \times 800 + 4 \times 30 + 4 \times 5$

6 A businesswoman travels 1284 miles every month. How far does she travel in 6 months?

Topic links: Measures, Area, Money, Mean

7 Work out

    a 162×28 **b** 284×21

    c 327×35 **d** 409×26

    e 1538×16 **f** 3745×24

Q7a hint

Use column multiplication.

    162
  ×   28

Or, use the grid method.

×	100	60	2
20			
8			

Worked example

$5.4 \times 28 = 151.2$

Use this fact to solve each calculation.

a 54×28

$\times 10 \left(\begin{array}{c} 5.4 \times 28 = 151.2 \\ 54 \times 28 = 1512 \end{array}\right) \times 10$ —— One of the numbers in the original calculation has been multiplied by 10, so the answer will be 10 times bigger.

b 0.54×2.8

$\div 10 \left(\begin{array}{c} 5.4 \times 28 = 151.2 \\ 0.54 \times 2.8 = 1.512 \end{array}\right) \div 10 \Big) \div 100$ —— Dividing by 10 and dividing by 10 again is the same as dividing by 100.

---

8 Use the fact that $12 \times 18 = 216$ to work out

    a 1.2×1.8 **b** 0.12×18

    c 0.18×1.2 **d** 0.018×120

9 Use the fact that $0.06 \times 70 = 4.2$ to work out

    a $0.06 \times 700 = 0.06 \times 70 \times 10 = \square$

    b $0.6 \times 70 = 0.06 \times \square \times 70 = \square$

    c 0.6×0.007

    d 60×0.7

10 **Real** A dress needs 2.85 metres of fabric. How much fabric is needed for 8 dresses?

Q10 hint

Estimate the answer first.

11 **STEM** A metal shelf in a warehouse is 3.45 metres long. What length of metal is needed for 15 shelves?

12 **Real** There are 12 songs on an album.

    a It costs £1.69 to download each song. How much will it cost to download 12 songs?

    b It costs £12.99 to download the whole album in one go. How much cheaper is this than downloading each song individually?

13 Theatre tickets cost £23.50 for an adult and £15.25 for children. How much will it cost to buy 5 adult and 7 children's tickets?

14 What is $0.65 \times 2.4 \, \text{m}$?

15 The mean of 6 masses is 45.68 kg. What is the total of the 6 masses?

16 **Explore** Does multiplying one number by another always make it bigger?

Choose some sensible numbers to help you explore this situation. Then use what you've learned in this lesson to help you answer the question.

17 **Reflect** In Q7 you had a choice of two methods. Which method did you choose and why? Would you always choose the same method, or does it depend on the calculation you are doing?

Explore

Reflect

1.3 Dividing

You will learn to:

- Divide by a decimal number.

Why learn this?
Dividing annual bills by 12 tells you how much something costs each month.

Fluency
Work out
- 350 ÷ 5
- 0.6 ÷ 2
- 4500 ÷ 90
- 45 ÷ 2

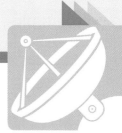

Explore
How do musicians and artists use division?

CONFIDENCE

Warm up

Exercise 1.3

1 Use a written method to work out
a 748 ÷ 4   b 925 ÷ 5   c 612 ÷ 6   d 4194 ÷ 9

2 Work out each calculation. Give your answer with a remainder.
a 573 ÷ 4   b 692 ÷ 5   c 548 ÷ 6   d 2174 ÷ 9

3 Round each number to the nearest 10.
a 2194   b 3546   c 2848   d 7009

Key point
If the answer to a division calculation has a remainder, it can also be written as a decimal.

Worked example

Work out 234 ÷ 8. Give your answer as a decimal.

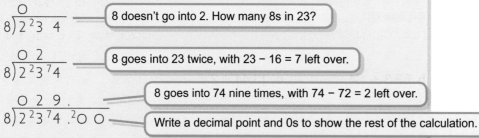

8 doesn't go into 2. How many 8s in 23?

8 goes into 23 twice, with 23 − 16 = 7 left over.

8 goes into 74 nine times, with 74 − 72 = 2 left over.

Write a decimal point and 0s to show the rest of the calculation.

8 goes into 20 twice, with 4 left over.

8 goes into 40 exactly 5 times.

4 Work out each division. Give your answer as a decimal.
a 736 ÷ 5   b 510 ÷ 4   c 251 ÷ 8

5 Finance A holiday apartment for 4 people costs £750. How much will each person pay?

Topic links: Inverse operations, Money, Multiplying and dividing by powers of 10, Estimation

6 Work out

    a $360 \div 15$ **b** $378 \div 21$ **c** $448 \div 14$

    d $792 \div 24$ **e** $800 \div 25$ **f** $400 \div 25$

7 Eggs are packed into trays of 12. How many trays are needed for 396 eggs?

8 How many pens costing 25p can be bought for £3.75?

9 Divide a restaurant bill of £512 between 16 people.

10 Write a division calculation to go with each multiplication.

    a $12 \times 22 = 264$ $264 \div \square =$

    b $15 \times 43 = 645$ **c** $25 \times 34 = 850$ **d** $18 \times 42 = 756$

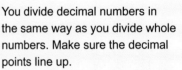

Worked example

Work out $34.52 \div 4$

$32 \div 4 = 8$ and $36 \div 4 = 9$, so answer is between 8 and 9.

$$4 \overline{)3\ 4\ .^2 5\ ^1 2} \quad \begin{array}{c} 8\ .\ 6\ 3 \end{array}$$

Use close multiples of 4 to estimate first.

Make sure you line the decimal points up.

$34.52 \div 4 = 8.63$

Check that your answer is close to your estimate.

> **Key point**
>
> You divide decimal numbers in the same way as you divide whole numbers. Make sure the decimal points line up.

11 Work out

    a $34.3 \div 7$ **b** $47.2 \div 8$ **c** $29.34 \div 9$

    d $71.04 \div 6$ **e** $57.24 \div 8$ **f** $56.4 \div 3$

> **Q11e hint**
>
> Write some extra zeros if you need more decimal places.

12 Six friends share a prize of £54.36. How much does each receive?

13 Divide a bill of £88.76 between 14 people.

> **Key point**
>
> To divide by a decimal number, multiply both numbers by a power of 10 (10, 100, 1000 and so on) so that you can divide by a whole number.

14 Work out

    a $48 \div 1.6$
       $\times 10 \left(\right) \times 10$
           $480 \div \square$

    b $75 \div 1.5$ **c** $56 \div 0.7$

    d $32.8 \div 0.8$ **e** $37.2 \div 0.6$

    f $72.5 \div 2.5$ **g** $252 \div 3.5$

15 Work out

    a $46.2 \div 1.2$
       $\times 10 \left(\right) \times 10$
           $462 \div \square$

    b $62.3 \div 1.4$ **c** $13.44 \div 2.4$

    d $88.05 \div 1.5$ **e** $131.84 \div 1.6$

16 There is 28.8 m of cable on a roll. How many 1.2 m lengths can be cut from the roll?

17 A regular **dodecagon** has a perimeter of 67.44 cm. What is the length of one of its sides?

> **Q17 Literacy hint**
>
> A **dodecagon** is a shape with 12 sides.

18 **Explore** How do musicians and artists use division? What further information do you need to be able to explore this question?

19 **Reflect** Sometimes division is called 'sharing'. How does the idea of sharing help you to visualise dividing one number by another?

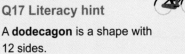

Reflect   Explore

1.4 Multiplying and dividing negative numbers

You will learn to:

- Multiply and divide with negative numbers.

CONFIDENCE

Why learn this?
Negative numbers are used when studying forces in physics.

Fluency
Count backwards in 2s from 5.
Count backwards in 5s from 11.

Explore
When and why did people first start using negative numbers?

Exercise 1.4

Warm up

1 Work out

   a -6×3 **b** 4×-5 **c** 7×-11

   d -12×4 **e** -7×8 **f** 2.5×-6

2 Continue each sequence.

   a 10, 6, 2, ..., ..., ...

   b 15, 10, 5, ..., ..., ...

   c 31, 21, 11, ..., ..., ...

3 Copy this table and continue the pattern.

Calculation	Answer
-5×3	-15
-5×2	-10
-5×1	
-5×0	
-5×-1	
-5×-2	
-5×-3	

$+5$
$+5$
$+5$
$+5$
$+5$
$+5$

4 Copy and complete the rules.

   positive × positive = positive

   positive × negative = _____

   negative × positive = _____

   negative × negative = _____

5 Work out

   a -4×-5 **b** -6×-7 **c** -5×-8

   d -12×-3 **e** -15×-4 **f** -20×-6

   g -7.2×-4 **h** -9.5×-3 **i** -6.1×10

Topic links: Sequences

6 Is the answer to each calculation 10 or −10?

   a −2 × 5
   b −2 × −5
   c −5 × 2
   d −5 × −2
   e 5 × 2
   f −1 × −10

7 Work out

   a −4 × 7
   b −3 × −8
   c 11 × −9
   d −12 × −2.2
   e 15.7 × −5
   f −4.2 × −4.2
   g −6.11 × 12.4
   h 16.5 × −1.1

8 Work out the missing numbers.

   a 5 × ☐ = −20
   b ☐ × 7 = −42
   c ☐ × −2 = 14
   d −6 × ☐ = −24
   e ☐ × − 5 = 30
   f 16 × ☐ = 1600

9 Fill in the missing number facts. The first one has been done for you.

   a −4 × 7 = −28   so   −28 ÷ −4 = 7   and   −28 ÷ 7 = −4
   b 3 × −4 = −12   so   −12 ÷ 3 = ☐   and   −12 ÷ −4 = ☐
   c −5 × −3 = 15   so   15 ÷ −5 = ☐   and   15 ÷ −3 = ☐

10 Copy and complete the rules.

   positive ÷ positive = positive
   positive ÷ negative = _____
   negative ÷ positive = _____
   negative ÷ negative = _____

11 Work out

   a −25 ÷ 5
   b −32 ÷ −4
   c 72 ÷ −9
   d −125 ÷ 5
   e −144 ÷ −6
   f 132 ÷ −4
   g −252 ÷ 8
   h −231 ÷ −6

12 Work out

   a −11 × 7
   b −3 × −9
   c −24 ÷ 8
   d −40 ÷ −5
   e 60 ÷ −2
   f −22 × 4
   g −15.3 × −3
   h −12.5 ÷ 2

13 Work out

   a −3 × (−4 × 5)
   b (−7 × −4) × −2
   c 4 × (−5 × 6)
   d (−27 ÷ 3) × 2
   e −40 ÷ (−2 × 4)
   f 100 ÷ −(2 × 25)

> **Q13 hint**
>
> Work out the part in brackets first.

14 **Explore** When and why did people first start using negative numbers?
   What have you have learned in this lesson to help you answer this question? How could you find out the other information you need?

15 **Reflect** Q4 asked you to complete some rules for working with positive and negative numbers. What other rules have you met in your maths lessons? How have they helped you?

1.5 Squares, cubes and roots

You will learn to:
- Know all square numbers to 16^2
- Find all positive and negative square roots of square numbers
- Work with cubes and cube roots
- Work out calculations involving squares and brackets.

CONFIDENCE

Why learn this?
Scientists can use square roots to estimate how long an object will take to fall.

Fluency
Work out
- 7^2
- 10^3
- $\sqrt{81}$
- 2^3

Explore
What happens when you multiply the square root of a number by itself?

Exercise 1.5

Warm up

1 Write these numbers in order from largest to smallest.
$$\sqrt[3]{729} \qquad 10^3 \qquad \sqrt{529} \qquad 25^2$$

2 Work out
 a $10^2 - 8^2$ **b** $\sqrt{64} \times \sqrt{25}$ **c** $6^2 \div \sqrt{4}$ **d** $\sqrt[3]{64} \times 3^3$

> **Q2 hint**
> Roots and indices first, then division, multiplication, addition and subtraction.

3 Work out
 a -5×-3 **b** -2×4 **c** -10×-10 **d** 10×10

4 Match the numbers in the red boxes with the numbers in the blue boxes.

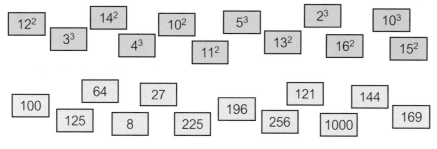

5 Work out
 a -8×-8 **b** $(-2)^2$ **c** $(-3)^2$ **d** $(-4)^2$
 Discussion What's the difference between -2^2 and $(-2)^2$?

> **Q5 Literacy hint**
> Sometimes you use brackets to show that the whole number, including its sign, needs to be multiplied by itself.

6 Write down the **positive** and **negative square roots** of
 a 100 **b** 49 **c** 121 **d** 36
 e 81 **f** 144 **g** 4 **h** 64

> **Key point**
> $6^2 = 36$ and $(-6)^2 = 36$.
> So 36 has two square roots, a positive and a negative.
> The **positive square root** of 36 is 6.
> The **negative square root** is −6.

7 Reasoning **a** Work out $5 \times 5 \times 5$.
 b Work out $-5 \times -5 \times -5$.
 c Explain why $(-5)^3$ is negative.

Topic links: Calculator skills, Priority of operations, Place value, Negative numbers

8 Use your calculator to work out

    a $\sqrt[3]{216}$ **b** 7^3 **c** $\sqrt[3]{1331}$ **d** 9.2^3

    e $\sqrt[3]{1728}$ **f** 10.5^3

9 Cube A has a volume of $4913\,\text{cm}^3$ and cube B has a volume of $2744\,\text{cm}^3$.
How much wider is cube A than cube B?

4913 cm³   2744 cm³

Cube A   Cube B

Investigation   **Reasoning**

1 a i Find $\sqrt{3}$ using your calculator.

    ii Square the answer. What do you notice?

  b Clear your calculator display. Repeat part **1a** for $\sqrt{7}$.

  c Copy and complete this sentence: If you square the square root of a number, _____

2 a Clear your calculator display. Write down $\sqrt{3}$ to one decimal place.

  b Square your answer.

  c What do you notice? Explain why this happens.

3 Repeat part **2** using

  i two decimal places

  ii three decimal places.

4 a Write down all the digits your calculator shows for $\sqrt{3}$.

  b Clear the display. Type in your answer on your calculator. Square this number.

  c Does your calculator give the exact value of $\sqrt{3}$? Explain.

---

10 Work out

    a $\sqrt{5} \times \sqrt{5}$ **b** $\sqrt{11} \times \sqrt{11}$ **c** $\sqrt{200} \times \sqrt{200}$

11 a Copy and complete this place-value table.

Million	Hundred thousand	Ten thousand	Thousand	Hundred	Ten	Units
☐	☐	☐	1000	☐	10	1
$10^{☐}$	$10^{☐}$	$10^{☐}$	$10^{☐}$	10^2	10^1	

  b Follow the sequence of powers. How do you write 1 as a power of 10?

> **Key point**
>
> Our place-value system can be written using powers of 10.
> Ten $= \;\; 10 = 10^1$
> Hundred $= \;\; 100 = 10^2$
> Thousand $= 1000 = 10^3$

> **Q11 hint**
>
> Use the patterns to help you.

12 Write these as numbers without powers.

    a 5×10^3 **b** 8×10^4 **c** 4.5×10^3 **d** 7.26×10^2

13 Write these numbers using powers.

    a $4000 = 4 \times 1000 = 4 \times 10^{☐}$ **b** 70   **c** 90 000

14 Explore What happens when you multiply the square root of a number by itself?
Choose some sensible numbers to help you explore this situation. Then use what you've learned in this lesson to help you answer the question.

15 Reflect Jamal says 'The investigation in this lesson shows that calculators can't be trusted to give the correct answer.' Do you think Jamal is right or wrong? Explain your answer.

1.6 More powers

You will learn to:
- Find the prime factor decomposition of a number
- Know and use the index notation and laws for positive powers
- Work out the LCM and HCF from prime factor decomposition.

CONFIDENCE

Why learn this?
Astronomers use the lowest common multiple to work out when orbiting satellites will line up.

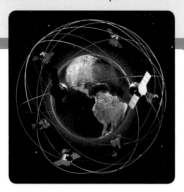

Fluency
Work out
- 2^3
- 4^3
- 5^3
- 10^5

Explore
How is doubling related to powers of 2?

Exercise 1.6

Warm up

1 Use a Venn diagram to find the highest common factor (HCF) of
  a 24 and 30
  b 32 and 48

2 a Draw a factor tree for
  i 24
  ii 28
  iii 32
  b Use your factor tree to write each number as a **product** of its prime factors.

> **Q2 Literacy hint**
> The **product** of numbers is the result of multiplying them.

3 Write the prime factor decomposition of 40.

4 Work out
  a $2^2 \times 3^2 = 4 \times 9 = \square$ **b** $2 \times 3 \times 5^2$
  c $3^2 \times 5^2$ **d** -11^2

5 Work out each number from their prime factor decomposition.
  a $2^2 \times 5 \times 11$
  b $2^3 \times 5^3$
  c $2 \times 3 \times 5^2$
  d $2^3 \times 3^2 \times 5$

6 Write the products using **powers**.
  a $3 \times 3 \times 3 \times 3 \times 3 \times 3 = 3^{\square}$
  b $4 \times 4 \times 4 \times 4 \times 4 = \square^{\square}$
  c $10 \times 10 \times 10 \times 10 \times 10 \times 10 \times 10 = \square^{\square}$
  d $2 \times 2 \times 2 \times 2 \times 5 \times 5 \times 5 \times 5 \times 5 = \square^{\square} \times \square^{\square}$
  e $3 \times 3 \times 4 \times 4 \times 4 \times 5 = \square^{\square} \times \square^{\square} \times \square^{\square}$

> **Key point**
> $2^5 = 2 \times 2 \times 2 \times 2 \times 2$
> 2^5 means '2 to the power 5'.
> The small number is called the **power** or **index** and tells you how many 2s to multiply together.

Investigation

1 Write each as a single power.

$2^2 \times 2^2 = 2 \times 2 \times 2 \times 2 = 2^{\square}$

$3^2 \times 3^3 = 3 \times 3 \times 3 \times 3 \times 3 = 3^{\square}$

$2^5 \times 2^3 =$

$5^2 \times 5^5 =$

Copy and complete: When you multiply numbers written as powers of the same number, you _____ the **indices**.

2 a Work out $\dfrac{2 \times 2 \times 2 \times 2}{2 \times 2}$ by cancelling.

b Write your answer to part **a** as a power of 2.

c Copy and complete $\dfrac{2 \times 2 \times 2 \times 2}{2 \times 2} = \dfrac{2^{\square}}{2^{\square}}$

$= 2^{\square}$

When you divide numbers written as powers of the same number, you _____ the indices.

7 Write each number as a product of prime numbers.

a 200

b 300

c 392

d 275

e 378

8 Write each product as a single power.

a $2^3 \times 2^2 = 2^{\square + \square} = 2^{\square}$

b $3^5 \times 3^5$

c $5^3 \times 5^4$

d 10×10^5

e $7^4 \times 7$

9 Write each division as a single power.

a $3^5 \div 3^3 = 3^{\square - \square} = 3^{\square}$

b $3^5 \div 3^2$

c $5^5 \div 5^4$

d $10^5 \div 10$

e $7^4 \div 7$

Worked example

Work out the HCF of 24 and 60.

Circle all the prime factors that appear in both lists.

$24 = ②\times②\times 2 \times ③$

$60 = ②\times②\times③\times 5$

The common prime factors are 2, 2 and 3.

HCF of 24 and 60 = $2 \times 2 \times 3 = 12$

10 Use the prime factor decompositions to work out the HCF of

a 20 and 48

b 56 and 48

c 40 and 32

d 112 and 88

Worked example

Work out the lowest common multiple of 24 and 80.

$24 = ②×②×②×③$ ——— Circle all the prime factors in the first number.

$8O = 2 × 2 × 2 ×②×⑤$

In the second number, circle any numbers you haven't yet included.
There are four 2s, but 3 were circled in the first number.

LCM of 24 and 8O = 2 × 2 × 2 × 2 × 3 × 5 = 24O

11 Use prime factor decomposition to find the **LCM** of each pair of numbers.
  a 20 and 36
  b 36 and 48
  c 40 and 60
  d 36 and 60

Q11a hint

Multiply together all the prime factors of 20, and any prime factors of 36 you haven't included.

12 Use prime factor decomposition to find the HCF and the LCM of 20, 30 and 40.

Q12 hint

Write all three numbers as products of their prime factors.

13 STEM / Problem-solving A shop sells bolts in packs of 24 and nuts in packs of 36. What is the least number of packs of each you can buy so that every bolt has a nut?

14 **Explore** How is doubling related to powers of 2?
Choose some sensible numbers to help you explore this situation. Then use what you've learned in this lesson to help you answer the question.

15 **Reflect** How would you explain what a 'power' or 'index' is to a classmate who has missed this lesson?

*Active*Learn   Pi 3, Section 1.6

1.7 Calculations

You will learn to:
- Work with calculations involving brackets, squares, cubes and square roots
- Estimate answers.

Why learn this?
Geographers estimate the volume of the sea and area of land using cubes and squares.

Fluency
Write each product as single power.
- $2 \times 2 \times 2 \times 2 \times 2 \times 2$
- $3 \times 3 \times 3 \times 3$

Explore
How could you estimate the volume of the Great Pyramid in Egypt?

Exercise 1.7

1 Work out

  a $2^3 + 5^2 - \sqrt{36}$ **b** $2 \times \sqrt{81} + 7^2$

  c $5^2 \div 5 \times 2$ **d** $2 \times 3^2 + \sqrt{36} \div 3$

  e $10^2 - 3 \times 5^2$ **f** $10^3 + \sqrt{25} - \sqrt{16}$

2 a Round each number to the nearest 10 to estimate an answer to each calculation.

  i 23.6×6.8

  ii 18.3×49

  iii 99×6.7

  iv $28.4 \div 5.76$

b Use your calculator to work out the actual answers to part **a**.

Discussion How accurate are your estimates? Why are some more accurate than others?

3 $p = 5$, $q = 4$ and $r = 3$. **Evaluate**

  a $p + q + r$ **b** $p \times q \times r$ **c** $p \times q - r$ **d** $p + q \times r$

4 Evaluate

  a $30 - (5 \times 7 - 15)$ **b** $24 \div (12 - 2 \times 4)$

  c $(20 - 3^2) \times 4$ **d** $(5^2 + 15) \div 5$

  e $10^2 + 6 \times 5 + 9$ **f** $(7^2 - 10) + 11$

  g $2 \times (5^2 - 10)$ **h** $(33 \div 11)^3 \div 9$

5 Evaluate

  a $\sqrt{45 + 36}$ **b** $(7 + 3)^2$

  c $(11 - 5 - 4)^3$ **d** $\sqrt{125 - 4}$

  e $(17 + 3 - 8)^2$ **f** $\sqrt{10^2 - 6^2}$

Key point

Use the priority of operations to do calculations.
Brackets.
Indices (powers).
Division and Multiplication.
Addition and Subtraction.

Q3 Literacy hint

Evaluate means work out.

Q5a hint

The square root sign acts like a bracket. Work out the calculation within the square root sign first.

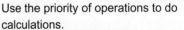

Warm up

6 Work out

  a -24^2 **b** 3.2^2

  c $\sqrt{4 \times 25}$ **d** $\sqrt{12 + 4}$

  e $\sqrt{40 - 4}$ **f** $\sqrt{36 \div 2^2}$

7 Evaluate

  a 2×5^3 **b** $3 \times \sqrt[3]{64}$

  c $4^2 + \sqrt{36} - 2$ **d** $10^3 \div 5^2$

  e $\sqrt{2 \times 32} \div \sqrt{4}$ **f** $\sqrt{100} \times \sqrt[3]{8}$

8 Evaluate

  a $(30 - 2 \times 7) \times (5 \times 3 - 4)$ **b** $(9 - 3)^2 \times 4$

  c $100 - (3 + 4)^2$ **d** $(3 + 2)^2 - (5 \times 3 + 2)$

9 Evaluate

  a $\sqrt{30 + 6} - 5$ **b** $\sqrt{20 - 4} + 3$

  c $8 + \sqrt{30 - 5}$ **d** $20 - \sqrt{60 - 11}$

  e $\sqrt{3 + 5 + 8} \times 2$ **f** $20 - \sqrt{9 \times 4}$

  g $(11 - \sqrt{9}) \times (12 - 3 + 1)$

10 Use the bracket keys on your calculator to work out

  a $4^3 \times \sqrt[3]{650 + 350}$ **b** $(20 \div 4)^3 + 5^2$

  c $8 - \sqrt[3]{3^2 \times 4 \times 6}$ **d** $600 - (32 \div 4)^3$

  e $(23 - 13 + 4 - 8)^3$ **f** $(115 \div 5)^2 + (13 + 8)^2$

11 Estimate each answer, then use your calculator to work it out.
Round decimal answers to 2 decimal places.

  a $3 \times (19.4 + 21.6)$ **b** $\dfrac{(29 \div 5)2}{2.7 \times 1.9}$

  c $(20.9 \div 4.5) + (43.8 \div 10.36)$ **d** $\dfrac{\sqrt{25.7 \times 3.99}}{15.6 \div 2.76}$

> **Q11a hint**
>
> Estimate by rounding to the nearest 10.
> $3 \times (19.4 + 21.6) \approx 3 \times (20 + 20)$

12 **Reasoning** **a** Work out

    i $(33 - \sqrt{25}) - \sqrt[3]{512}$ **ii** $250 - (122 + 6)$

    iii $(22.5 + 27.5) \times 2$ **iv** $(15^2 - \sqrt[3]{343}) + 21.5$

    v $(6 + \sqrt{196})^2 \times 2^3$ **vi** $(16.2 - 3.5)^2 \div 1.7$

  b What happens to each calculation if you don't use the bracket keys?

> **Q12 hint**
>
> If there is a bracket in the calculation you can use the bracket keys on your calculator.
> Make sure you type in the correct order on your calculator.

13 $a = 10$ and $b = 6$. Work out the value of

  a a^2 **b** b^2

  c $a^2 - b^2$ **d** $(a - b)^2$

  e $\sqrt{(a + b)}$ **f** $a^3 + (2a + 3b)$

14 **Explore** How could you estimate the volume of the Great Pyramid in Egypt?
Is it easier to explore this question now you have completed the lesson?
What further information do you need to be able to answer this?

15 **Reflect** Q2 and Q11 asked you to estimate answers. How does estimating help you when working out calculations in maths, in other subjects and everyday life?

1 Check up

Log how you did on your Student Progression Chart.

Integer calculations

1 24 friends go out for a meal. The total bill is £432. How much does each person pay?

2 Work out
  a 1745×8
  b 8234×16
  c $12856 + 459 - 6741 - 75$
  d $3850 \div 5$

3 Use a mental method to work out 25×28.

4 Work out
  a -4×5
  b -9×-11
  c $-21 \div 7$
  d $-56 \div -8$
  e $-5 \times (-3 \times 4)$
  f $(-4 \div -2) \times 15$

5 Copy and complete
  a $1200000 = \square$ million
  b $3450000 = \square$ million
  c 4.2 million $=$
  d 2.09 million $=$

Decimal calculations

6 Work out
  a $452.08 - 62.9 + 633.2$
  b $720 - 456.78 + 24.6$
  c $38.9 + 29.2 - 22.4$
  d 3.4×56
  e 7.2×3.8
  f $4.6 \times 2 - 1.1$

7 This is Henry's shopping bill. He pays with two £50 notes. How much change does he get?

```
£12.50
£ 4.99
£17.05
£42.00
```

8 $136 \times 82 = 11152$. Work out
  a 1.36×82
  b 13.6×8.2

9 Work out £734.64 ÷ 24

10 Work out
  a $362.95 \div 5$
  b $132 \div 0.6$
  c $12.8 \div 0.8$
  d $364.5 \div 1.5$

11 Work out -5.2×0.8

Powers and roots

12 Evaluate $(50 - 5^2) \times 10$

13 Work out
  a $\sqrt{3 \times 27}$
  b $\sqrt{30 - 5}$

14 Work out

a 3^3

b $\sqrt[3]{125}$

15 Write the products using powers.

a $7 \times 7 \times 7 \times 7 \times 7$

b $4 \times 4 \times 5 \times 5 \times 5 \times 5$

16 Write as a single power.

a $4^3 \times 4^2$

b $7^4 \times 7$

c $2^5 \div 2^2$

d $9^5 \div 9$

17 **a** Write 28 as a product of its prime factors.

b Write 36 as a product of its prime factors.

c Work out the highest common factor of 28 and 36.

d Work out the lowest common multiple of 28 and 36.

18 Write 860 as a product of its prime factors.

19 Work out $(-7)^2$.

20 Give the positive and negative square root of 64.

21 Evaluate

a $5^3 \times \sqrt[3]{9261}$

b $(72 \div 18)^3 + 8^2$

c $(47.1 + 12.09) \times 4$

d $(17^2 - \sqrt[3]{4913}) \times 7.5$

22 **How sure are you of your answers? Were you mostly**

😞 **Just guessing**   😐 **Feeling doubtful**   🙂 **Confident**

What next? Use your results to decide whether to strengthen or extend your learning.

Challenge

23 Write four related multiplications and their answers using decimal numbers.

a $345 \times 16 = 5520$

b $742 \times 23 = 17\,066$

c $2.8 \times 61.2 = 171.36$

1 Strengthen

You will:
• Strengthen your understanding with practice.

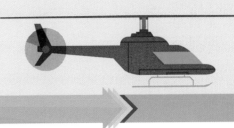

Integer calculations

1 Work out the sum of
  a 28 506   4501   36 819   99   672
  b 73 590   379   4999   85   12 069

2 Work out
  a 37 605 − 22 756 + 463 − 2105
  b 16 700 − 5781 + 3765 − 904
  c 783 − 3756 − 8104 + 45 962

3 Match each number to a word from the cloud.

  100
  1000
  10 000
  1 000 000

  one hundred
  one million   *ten thousand*
  one thousand

4 Write each as ☐ million.
  a 7 000 000
  b 24 000 000
  c 9 500 000
  d 3 905 000
  e 900 000
  f 980 000
  g 550 000

5 Write each number using only digits.
  a 5 million
  b 6.9 million
  c 5.21 million
  d 0.4 million
  e 0.39 million

6 Work out
  a 3867 × 8
  b 3792 × 6
  c 7 × 2047

7 Work out
  a 2754 × 16
  b 3856 × 21
  c 2716 × 32
  d 1073 × 24

Q1a hint

Write each number in a place value table. Line up the units, tens, hundreds, etc.

Ten thousands	Thousands	Hundreds	Tens	Units
2	8	5	0	6
	4	5	0	1

Q2a hint

Work out 37 605 − 22 756. Then add 463. Then subtract 2105.

Q4a hint

1 000 000 is 1 million.
7 000 000 is 7 lots of 1 million.

Q7a hint

Split both numbers into thousands, hundreds, tens and units.

×	2000	700	50	4
10				
6				
Totals				

8 a Write the multiples of 12 up to 10 × 12.
  b Use the multiples to work out
    i 684 ÷ 12
    ii 1128 ÷ 12
    iii 1452 ÷ 12

9 Work out
  a 752 ÷ 16
  b 550 ÷ 22
  c 725 ÷ 25

Q8b i hint

Subtract multiples of 12 from 684 until you can't subtract any more.
5 × 12 = 60 so 50 × 12 = 600

$$\begin{array}{rl} 6\,8\,4 & \\ -6\,0\,0 & \quad 50 \times 12 \\ \hline 8\,4 & \quad \square \times 12 \\ \hline 0 & \end{array}$$

684 ÷ 12 = 50 + ☐ = ☐

10 Copy and complete the rules on multiplying and dividing negative numbers. Look at the calculations to help.
    negative × negative = _____
    positive × negative = _____
    negative × positive = _____
    negative ÷ negative = _____
    positive ÷ negative = _____
    negative ÷ positive = _____
    Two signs the same = _____
    Two different signs = _____

$-4 \times 6 = -24$

$-32 \div -4 = 8$

$45 \div -9 = -5$

$-15 \div 5 = -3$

$-5 \times -10 = 50$

$6 \times -5 = -30$

11 Work out
  a −10 × 6
  b −10 × −6
  c 60 ÷ −10
  d −60 ÷ −10

Decimal calculations

1 Work out
  a 6 × 0.07 = 6 × 7 ÷ 100 = ☐
  b 0.4 × 6 = 4 × 6 ÷ 10 = ☐
  c 7 × 0.8
  d 5 × 0.6
  e 0.08 × 4
  f 0.05 × 6

Q1b hint

You can do multiplication in any order, so
0.4 × 6 = 4 × 6 ÷ 10

2 152 × 15 = 2280. Use this fact to work out
  a 152 × 1.5
  b 15.2 × 15
  c 1.52 × 15
  d 1.52 × 1.5

Q2a hint

152 × 1.5 = 152 × 15 ÷ 10
         = 2280 ÷ 10
         = ☐

3 Work out
  a 84.32 × 9
  b 46.5 × 6
  c 67.8 × 5

Q3a hint

84.32 × 9 = 8432 × 9 ÷ 100

4 Work out
  a 1.2 × 4.6
  b 5.7 × 2.1
  c 2.5 × 7.4
  d 3.8 × 8.3

Q4a hint

1.2 × 4.6 = 12 ÷ 10 × 46 ÷ 10
         = 12 × 46 ÷ 100

5 Work out

   a $27.9 \div 3$

   b $74.1 \div 3$

   c $42.84 \div 6$

   d $83.16 \div 9$

Q5a hint

$27.9 \div 3 = 279 \div 10 \div 3$
$= 279 \div 3 \div 10$

Powers and roots

1 Work out

   a 8^2

   b 15^2

   c 11^2

   d 14^2

2 Work out

   a $(-5)^2$

   b $(-10)^2$

   c $(-12)^2$

   d $(-21)^2$

Q2a hint

Use the rule for multiplying negatives.
$(-5)^2 = -5 \times -5$

3 Work out

   a $\sqrt{25} + 3^2$

   b $8^2 - \sqrt{100}$

   c $4^2 \div 2^2$

   d $4^2 \times \sqrt{36}$

Q3 hint

Work out squares and roots before adding, subtracting, multiplying and dividing.

4 Which pairs of calculations have the same answer?

$5^2 \times 2$ $50 - (2^2 + 4^2)$ $2 \times (8 - 3)^2$

$(10^2 - 4 \times 5) \div 2$ $(4 + 6^2) - 10$ $10 \times (30 - 5^2) - 10$

Q4 hint

Work out the calculation inside the brackets first.

5 Work out

   a $6^3 = (6 \times 6) \times 6 = \square \times 6 = \square$

   b 9^3

   c 11^3

   d 14^3

6 Work out

   a $\sqrt[3]{1000}$

   b $\sqrt[3]{216}$

Q6 Literacy hint

$\sqrt{}$ means 'square root'.
$\sqrt[3]{}$ means 'cube root'.

7 Copy and complete.

   a $3^3 \times 3^2 = 3 \times 3 \times 3 \times 3 \times 3 = 3^\square$

   b $4^2 \times 4^3 = 4 \times 4 \times 4 \times 4 \times 4 = 4^\square$

   c $5^4 \times 5 = \square \times \square \times \square \times \square \times 5$

   d $6^5 \div 6^2 = \dfrac{\cancel{6} \times \cancel{6} \times 6 \times 6 \times 6}{\cancel{6} \times \cancel{6}} = \square^\square$

   e $7^4 \div 7^3 = \dfrac{7 \times 7 \times 7 \times 7}{7 \times 7 \times 7} = \square^\square$

   f $10^5 \div 10 = \square^\square$

Q7 hint

Add the indices for multiplication.
Subtract the indices for division.
$5 = 5^1$

8 Phil says, 'I multiply a number by itself and get the answer 64.
What number did I start with?'
There are two numbers Phil could have started with. What are they?

9 Give the positive and negative square root of each number.

   a 16

   b 100

   c 169

10 a Complete the factor tree for 360.

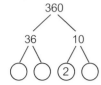

   b Write 360 as a product of its prime factors.

11 a Write each number as a product of prime factors.

    i 40

    ii 56

   b Find the HCF and LCM of 40 and 56.

> **Q11 hint**
>
> Check your answers.
> When you multiply the numbers in the prime factor decomposition you should get the original number.
> The HCF is smaller than both numbers.
> The LCM is bigger than both numbers.

Enrichment

1 Choose some numbers to see how to complete these rules.

   negative × negative × negative = _____

   positive × negative × negative = _____

   negative × positive × negative = _____

   negative × negative × positive = _____

   negative × positive × positive = _____

   positive × negative × positive = _____

   positive × positive × negative = _____

2 a Predict how many cube numbers there are up to 1000.

   b Work out the exact answer. Is it more or less than you thought?

> **Q2b hint**
>
> Start with $1^3 = 1 × 1 × 1 = \square$
> $2^3 = 2 × 2 × 2 = \square$

3 Reflect Write down five strategies you have used in this unit that helped you work out answers to calculations, for example, *doubling and halving, estimating*
Give an example of each.

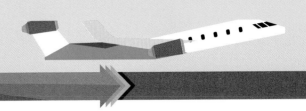

1 Extend

You will:
- Extend your understanding with problem-solving.

1 **Reasoning** Jakob finds multiples of 25 by first dividing the number by 4 and then multiplying by 100.
  a Copy and complete each calculation, using Jakob's method.
    i 28×25 $28 \div 4 = 7$ $7 \times 100 = \Box$
    ii 32×25 $32 \div 4 = \Box$
    iii 20×25
  b Explain why Jakob's method isn't the easiest method for multiplying any number by 25.

2 There are 375 ml of medicine in a bottle. How many 25 ml doses are in the bottle?

 3 Write these in order from smallest to largest.
  3.4^2 $\sqrt[3]{216}$ 2.4^3 $\sqrt{256}$

4 Work out
  a $12\,456 \times 8$ **b** 7261×15 **c** 3756×23
  d 345×321 **e** 709×264 **f** 4502×18

5 Use your answers to Q4 to work out
  a 12.456×8 **b** 7261×1.5 **c** 37.56×2.3
  d 3.45×3.21 **e** 709×0.264 **f** 45.02×1.8

> **Q5 hint**
>
> Number of decimal places in calculation = Number of decimal places in the answer

6 Use a written method to work out
  a 42.135×9 **b** 324.2×4.5
  c 62.89×0.54 **d** 25.2×14.6

7 **Modelling** Ali flies 2354.78 miles every month on business. How far does he fly in a year?

8 Evaluate
  a 0.9×0.8 **b** 0.4×0.2 **c** 0.6×0.5
  d 0.4×0.03 **e** 0.04×0.8

9 **Reasoning** Work out
  a **i** 68×0.1 **ii** $68 \div 10$
  b **i** 72×0.1 **ii** $72 \div 10$
  c **i** 56×0.1 **ii** $56 \div 10$
  d Explain how $\times\, 0.1$ and $\div\, 10$ are related.

10 Evaluate
  a **i** $68 \div 0.1$ **ii** 68×10
  b **i** $72 \div 0.1$ **ii** 72×10
  c **i** $56 \div 0.1$ **ii** 56×10
  d Explain how $\div\, 0.1$ and $\times\, 10$ are related.

11 **Reasoning** 56 × 93 = 5208. Use this fact to work out
    a 5.6 × 93   **b** 0.56 × 93   **c** 0.56 × 9.3
    d 0.56 × 0.93   **e** 52.08 ÷ 930   **f** 5.208 ÷ 0.56

Q11e hint

Rearrange the original calculation.

5208 ÷ 93 = 56

÷100 ( )×10 ÷100 ÷10

52.08 ÷ 930 = ☐

The dividend is 100 times smaller and the divisor is 10 times bigger, so the whole answer will be 1000 times smaller.

12 Calculate
    a 0.12 × 0.45   **b** 0.08 × 0.91   **c** 0.42 × 0.06
    d 0.35 × 0.49   **e** 0.76 × 0.25

13 Work out
    a 0.32^2 **b** 0.48^2 **c** 0.75^2

14 What is the area of a cupboard 0.82 m by 0.65 m?

15 **Problem-solving** What is the area of a square tray with a perimeter of 1.44 m?

Q15 hint

Work out the length of one side using the perimeter.

16 Work out each division, give your answers as decimal numbers.
    a 12 345 ÷ 6   **b** 24.768 ÷ 8   **c** 294 ÷ 12
    d 431.2 ÷ 28   **e** 604.8 ÷ 32   **f** 73.36 ÷ 14

17 **Modelling / Problem-solving** Kristen drove 2949 miles last year for work.
    a What is the mean number of miles per month?
    b She worked 48 weeks last year. What is the mean number of miles per week?
    c She works 3 days a week. How far does she travel to get to work?

18 Calculate
    a −6 × −3 × −5 = (−6 × −3) × −5 = ☐ × −5 =
    b 8 × −5 × 4
    c −10 × −7 × 6
    d −15 ÷ 3 × −2
    e 24 ÷ −8 × −5
    f −30 ÷ −5 ÷ −3

Q18 hint

Use the rules for multiplying and dividing negative numbers.

19 Martin multiplies 3 numbers together.
    Say whether the answer will be positive or negative if the numbers are
    a negative, positive, positive
    b negative, negative, positive

20 Use an estimate to write < or > between each pair.
    a 11.7^2 $\sqrt{14\,400}$
    b $\sqrt[3]{120}$ 3.4^2

Q20a hint

$\sqrt{14\,400} = \sqrt{120 \times 120}$

21 **Reasoning** **a** Work out $\sqrt{16} \times \sqrt{4}$ and $\sqrt{(16 \times 4)}$
    b What do you notice about your answers to part **a**?
    c Given that 25 × 9 = 225, what is $\sqrt{225}$?
    d Given that 9 × 81 = 729, what is $\sqrt{729}$?
    e Given that 64 × 49 = 3136, what is $\sqrt{3136}$?
    f Check each answer in parts **c**–**e** using your calculator.

Q21c hint

Work out $\sqrt{25} \times \sqrt{9}$.

22 Work out the square roots of each number.
    a $\sqrt{625} = \sqrt{25} \times \sqrt{25} = ☐ \times ☐ = ☐$ **b** $\sqrt{144} = \sqrt{4} \times \sqrt{36}$
    c $\sqrt{256} = \sqrt{4} \times \sqrt{64}$ **d** $\sqrt{196} = \sqrt{4} \times \sqrt{49}$
    e $\sqrt{900} = \sqrt{☐} \times \sqrt{100}$ **f** $\sqrt{2500}$

23 Write each expression as a single power.

   a $6^2 \times 6^4 \times 6 = 6^{2+4+1} = 6^{\square}$ **b** $2^5 \times 2 \times 2^3$

   c $10^6 \times 10^4 \times 10$ **d** $4^8 \div 4^2 \div 4 = 4^{8-2-1} = 4^{\square}$

   e $5^5 \div 5^2 \div 5$ **f** $7^7 \div 7^3 \div 7$

   g $10^6 \div 10^3 \times 10^2 = 10^{6-3+2} = 10^{\square}$ **h** $9^8 \times 9^2 \div 9^7$

   i $8^5 \times 8 \div 8^6$ **j** $3 \times 3^3 \div 3^2 \times 3$

24 **Reasoning** Work out the value of each letter.

   a $9^4 \times 9^a = 9^7$ $a =$

   b $10^4 \times 10^b = 10^5$ $b =$

   c $4^6 \div 4^c = 4^2$ $c =$

   d $5^d \div 5 = 5^4$ $d =$

> **Q24a hint**
>
> $4 + a = 7$

25 Find both square roots of the following numbers. Round your answers to 2 decimal places.

   a 80   **b** 175

   c 240   **d** 872

   e 1001   **f** 40

26 **Reasoning** The square root of a number is 3.5. What is the number?

27 **Reasoning** Solve each equation.

   a $r^3 = 3375$ $\sqrt[3]{3375} = \square$ $r = \square$

   b $g^4 = 10\,000$

   c $\sqrt{b} = 13$

   d $\sqrt[3]{c} = 1728$

   e $10^y = 100\,000$

   f $8^r = 512$

> **Q27 hint**
>
> Check your answer using the inverse operation.

28 **Reasoning** **a** Use factors of each number to work out the square root.

   i $\sqrt{1024} = \sqrt{16} \times \sqrt{64} = 4 \times \square = \square$

   ii $\sqrt{256} = \sqrt{16} \times \sqrt{\square} = \square \times \square = \square$

   iii $\sqrt{1764} = \sqrt{36} \times \sqrt{\square} = \square \times \square = \square$

   iv $\sqrt{2500} = \sqrt{\square} \times \sqrt{\square} = \square \times \square = \square$

   b Check your answers to part **a** with your calculator.

> **Q28 hint**
>
> Divide the number to be square rooted by the factor given to find the factor pair.
>
> $1024 \div 16 = 64$

29 **Reasoning** Work out

   a 3.5×10^3 and 35×10^2

   b 5.6×10^3 and 56×10^2

   c 7.2×10^3 and 72×10^2

   d What do you notice about the answers?

   e Re-write each number using 10^3 then work out the answer.

     i $7 \times 10^2 = \square \times 10^3 =$ **ii** 45×10^2 **iii** 75×10^2

30 **a** Write 200 and 300 as a product of their prime factors.

   b Use the prime factor decomposition to find the HCF of 200 and 300.

   c Use the prime factor decomposition to find the LCM of 200 and 300.

31 **a** Write 350 and 500 as a product of their prime factors.

   b Use the prime factor decomposition to find the HCF of 350 and 500.

   c Use the prime factor decomposition to find the LCM of 350 and 500.

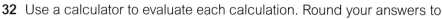

32 Use a calculator to evaluate each calculation. Round your answers to 1 decimal place.

   a $2.8^2 \times (4.5 + 3 \div 5)$ **b** $3 \div 4 \times 7.2 - 3.09$

   c $2.5^3 \div 7 \div 8 + \sqrt{12.6}$ **d** $15.4^2 \div (4 \div 5)^3 + \sqrt[3]{156}$

33 Evaluate

   a $5 \times (\sqrt{144} - 6)$ **b** $8^2 \div (4 \times \sqrt{16})$

   c $(2^3 - \sqrt{25})^3$ **d** $4^3 - (\sqrt{36} \times \sqrt{49})$

   e $\sqrt[3]{1000} \times (5^3 \div 5^2)$ **f** $\sqrt{3^3 \times 3} + 12^2$

> **Q33 hint**
>
> Make sure you use the correct priority of operations.

34 Work out

   a $\sqrt{56 \times 2 - 3 \times 4}$

   b $\sqrt[3]{3^3 \times 10^3}$

   c $(5^2 - 20 + 4)^3$

35 Work out

   a $\left(\dfrac{1}{3}\right)^2 = \dfrac{1^2}{3^2} = \dfrac{1}{\square}$ **b** $\left(\dfrac{1}{5}\right)^2$

   c $\left(\dfrac{1}{6}\right)^2$ **d** $\left(\dfrac{2}{3}\right)^2$

   e $\left(\dfrac{3}{5}\right)^2$ **f** $\left(\dfrac{7}{10}\right)^2$

36 Calculate the cube of each fraction.

   a $\left(\dfrac{2}{3}\right)^3 = \dfrac{2^3}{3^3} = \dfrac{\square}{\square}$ **b** $\left(\dfrac{1}{3}\right)^3$

   c $\left(\dfrac{2}{5}\right)^3$ **d** $\left(\dfrac{3}{10}\right)^3$

37 Simplify each fraction.

   a $\dfrac{20 - 16}{4 \times 5}$ **b** $\dfrac{6^2}{2^3}$

   c $\dfrac{4^2 - 10}{\sqrt{25} \times 2}$ **d** $\dfrac{\sqrt{49} \times 2^2}{2^3 \times \sqrt{36}}$

Investigation   **Reasoning**

   1 Work out 11^2, 101^2, 1001^2.

   2 What patterns emerge? Predict the answer to $10\,001^2$ and check it using your calculator.

   3 Work out 12^2, 102^2, 1002^2 and 13^2, 103^2, 1003^2. Predict $10\,002^2$ and $10\,003^2$.

   4 Investigate the patterns for some other numbers.

38 Reflect Q20 asked you to estimate numbers.

   a Explain in your own words what is meant by 'estimate'.
      You can also estimate to check your answers are sensible.

   b Choose an example of a question where this would be a good idea.

Reflect

1 Unit test

Log how you did on your Student Progression Chart.

1 Dan is counting his stamp collection. He has 1823 British stamps, 286 from France, 99 from Germany and 1002 from the rest of the world.
 a How many stamps does he have altogether?
 b He sells 189 British stamps and buys 84 French and 15 German ones. How many stamps does he have now?

2 Work out
 a 7200×5 b 370×25
 c 185×20 d 23^2

3 Work out the area of each shape.

a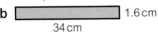
14 cm
14 cm

b 1.6 cm
34 cm

4 Use a written method to work out
 a $8142 \div 6$ b $3754 \div 8$ c $26.4 \div 0.8$

5 Use a written method to work out
 a $578 \div 17$ b $675 \div 25$ c $4000 \div 32$

6 a Write 65 as a product of its prime factors.
 b Write 80 as a product of its prime factors.
 c Work out the HCF of 65 and 80.
 d Work out the LCM of 65 and 80.

7 Write 275 as a product of its prime factors.

8 Copy and complete
 a $6\,500\,000 = \square$ million
 b $14\,750\,000 = \square$ million
 c $100\,000 = \square$ million

9 Write each number using digits only.
 a 7.8 million b 0.2 million

10 Write each number as a power of 10.
 a 10 000
 b one thousand
 c one million

11 Give both square roots of
 a 16 b 400 c 1

12 Evaluate
 a $\sqrt{81} + 4^2$ b $7^2 - \sqrt{49}$
 c $(25 - 16 + 2)^2$ d $\sqrt{19} \times \sqrt{19}$

13 Work out
  a 42.56×7 **b** 12.05×18 **c** 8.6^2

14 $24 \times 36 = 864$. Use this fact to work out
  a 2.4×3.6 **b** 0.24×0.36

15 Evaluate
  a -12×-8 **b** $-45 \div 9$ **c** $-3 \times -6 \times 2$
  d $-36 \div -4$ **e** $-24 \div 6 \times -3$ **f** $(-11)^2$

16 Write as a single power.
  a $3^2 \times 3^5$
  b $5^6 \div 5$
  c $10^5 \div 10^3 \times 10$

17 Work out
  a $8 \times (\sqrt{400} - 50)$ **b** $\sqrt[3]{125} \times (5^3 \div 5^2)$
  c $\sqrt{(3^3 \times 3)} + 12^2$ **d** $\dfrac{8^2}{2^3}$
  e $\dfrac{\sqrt{144} \div 2^2}{4^2 \times \sqrt{36}}$ **f** $(6^2 - 35 + 3)^3$

18 Evaluate
  a 25×0.1 **b** $62 \div 0.1$
  c 38×0.01 **d** $27 \div 0.01$

19 Work out each square root by factorising. Check your answer using your calculator.
  a $\sqrt{1600} = \sqrt{16} \times \sqrt{100} =$ **b** $\sqrt{2916} = \sqrt{36} \times \sqrt{\square} =$

Challenge

20 a Work out the area of each square.

5 cm A   6 cm B

  b Caitlyn says, '$5^2 + 6^2 = (5 + 6)^2$'.
    Use the squares to show that Caitlyn is wrong.
  c Are there any squares for which Caitlyn's statement is true?

21 Reflect Look back at this test. Which questions took the shortest time to answer, and which took the longest? Suggest why you could answer some questions more quickly than others.

2 Sequences and equations

2.1 Algebraic expressions

You will learn to:
- Write expressions given a description in words
- Simplify expressions.

$2m + 3n = ?$

Why learn this?
Describing a calculation using algebra is much quicker than using words.

Fluency
Work out
- $5 \times 2 - 3$
- $4 + 8 \div 2$
- $10 - 2 \times 3$
- $2 + 3^2$

Explore
Is it possible to simplify algebraic expressions?

Exercise 2.1

1 Write an expression for

  a 5 more than x

  b 2 fewer than n

  c 3 lots of y

  d the sum of m and 4.

2 Simplify each expression.

  a $4p + 2p + 5t - 2t$

  b $6m + 2n - m - n$

  c $2d + 5d + 3$

  d $4 \times 3a$

  e $10c \div 2$

  f $\dfrac{6k}{3}$

3 The total weight of n compact discs is $5n$ grams. Work out the total weight of

  a 6 discs

  b 20 discs

  c one disc.

4 Write an algebraic expression for each length.

  a Stephen cuts x cm of ribbon from a length of y cm. How much does he have left?

  b Paul cuts a chain of length p metres in half. What is the length of each piece?

  c Lucy cuts 50 metres of rope into n pieces. What is the length of each piece?

  d Two lengths of twine are each t cm long. Madison joins them to a 10 cm piece. What is the total length?

Q4a hint

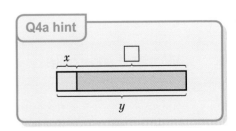

Warm up

Worked example

A pack contains n tangerines. Sandra buys 2 packs of tangerines and 3 loose tangerines.

a Write an expression for the total number of tangerines Sandra buys.

b Work out the total number of tangerines when $n = 8$.

a 2 packs = $2n$

Plus 3

$2n + 3$

b $2 \times 8 + 3 = 16 + 3 = 19$ ——— Substitute $n = 8$ into your expression.

5 a Write an expression for each case.

   i Marion buys 3 packs of n stamps. She adds them to her collection of 20 stamps.

   ii James buys 2 packs of n stamps. He gives 7 stamps away.

   iii Karen has 12 stamps. She is given $\frac{1}{2}$ a pack of n stamps.

   iv Pat has 40 stamps. She gives away 2 packs of n stamps.

b Work out the number of stamps each person has in part **a** when $n = 10$.

Q5a iii hint

$\square + \square \div 2$

6 a These shapes are made using rectangles. All lengths are in metres. Write an expression for the area of each shape.

   i 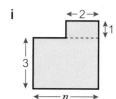   **ii** 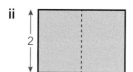   **iii**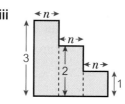

b Work out the area of each shape when $n = 4$.

7 Rachel did x press-ups each day for 5 days. Ziona did y press-ups each day for 7 days.

a Write an expression for the total number of press-ups they did.

b Work out the total when $x = 15$ and $y = 20$.

 8 Work out the value of a^2 when

   a $a = 12$

   b $a = 1.5$

   c $a = 22$

Key point

You can write $n \times n$ as n^2.

Worked example

Simplify $5m \times 3m$

$5 \times m \times 3 \times m = 5 \times 3 \times m \times m$

$= 15 \times m^2$ Rewrite the expression so numbers and letters are together, then simplify.

$= 15m^2$

Topic links: Area

9 Simplify each expression.

   a $m \times m$

   b $2 \times a \times a$

   c $t \times 4 \times t$

   d $3y \times 5y$

   e $4p \times 2q$

   f $-3m \times 4n$

10 Write an expression for the area of each rectangle.

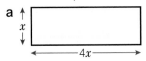

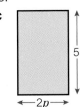

11 Simplify each expression by collecting like terms.

   a $-3u - 2u + 4v - 7v$

   b $5m + 2n - 3p - 7m$

   c $9 - 5a + 2b + 6a$

   d $d - e - f - 2e - 1 + 3d - e$

   e $5 \times 2n + 3 \times 4m$

Investigation   Reasoning

Jemma writes $2m + 3n = 5mn$

a Work out the value of $2m + 3n$ when $m = 4$ and $n = 3$.

b Work out the value of $5mn$ when $m = 4$ and $n = 3$.

c Is Jemma correct?

$6p - 2q$ cannot be simplified further.

d Write down another expression which cannot be simplified further.

e Write down an expression which can be simplified, and simplify it.

Compare your answers with your classmates.

---

12 Explore Is it possible to simplify algebraic expressions? Look back at the maths you have learned in this lesson. How can you use it to answer this question?

13 Reflect Do you prefer answering questions that have a diagram (like Q6) or those that are just words (like Q7)? If you prefer diagrams, can you always draw a diagram to help? Give an example of one from this lesson.

Explore

Reflect

2.2 Using the nth term

You will learn to:
- Use algebra to generate the terms of a sequence
- Solve problems involving sequences.

CONFIDENCE

Why learn this?
When you know the nth term, you can generate any term of a sequence.

Fluency
What is the next term in each sequence?
- 3, 5, 7, ...
- 3, 6, 12, 24, ...
- 20, 16, 12, ...
- 32, 16, 8, ...

Explore
What rules generate a sequence where all the terms are identical?

Exercise 2.2

Warm up

1 a Write the first three terms of the sequence with nth term
  i $n + 7$
  ii $4n$
  iii $n - 10$
 b Work out the 20th term of each sequence.

2 Work out the value of each expression when
   i $n = 3$ **ii** $n = 10$
 a $3n + 2$
 b $4n - 5$
 c $-2n + 1$
 d $6 - 5n$

Worked example

The nth term of a sequence is $2n - 1$.
Work out the first five terms.

Position (n)	1	2	3	4	5
Term ($2n - 1$)	$2 \times 1 - 1$ $= 1$	$2 \times 2 - 1$ $= 3$	$2 \times 3 - 1$ $= 5$	$2 \times 4 - 1$ $= 7$	$2 \times 5 - 1$ $= 9$

Substitute the position number into the expression $2n - 1$.

Literacy hint

The nth term of a sequence tells you how to work out a term in position n.

3 Copy and complete the tables to work out the first five terms of each sequence.
 a nth term $= 2n + 1$

Position (n)	1	2	3	4	5
Term ($2n + 1$)	$2 \times 1 + 1 = 3$	$2 \times \square + 1 = \square$			

Topic links: Negative numbers

Subject links: Computing (spreadsheets) Q9

b nth term $= 10n - 10$

Position (n)	1	2	3	4	5
Term ($10n - 10$)	$10 \times 1 - 10 = \square$	$10 \times \square - \square = \square$			

c nth term $= 3n - 9$

Position (n)	1	2	3	4	5
Term ($3n - 9$)					

d nth term $= 2n - 0.5$

Position (n)	1	2	3	4	5
Term ($2n - 0.5$)					

4 Work out the 10th term of the sequence with nth term
   a $4n + 3$ **b** $7n - 2$ **c** $5n + 9$
   d $6n - 18$ **e** $3n - 1.5$ **f** $2n + 0.5$

5 Problem-solving The nth term of a sequence is $6n - 20$.
   What is the smallest positive term?

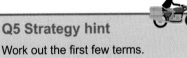

Q5 Strategy hint

Work out the first few terms.

6 Reasoning **a** Draw the next two patterns in this sequence.

Pattern 1   Pattern 2   Pattern 3

   b Copy and complete the table to show the number of lines in each
   pattern.

Pattern number (n)	1	2	3	4	5
Number of lines					

   c Kalsi thinks that the nth term is $3n + 1$.
   Leroy thinks that the nth term is $n + 3$.
   Who is correct? How do you know?

7 Problem-solving / Reasoning
   a There are 2 chairs in a room. Terry and Alan sit on a chair. In how
   many different ways can this happen?
   b There are 3 chairs in a room. How many different ways can Terry
   and Alan sit on a chair?
   c Copy and complete this table.

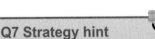

Q7 Strategy hint

Draw a box for each chair, and write
T or A to show where they sit.

Number of chairs	2	3	4	5
Number of ways to sit				

   d How many ways can they sit on 10 chairs?

8 Reasoning The nth term of a sequence is $-2n + 10$
   a Work out the first five terms.

Position (n)	1	2	3	4	5
Term ($-2n + 10$)	$-2 \times 1 + 10 = 8$	$-2 \times 2 + 10 = \square$			

   b Is the sequence ascending or descending? Why?
   c Decide whether each of these sequences is ascending or
   descending.
      i $4n - 20$ **ii** $-n + 10$ **iii** $15 - 3n$ **iv** $-5n - 10$

9 **Finance** Barry has £220 in his savings account. Each week he spends the same amount.
The spreadsheet shows the amount left in his account after each week.

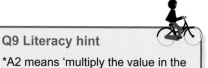

	A	B
1	Week	Savings
2	1	=220–20*A2
3	2	=220–20*A3
4	3	=220–20*A4
5	4	

Q9 Literacy hint

*A2 means 'multiply the value in the cell A2'.

a Work out the values in cells B2, B3 and B4.
b How much does he spend each week?
c What formula should Barry enter into cell B5?
d Write an expression to show how much money he will have left after n weeks.

Investigation   Reasoning

1 Write the first five terms of the sequence with nth term
 a $2n$
 b $3n + 4$
2 Make a new sequence by adding the two sequences in part **1**.
3 Write the nth term of the new sequence.
4 Write two more sequences using your own nth terms. Repeat parts **1–3**.
5 Write a rule to find the nth term for the sum of two sequences.

---

10 **Explore** What rules generate a sequence where all the terms are identical?
Choose some sensible numbers to help you explore this situation.
Then use what you've learned in this lesson to help you answer the question.

11 **Reflect** Stacey says, 'Sequences are just about substituting into expressions.'
Do you agree or disagree? Explain.

2.3 Finding the nth term

You will learn to:
- Work out the nth term of a linear sequence.

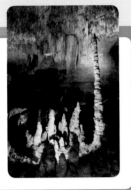

Why learn this?
If you measure the height of a stalagmite in 2015 and 2016 you can estimate its height 100 years later.

Fluency
What is the term-to-term rule of each sequence?
- 4, 7, 10, 13, ...
- 50, 45, 40, 35, ...
- −3, −4, −5, −6, ...
- 2, 2.1, 2.2, 2.3, ...

Explore
The 4th term of a sequence is 25.
What could be the nth term?

Exercise 2.3

1 Find the nth term of each sequence. Use your answer to find the 10th term.
  a 4, 8, 12, 16, ...   **b** 100, 200, 300, 400, ...
  c −3, −6, −9, −12, ...   **d** 0.1, 0.2, 0.3, 0.4, ...

Q1 hint
nth term is $\square n$

2 Find the nth term of each sequence. Use your answer to find the 10th term.
  a 4, 5, 6, 7, ...   **b** 100, 101, 102, 103, ...   **c** −5, −4, −3, −2, ...

Q2a hint
nth term is $n + \square$

Worked example
Work out the nth term of this sequence.
7, 9, 11, 13 ...

7   9   11   13
  +2 +2 +2

First work out the common difference.

Position, n	1	2	3	4
$2n$	2	4	6	8
$2n + 5$	7	9	11	13

+5 +5 +5 +5

The common difference is 2, so compare it to the multiples of 2. (The nth term for multiples of 2 is $2n$.)

Add 5 to get the sequence.

The nth term is $2n + 5$

3 Find the nth term of each sequence. The first one has been started for you.
  a 11, 16, 21, 26, ...

11   16   21   26
  +□ +□ +□

Position, n	1	2	3	4
$\square n$	□	□	□	□
$\square n + \square$	11	16	21	26

+□ +□ +□ +□

  b 7, 11, 15, 19, ...   **c** 1, 4, 7, 10, ...   **d** 20, 18, 16, 14 ...
  e 7, 6, 5, 4 ...   **f** 100, 90, 80, 70 ...   **g** −4, −2, 0, 2, ...

Warm up

4 Pasha pours 2.5 litres of sparkling water into a jug.
She then pours 500ml cartons of juice into the jug, one at a time.
   a Write a sequence to show how the volume of drink increases.
   b Work out the nth term of the sequence.
   c Work out the volume of drink after Pasha added 7 cartons of juice.

5 Modelling / STEM
The table shows the length of a piece of rope after weights are attached to it.

Mass (kg)	Length (cm)
1	13
2	16
3	19
4	22

   a Work out the length of the rope when n kg is attached.
   b Do you think your answer to part **a** is a good model? Explain.

6 Match each sequence to its nth term.

A 8, 12, 16, 20, ...	**i** $2n + 2$
B 0, 4, 8, 12, ...	**ii** $-n + 5$
C 4, 6, 8, 10, ...	**iii** $4n + 4$
D 4, 3, 2, 1, ...	**iv** $3n + 5$
E 8, 11, 14, 17, ...	**v** $-2n + 4$
F 2, 0, −2, −4, ...	**vi** $4n - 4$

7 For each sequence, work out
   i the nth term for the number of lines
   ii the number of lines in the 20th pattern.

   a

   b

8 **Explore** The 4th term of a sequence is 25. What could be the nth term?
Look back at the maths you have learned in this lesson.
How can you use it to answer the question?

9 **Reflect** In this lesson, Q5 is tagged as 'Modelling'. Which part do you think makes it a Modelling question? Explain why modelling is a useful skill to develop in answering this type of question.

Q4a hint

Start your sequence with 2.5 litres.
2.5, 2.5 + ☐, ...

Q4c hint

How many times has juice been poured into the bowl to empty 7 cartons?

Q5a hint

Work out the nth term of the sequence of lengths.

Topic links: Negative numbers   Subject links: Science (Q5)   *Active*Learn   Pi 3, Section 2.3

Explore

Reflect

2.4 Solving equations

You will learn to:
• Solve more complex equations.

Why learn this?
Scientists work out the amount of fuel needed to launch a rocket by solving a complex equation.

Fluency
What is the inverse of each of these operations and calculations?
• add
• subtract
• − 5
• − 10
• multiply
• divide
• ÷ 2
• × 3

Explore
Which linear sequences contain the number 101?

Exercise 2.4

1 Draw the inverse of each function machine.

a 7 → −3 → 4

7 ← ☐ ← 4

b 4 → ×2 → 8

4 ← ☐ ← 8

c ☐ ☐ → +5 → 7, 10

d ☐ ☐ → ÷3 → 2, 10

2 Draw a function machine for each equation and use it to solve the equation.

a $x + 7 = 12$

b $4y = 20$

c $m - 3 = 7$

d $10t = 60$

Q2a hint

x → +7 → 12

☐ ← ☐ ← 12

3 Work out the nth term for each sequence.

a 4, 6, 8, 10, ...

b 0, 5, 10, 15, ...

c 15, 14, 13, 12, ...

4 Work out the missing output for each function machine.

a 4 → ×2 → +3 → ☐

b 5 → ×3 → +12 → ☐

c 10 → ×10 → −50 → ☐

d 3 → ×6 → +11 → ☐

Warm up

5 Draw the inverse of each function machine to find the missing input.

a Input

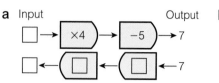

Output

$\square \rightarrow \boxed{\times 4} \rightarrow \boxed{-5} \rightarrow 7$

$\square \leftarrow \boxed{} \leftarrow \boxed{} \leftarrow 7$

b Input

Output

$\square \rightarrow \boxed{\times 2} \rightarrow \boxed{+10} \rightarrow 22$

$\square \leftarrow \boxed{} \leftarrow \boxed{} \leftarrow 22$

Q5a hint

The inverse of −5 is $\square$
The inverse of ×4 is $\square$

c Input

Output

$\square \rightarrow \boxed{\times 6} \rightarrow \boxed{-4} \rightarrow 20$

d Input

Output

$\square \rightarrow \boxed{\times 20} \rightarrow \boxed{+30} \rightarrow 90$

6 Solve these equations.
- **a** $5x + 10 = 25$
- **b** $2y + 4 = 16$
- **c** $3m - 4 = 11$
- **d** $4n - 1 = 23$
- **e** $10c + 10 = 40$
- **f** $8s - 20 = 44$

Q6a hint

$x \rightarrow \boxed{\times 5} \rightarrow \boxed{+10} \rightarrow 25$

$\square \leftarrow \boxed{} \leftarrow \boxed{} \leftarrow 25$

7 Check each of your solutions to Q6 by substituting your answer back into the equation.

Worked example

The nth term of a sequence is $4n + 5$.
a What position is the term 33?
b Mike says, '44 is a term of this sequence.' Is he correct? Explain.

a $4n + 5 = 33$

$n \rightarrow \boxed{\times 4} \rightarrow \boxed{+5} \rightarrow 33$

$7 \leftarrow \boxed{\div 4} \leftarrow \boxed{-5} \leftarrow 33$

> Solve the equation to find n, the position number.

$n = 7$

The 7th term = $4 \times 7 + 5 = 28 + 5 = 33$ ✓

> Check your answer by substituting $n = 7$ into $4n + 5$.

b $4n + 5 = 44$

$n \rightarrow \boxed{\times 4} \rightarrow \boxed{+5} \rightarrow 44$

$9.75 \leftarrow \boxed{\div 4} \leftarrow \boxed{-5} \leftarrow 44$

> Solve the equation $4n + 5 = 44$

9.75 is not an integer, so 44 cannot be a term of the sequence.

> Position numbers are always **integers**.

Literacy hint

An **integer** is a whole number.
It can be positive, negative or 0.

8 Reasoning For each sequence, decide if 42 is one of its terms. State its position in the sequence if it is.
- **a** $2n + 12$
- **b** $5n - 3$
- **c** $4n + 4$
- **d** $10n + 2$
- **e** $6n - 1$
- **f** $9n + 8$

9 Problem-solving Is the number inside the brackets a term of the linear sequence?
Explain your answer.
a 5, 8, 11, ...   (32)
b 10, 17, 24, ...   (77)
c 2, 6, 10, ...   (48)
d −23, −20, −17, ...   (10)

Q9 Strategy hint
Work out the nth term. Then solve an equation.

10 Problem-solving / Finance The balance of Olivia's savings account for each of the last three months was £130, £145 and £160.
At this rate, how long will it take for her savings to reach £400?

Q10 Strategy hint
Find the nth term of the sequence 130, 145, 160, ...

Investigation   Problem-solving

1 The nth term of a sequence is $2n + a$, where a is an integer.
One of its terms is 20.
  a Choose a value for a.
  b What position is the term 20 with your choice of a?
  c How can you make the term 20 appear earlier in the sequence?
2 The nth term of a sequence is $an + 4$, where a is an integer.
One of its terms is 20.
  a Choose a value for a.
  b What position is the term 20 with your choice of a?
  c How can you make the term 20 appear earlier in the sequence?
3 The nth term of a sequence is $an + b$, where a and b are integers.
One of its terms is 20.
  a Choose a value for a.
  b What position is the term 20 with your choice of a?
  c How can you make the term 20 appear earlier in the sequence?

11 **Explore** Which linear sequences contain the number 101?
Choose some sensible numbers to help you explore this situation.
Then use what you've learned in this lesson to help you answer the question.

12 **Reflect** In this lesson you created and solved equations. In your own words, explain the difference between an expression and an equation.

Q12 hint
Look back at lesson 2.1 if you need a reminder about expressions.

Explore

Reflect

Master
P28

CHECK

Strengthen
P41

Extend
P45

Test
P49

2 Check up

Log how you did on your
Student Progression Chart.

Algebraic expressions

1 Write an algebraic expression for each length.

a Rebecca cuts a piece of wool w cm long into 3 equal pieces.
What is the length of each piece?

b Alex ties a piece of string s cm long to a 20 cm piece of string.
What is the total length of the string?

2 A box contains 3 strips of plasters.
Each strip is made of n plasters.

a Margaret takes 5 plasters from a full box. Write an expression for
the number of plasters left in the box.

b Margaret buys 2 more boxes of plasters.

i Write an expression for the total number of plasters she has now.

ii Work out the number of plasters she has when $n = 8$.

3 Simplify

a $4d \times 5d$

b $5t + u - 4a - 2u - 6t + 5a$

4 The diagram shows two rectangles.

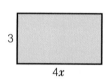

a Write an expression for the total area of the two rectangles.

b Work out the total area when $x = 4$ and $y = 5$.

Sequences

5 The nth term of a sequence is $5n - 22$.

a Work out

i the first five terms

ii the largest negative term.

b Is the sequence ascending or descending?

6 The nth term of a sequence is $-4n + 10$.

a Copy and complete the table of values.

Position (n)	1	2	3	4	5
Term ($-4n + 10$)					

b Work out the 15th term.

7 a Draw the next two patterns in this sequence.

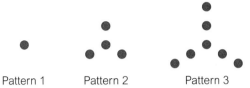

Pattern 1   Pattern 2   Pattern 3

b Copy and complete the table to show the number of dots in each pattern.

Pattern number (n)	1	2	3	4	5
Number of dots	1	4	7		

c What is the 12th term of the sequence?

d What is the nth term of the sequence?

8 a Work out the nth term of each sequence.

   i 7, 10, 13, 16, …

   ii 2, 1, 0, −1, …

b Work out the 20th term of each sequence.

Equations

9 Solve $5x - 10 = 20$.

10 The nth term of a sequence is $5n - 12$.
Decide if each number is a term of the sequence. Show how you made your decision.

a 33

b 15

11 Is 47 a term of the sequence 3, 7, 11, 15, …?
Explain.

12 How sure are you of your answers? Were you mostly

😟 **Just guessing**   😐 **Feeling doubtful**   🙂 **Confident**

What next? Use your results to decide whether to strengthen or extend your learning.

Challenge

13 The patterns in this sequence are made from squares.

Pattern 1   Pattern 2   Pattern 3

> **Q13 hint**
>
> Don't forget that a square is also a special kind of rectangle.

a Draw the fourth pattern in the sequence.

b Count the number of rectangles you can see in each pattern.

c Copy and complete the table.

Pattern number (n)	1	2	3	4
Rectangles				

d Continue the sequence to find the number of rectangles in pattern 6. Check your answer by drawing the pattern.

e How will your answers change if you only count rectangles that are not squares?

Master
P28

Check
P39

STRENGTHEN

Extend
P45

Test
P49

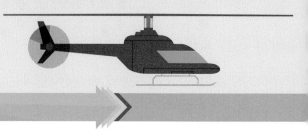

2 Strengthen

You will:

• Strengthen your understanding with practice.

Algebraic expressions

1 Write an algebraic expression for each length.

a A plank of wood is x metres long. Andy cuts off y metres.
How much is left?

b Elspeth has a rod of length r cm.
  i She cuts it into 3 equal pieces.
  How long is each piece?
  ii Shaif also has a rod of length r cm.
  He cuts it into n equal pieces.
  How long is each piece?

c A brick has length b cm.
  i Simon makes a row of 6 bricks. How long is the row?
  ii He cuts 3 cm off another brick and adds it to the end of the row.
  How long is the row now?

d 2 sections of a rail are each a metres long.
3 other sections are each b metres long.
Lopa joins the sections together.
What is the total length?

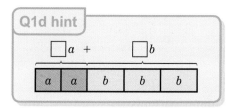
Q1a hint

2 Simplify each expression.
  a $5a \times 2b$
  b $4f \times 5g$
  c $2p \times 8p$
  d $3c \times 5c$
  e $4g + 2h + 3i - 2g - 3h - i$
  f $2a + 3b - 4c - a + 5b + 7c$
  g $-4m + 2n - p - 2m + n - m$

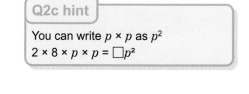
Q1d hint

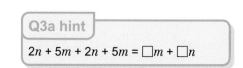
Q2c hint
You can write $p \times p$ as p^2
$2 \times 8 \times p \times p = \square p^2$

3 Write an expression for the perimeter of each rectangle.
Simplify your expression.

a
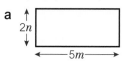
2n
5m

b
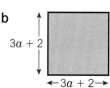
3a + 2
3a + 2

Q3a hint
$2n + 5m + 2n + 5m = \square m + \square n$

c
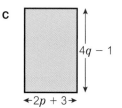
4q − 1
2p + 3

d
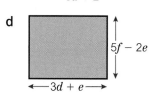
5f − 2e
3d + e

4 a Write an expression for the final number of biscuits in each case.

   i Martha bakes 1 tin of n biscuits. She adds them to her first batch of 10 biscuits.

   ii Richard bakes 3 tins of n biscuits. He eats 5 of them.

   iii Ismat has 8 biscuits. She then bakes $\frac{1}{2}$ a tin of n biscuits.

   iv Brendan has 60 biscuits. He gives away 2 tins of n biscuits.

b Work out the number of biscuits each person has when $n = 20$.

Sequences

1 a Copy and complete the tables to show the first five terms of each sequence. The first is partly done for you.

   i $6n - 2$

Position number (n)	1	2	3	4	5
$6n$	6				
-2	-2	-2			
Term	4				

$\leftarrow$ Work out $6 \times n$ for each value of n.

$\leftarrow$ Subtract 2.

$\leftarrow$ Add the numbers in the middle two rows to find each term.

   ii $4n - 10$

Position number (n)	1	2	3	4	5
$4n$					
-10					
Term					

b Work out the 10th term of each sequence.

2 a Copy and complete the table to show the first five terms of the sequence $-3n + 12$.

Position number (n)	1	2	3	4	5
$-3n$	-3				
$+12$	$+12$	$+12$			
Term	9				

> **Q2a hint**
>
> Work out $-3 \times n$ for each value of n.
> Then add 12.
> Then add the numbers in the middle two rows to find each term

b Work out the 10th term of the sequence.

3 Copy and complete this method to work out the nth term of the sequence 6, 11, 16, 21, …

   a Sequence   6   11   16   21

    Differences $+\square$ $+\square$ $+\square$

   The sequence goes up in $\square$.

   b The $\square$ times table is: $\square$, $\square$, $\square$, $\square$, … $\square n$.

   c Each term in the sequence is $\square$ more than $\square n$.

   d The nth term is $\square n + \square$

> **Q3d hint**
>
> Substitute $n = 1$ into your nth term.
> Do you get 6 (the first term)?

4 a Draw the next two patterns in this sequence.

   b Copy and complete the table to show the number of squares in each pattern.

Position number (n)	1	2	3	4	5
Number of squares	5	9			

   c What is the term-to-term rule?

   d Use your term-to-term rule to work out the nth term.

5 Work out the nth term of each sequence.

a 7, 10, 13, 16, ...

b 10, 14, 18, 22, ...

c 2, 7, 12, 17, ...

d 5, 15, 25, 35, ...

e 1, 7, 13, 19, ...

f 10, 8, 6, 4, ...

g 25, 20, 15, 10, ...

h −5, −7, −9, −11, ...

i 2.5, 3, 3.5, 4, ...

Q5f hint

The sequence is descending, so the common difference is −☐
The nth term is −☐n + ☐

Equations

1 Work out n using these function machines.

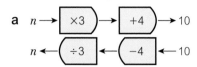

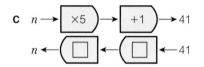

2 Use the function machines to help solve these equations. Check your solutions.

a $3n - 2 = 19$

b $2n + 7 = 23$

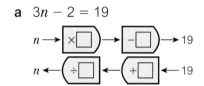

c $10n - 8 = 32$

d $4n + 9 = 41$

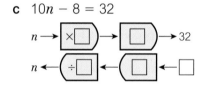

3 Solve each equation.

a $2n + 5 = 27$

b $6n - 5 = 43$

$$n \rightarrow \boxed{\times 2} \rightarrow \boxed{+5} \rightarrow 27 \qquad n \rightarrow \boxed{\times \square} \rightarrow \boxed{-\square} \rightarrow 43$$

c $5n - 8 = 27$

d $3n + 8 = 35$

4 The nth term of a sequence is $2n + 9$.
Work out the position number n for each of these terms.

a 25

b 31

c 55

Q4a hint

Solve the equation $2n + 9 = 25$

5 Reasoning The nth term of a sequence is $5n - 1$.

a Copy and complete the table for the first five terms.

Position (n)	1	2	3	4	5
Term ($5n - 1$)					

b Look at the numbers in the sequence. Explain why 16 cannot be a term of the sequence.

c i Solve the equation $5n - 1 = 16$.

ii How does your answer show that 16 is not a term of the sequence?

Q5c ii hint

Position numbers n are whole numbers.

Topic links: Negative numbers, Perimeter

Enrichment

1 Oprah sticks one square mosaic tile at a time on to a box lid.

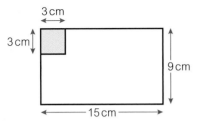

  a Work out the area of the box lid.

  b Work out the area of a tile.

  c Work out the uncovered area of the box lid in the diagram.

  d Oprah sticks n mosaic tiles to the box lid. Write an expression for the uncovered area.

2 Problem-solving Complete this function machine in as many ways as possible.

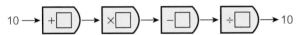

3 **Reflect** Some of the hints in the 'Algebraic expressions' section used bar models. Did these help you work out the answers?
Explain how they helped you, or if you used a different method, explain how that worked instead.

2 Extend

You will:
- Extend your understanding with problem-solving.

1 Write an algebraic expression for each mass.
  a Carrie divides D grams of dough into 10 equal balls.
    What is the mass of each ball?
  b Tom melts 20 kg of lead into n equal blocks.
    What is the mass of each block?
  c Sue forms B grams of butter into n equal packs.
    What is the mass of each pack?
  d A bag of sugar has a mass of 2 kg. David uses n bags to fill m bowls equally.
    How much sugar is in each bowl?

2 Solve these equations.
  a $2x + 7 = 1$ **b** $5m - 20 = -5$ **c** $-3t + 2 = 17$
  d $-2n + 5 = 11$ **e** $-3d + 7 = 1$ **f** $-10e - 30 = 10$

Q2c hint

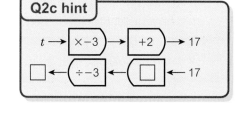

3 a These shapes are made by cutting rectangles from a larger rectangle. All lengths are in centimetres.
    Write an expression for the area of each shaded shape.

i 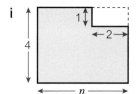   **ii** 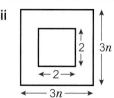   **iii**

iv 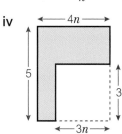   **v** 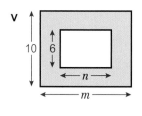   **vi**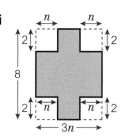

  b Work out the shaded area of each shape when $n = 2$ and $m = 5$.

4 Copy and complete the tables to work out the first five terms of each sequence.
  a nth term $= \dfrac{n}{2} + 1$

Position (n)	1	2	3	4	5
Term $\left(\dfrac{n}{2} + 1\right)$	$\frac{1}{2} + 1 = 1.5$				

  b nth term $= 1 - \dfrac{n}{10}$

Position (n)	1	2	3	4	5
Term $\left(1 - \dfrac{n}{10}\right)$	$1 - \frac{1}{10} = \square$				

45

5 The graphs show the terms of two sequences.

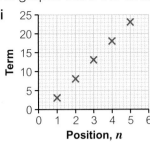
i

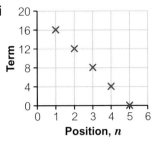
ii

   a Work out the nth term of each sequence.

   b Work out the 20th term of each sequence.

Q5 Strategy hint

Make a table of values.

6 Work out the nth term and 20th term of each sequence.

   a 3, 1, −1, −3, ...   b −15, −20, −25, −30, ...

   c −7, −4, −1, 2, ...   d 0.5, 0, −0.5, −1, ...

7 **Problem-solving** Here are some **arithmetic** sequences.

   a 1, □, □, 10, 13, ...   b 2, □, □, 14, ...

   c 12, □, 8, 6, ...   d □, 5, □, 9, ...

   For each sequence, work out

    i the missing terms

    ii the nth term

   iii the 20th term.

Q7 Literacy hint

An **arithmetic** sequence has a constant difference between terms.

8 **Problem-solving** For each part, make an equation and solve it.

   a Marion thinks of a number n. She doubles it and adds 12. Her answer is 28. What was the number, n, she first thought of?

   b Ollie hired a cement mixer for n hours at £4 per hour plus a fixed charge of £15. His total bill was £43. How long did he hire the cement mixer for?

   c Naeem's bucket holds 5 litres of water. She used n bucketfuls of water to fill a paddling pool. After 10 litres of water leaked out, the pool contained 80 litres. How many bucketfuls did Naeem need to fill the pond?

Q8a hint

Write the information using algebra. Write $n \times 2$ as $2n$.

9 Matthew solves equations using inverse operations like this.

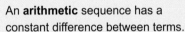

$$3y + 5 = 17$$
$$(-5) \qquad (-5)$$
$$3y = 12$$
$$(\div 3) \qquad (\div 3)$$
$$y = 4$$

   Use Matthew's method to solve

   a $2m + 5 = 21$ b $4u + 3 = 27$

   c $5n − 2 = 23$ d $3w − 4 = 26$

   e $2y + 9 = 5$ f $−4t + 1 = −7$

10 **Reasoning**

   a Make x the subject of each formula.

    i $3x + 2r = 2x + r$

    ii $5x + 3c = 9c − 4x$

   iii $x^2 = r$

   b Solve these equations.

    i $3x + 4 = 2x + 2$

    ii $5x + 9 = 27 − 4x$

   iii $x^2 = 25$

   c Mariana says, 'Solving equations is a bit like changing the subject of a formula.' Do you agree? Explain.

Q10a Literacy hint

The subject of a formula is the variable on its own on one side of the equals sign.

11 Solve each equation.

 a $6x + 1 = 4x + 13$
 b $5m + 3 = 4m + 5$
 c $3y - 2 = y + 8$
 d $10t - 3 = 7t + 9$
 e $4p + 9 = 2p + 1$
 f $x^2 = 100$
 g $x^2 - 5 = 31$

12 Solve each equation.

 a $\dfrac{g + 5}{4} = 2$

 b $\dfrac{h - 1}{10} = 6$

 c $\dfrac{2d + 3}{4} = 1$

 d $\dfrac{6t - 9}{5} = 3$

Q12 hint

$\dfrac{g + 5}{4} = 2$ means $(g + 5) \div 4 = 2$.
Rearrange to get g on its own on one side.

13 **Problem-solving a** Work out the nth term for each arithmetic sequence.

 i 1, 4, 7, ...
 ii 9, 11, 13, ...
 b Find the position number n for which the terms in each sequence are equal.

Q13b Strategy hint

When the terms are equal, the nth term for the first sequence equals the nth term for the second sequence. Put the terms equal to each other and solve the equation.

14 a Copy and complete this table.

n	1	2			7			11	12
$2n$				8			20		
n^2			9			64			

 b Use your table to solve the equation $n^2 = 2n$.
 Discussion There is another value for which $n^2 = 2n$. What is it?

15 a Write the first five terms of the sequence of square numbers.
 b Write the nth term of the sequence.

16 Work out the first five terms of each sequence.
 a nth term $= n^2 + 5$

Position (n)	1	2	3	4	5
Term ($n^2 + 5$)	$1^2 + 5 = 1 + 5 = 6$				

 b nth term $= n^2 - n$

Position (n)	1	2	3	4	5
Term ($n^2 - n$)			$3^2 - 3 = 9 - 3 = 6$		

 c nth term $= n^2 + 2n$

Position (n)	1	2	3	4	5
Term ($n^2 + 2n$)					

 d nth term $= 2n^2 + 1$

Position (n)	1	2	3	4	5
Term ($2n^2 + 1$)				$2 \times 4^2 + 1 = 2 \times 16 + 1 = 33$	

Topic links: Area, Graphs

17 Problem-solving / Reasoning Is 210 a term in the sequence with nth term $2n^2 + 1$? Explain.

18 Simplify each expression by collecting like terms.
- **a** $3n^2 + 2n^2$
- **b** $4p^2 - 2p^2$
- **c** $m^2 + m^2 + m^2$
- **d** $2e^2 + e^2 + 5e^2$
- **e** $5r^2 - r^2$
- **f** $-3a^2 + 7a^2$
- **g** $4k^2 - 10k^2 - 3k^2$
- **h** $-w^2 - 2w^2$

> **Q18a hint**
>
> How many lots of n^2 are there altogether?
> $3n^2 + 2n^2 = \square n^2$

19 Find the missing outputs of this function machine.

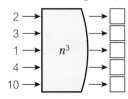

> **Q19 hint**
>
> n^3 means $n \times n \times n$

20 Reflect Wai Yee says, 'Maths is just solving puzzles.'
Kuldip says, 'Maths is all about organising data.'
Which of these statements do you agree with: both, one of them, or neither?
If neither, make a statement to describe what you think maths is about.

Reflect

Master
P28

Check
P39

Strengthen
P41

Extend
P45

TEST

2 Unit test

Log how you did on your
Student Progression Chart.

1 Draw the inverse of this function machine to work out n.

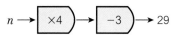

$n \rightarrow \boxed{\times 4} \rightarrow \boxed{-3} \rightarrow 29$

2 Solve
  a $4x + 5 = 33$
  b $-3m + 2 = 14$

3 Work out the first five terms of each sequence.
  a $4n + 7$
  b $3n + 0.5$
  c $6n - 8$
  d $2n - 9$

4 The nth term of a sequence is $-3n + 4$.
  a Is the sequence ascending or descending?
  b Work out the 12th term.

5 The nth term of a sequence is $6n + 2$.
  a Write the first five terms of the sequence.
  b Is 52 a term of the sequence? Explain.

6 Work out the nth term of each sequence.
  a 7, 12, 17, 22, …
  b 0, −2, −4, −6, …

7 a Draw the next two patterns in this sequence.

Pattern 1   Pattern 2   Pattern 3

  b Copy and complete the table to show the number of dots in each
     pattern.

Pattern number (n)	1	2	3	4	5
Number of dots					

  c Work out the nth term.
  d Work out the number of dots in the 10th pattern.

8 Simplify each expression.
  a $2t \times 10t$
  b $m - n + 2p - n + 3 + 7m - 4p$

9 A shop sells first class stamps in books of n stamps.
It sells second class stamps in sheets of m stamps.
Poppy bought 4 books of first class stamps and $\frac{1}{2}$ a sheet of second
class stamps.
  a Write an expression for the total number of stamps she bought.
  b Work out the total number of stamps she bought when $n = 12$ and
  $m = 60$.

10 Paul thinks of a number n. He multiplies it by 4 and subtracts 7.
  a Write an expression for his calculation.
  b Paul says that his answer is 29.
    i Write an equation involving n.
    ii Solve your equation to find the number Paul first thought of.

11 Solve
  a $5m - 4 = 2m + 17$
  b $n^2 + 3 = 67$

12 The nth term of a sequence is $n^2 + n$.
Copy and complete the table.

Position (n)	1	2	3	4	5
Term ($n^2 + n$)					

13 Simplify $4x^2 - x^2$.

14 The nth term of a sequence is n^3.
Work out the 3rd term.

Challenge

15 a Make up four different sequences, each with 4th term 10. Try to
    include a decreasing sequence.
  b Write the nth term next to each sequence.
  c How many different sequences with 4th term 10 can you make?
  d What type of sequences have you used?

16 Reflect In this unit you have studied equations, sequences and
expressions. Which topic did you find easiest and which did you
find hardest? For the one you found hardest, make up some hints or
practice questions to help you.

3.1 Planning a survey

You will learn to:
- Plan and collect data.

Why learn this?
Local councils collect data to plan what services they will offer.

Fluency
Work out
- 10% of 50
- 10% of 120
- 10% of 500
- 10% of 1000

Explore
How can you make sure your data is accurate when you do a survey?

CONFIDENCE

Exercise 3.1

1 What unit would you use to measure
  a the height of a giraffe
  b the width of a fingernail
  c the length of a river
  d the mass of a shopping bag?

2 Michelle wants to test whether a dice is **biased**.
Should she roll it 5, 30 or 100 times?

Q2 Literacy hint

Biased means it is more likely to land on one number than another.

3 Alpita wants to find out if young people use the swimming pool at her local sports centre more than adults.
Which of these pieces of information should she collect?
A Gender
B Age
C Distance of travel to sports centre
D Activity chosen at the sports centre
E Length of time spent in the sports centre

Key point

Primary data is data you collect yourself.
Secondary data is collected by someone else.

4 A journalist wants to find out information about the number of people in each household in the UK.
Decide whether each method will produce **primary** or **secondary** data.
  a She carries out a survey of the number of people in her town.
  b She looks at the most recent **census** results.

Q4b Literacy hint

In a **census**, data is collected from the whole population. The UK Government carries out a census every 10 years.

5 Reasoning Match each investigation to the best way to obtain relevant data.
  i the age of students in your class   **A** experiment
  ii who uses the local supermarket   **B** survey
  iii the number of times an even number is rolled on a dice   **C** questionnaire

Warm up

6 **Real** Choose the most suitable unit for investigating
   a the lengths of leaves from a tree
   b the lengths of different classrooms
   c the distances between your school and other schools
   d the heights of buildings in your town.

mm	
cm	metre
	kilometre

7 **Reasoning** For each survey select the most appropriate **sample** size. Explain your choices.
   a There are 1000 students in a school. Peter wants to find out students' favourite drinks. How many students should he ask?
   A 4   **B** 100   **C** 500
   b A café gets 700 customers each week. The owner thinks most customers order food to take away. How many customers should she sample?
   A 7   **B** 70   **C** 350

Key point

The total number of items your survey relates to is called the population.
Sometimes you can't test every single item in a set of data, so you collect a **sample**.
A good-sized sample is usually about 10% of the population.
For a sample to be suitable it needs to be unbiased.

8 **Reasoning** Callum wants to find out the favourite TV programme of people in his school. He asks his friends what their favourite TV show is. Explain why Callum's results will be biased.

9 **Reasoning** A school wants to find out how long students take to travel to school. There are 500 students in the school.
   Which of these sampling methods will give an unbiased sample?
   A Standing at the gates of the school to collect the data
   B Standing by a bus stop to collect the data
   C Asking only boys in the school
   D Asking only students who arrive at school early
   E Asking only students who arrive at school late

Key point

If a sample is **random**, everyone in the group has the same chance of being chosen.

10 **Reasoning** Four people carry out a survey to find out the favourite food of people in their town.
   • Sophie interviews 100 students chosen at **random** in her school.
   • Paul asks everyone coming out of an Italian restaurant.
   • Jamie asks his friends, family and neighbours.
   • Pamela stands in the centre of a town on Saturday and asks 500 people that she chooses at random.
   a Whose survey will give the most reliable results? Explain your answer.
   b For each method, is the data primary or secondary data?

11 **Explore** How can you make sure your data is accurate when you do a survey?
   Look back at the maths you have learnt in this lesson. How can you use it to answer this question?

12 **Reflect** Make a list of all the new terms you have met in this lesson. In your own words, write a sentence using each of these terms that shows its meaning. For example, you could write, 'For her primary data, Alice counted all the daisy plants in 1 square metre of the school field.'

3.2 Statistics from tables

You will learn to:
- Interpret frequency tables
- Find the range and mean from a frequency table.

Why learn this?
We use weather averages when going on holiday so we can plan the clothes we will take.

Fluency
Calculate
- 12 × 3
- 24 × 5
- 384 ÷ 12
- 558 ÷ 9

Explore
Choose a holiday destination and a time of year. What should you pack?

Exercise 3.2

1 Look at this set of data.

1   7   3   3   9   5   6   1   1

a Order the numbers from smallest to largest.

b What is the **median**?

c What is the **mode**?

d What is the **range**?

e Work out the **mean**.

> **Q1 hint**
>
> The **median** is the middle data item when the data is written in order.
> The **range** is the difference between the smallest and largest values.
> The **mode** is the most common value. It is also called the modal value.
>
> **Mean** = $\dfrac{\text{sum of values}}{\text{total number of values}}$

2 The table shows the number of spectators at a school's netball matches.

Number of spectators	Frequency
0–9	5
10–19	8
20–29	10
30–39	2

a How many netball matches were played?

b What is the modal **class**?

> **Q2 Literacy hint**
>
> Data is sometimes organised into **classes** or class intervals.

3 The table shows the shoe size of Year 9 girls.

a What is the modal shoe size?

b What is the range of shoe sizes?

Shoe size	Number of girls
4	4
5	5
6	7
7	5
8	3

> **Q3b hint**
>
> What is the largest shoe size in the table? What is the smallest?

Worked example

In a game a 4-sided spinner is spun 20 times.
The frequency table shows the results.
Work out the mean score.

Score	Frequency	Total score
1	4	1 × 4 = 4
2	3	2 × 3 = 6
3	8	3 × 8 = 24
4	5	4 × 5 = 20
Total	20	54

Draw a third column to work out the total score for the whole game.
Work out score × frequency for each row.

Mean = 54 ÷ 20 = 2.7

Divide the total score by the number of times the spinner was spun.

4 The table shows the numbers of siblings of students in a Year 9 class.
   a How many students are there in the class?
   b How many siblings were counted altogether?
   c Work out the mean number of siblings.

Siblings	Frequency
0	2
1	3
2	4
3	1
4	3

5 This frequency table shows the number of novelty erasers children in a Year 6 class had in their pencil cases. Work out the mean number of novelty erasers.

Number of erasers	Frequency
0	2
1	3
2	7
3	5
4	1

Investigation
Reasoning / Problem-solving

The table shows the number of goals a hockey team scored in one season.

1 What is the mode?
2 What is the range?
3 Work out the mean number of goals per match.
4 Work out the median number of goals.
5 The hockey team said that their average number of goals was 3. Is this correct? Explain your answer.
6 Use the averages and the range to write a sentence commenting on the team's performance.

Number of goals scored	Frequency
0	2
1	1
2	5
3	10
4	2

Part 4 hint

In order, write out the number of goals scored for each match. What is the middle value?

6 **Explore** Choose a holiday destination and a time of year.
   What should you pack?
   How can you use the maths you have learned in this lesson to explore this?

7 **Reflect** In this lesson, the investigation asked you to use your reasoning skills. This meant that you had to find an answer and also explain it. How do you feel about questions that ask you to explain – do they help you to understand the maths you have used? If so, how?

3.3 Comparing data

You will learn to:

* Use median, mean and range to compare sets of data.

CONFIDENCE

Why learn this?
Averages are used in sports to analyse performance.

Fluency
* For which of these sets of data can you not find the range?
* Which set of data does not have a mode?
A Scores in a test:
  2, 4, 12, 6, 10, 5, 9, 10, 7
B Favourite colour: brown, red, white, red, yellow, red, pink, orange

Explore
What averages are used in car racing?

Exercise 3.3

Warm up

1 For each set of data, work out
   i the median   **ii** the mode   **iii** the mean   **iv** the range.
  a 31   25   25   36   58
  b 4   8   2   5   8   9

2 **Reasoning** Here are the scores of two different teams in 7 rounds of a quiz.
  Team A   12   20   24   25   25   25   26
  Team B   23   24   24   25   25   27   27
  a Work out the median score for each team.
  b Work out the range of scores for each team.
  c Write two sentences to compare the median and the range.
  Discussion Which team do you think did better? Explain.

3 Here are the scores that Nathaniel and Caitlin achieved when playing a computer game.
  Nathaniel   20   15   8   14   13
  Caitlin   16   16   17   16   15
  a Work out the mean score for each player.
  b Work out the range of scores for each player.
  c Write two sentences to compare the mean and the range.

4 **Reasoning** The table shows the median and the range of the numbers of goals scored by two netball teams in a tournament. Copy and complete these sentences comparing the two teams.

	Median	Range
Team A	4	4
Team B	6	2

  Team A has a _____ median than Team B.
  Team B has a _____ range than Team A.
  This means Team B was more _____
  Discussion Is a large median or a small range better?

5 Here are the times, in seconds, of two 100 m sprinters in one season.

Sprinter A   11.1   11.2   11.6   11.6   11.7
Sprinter B   11.2   11.3   11.4   11.1   11.4

  a Calculate the range of times for each sprinter.
  b Which of the sprinters was more **consistent** in their times?
  c Which sprinter has a smaller median?

Key point

A small range shows the data items are close together. This means the data is more **consistent**.

6 **Finance / Reasoning** Here are the salaries of workers in a small company.

£5000   £8000   £10 000   £10 000   £42 000

  a Work out the range of the salaries.
  b Work out the mean, median and modal salary.
  c The boss says that the average salary is £15 000.
     Do you think this is a fair statement? Explain your answer.

Investigation   **Reasoning / Problem-solving**

1 For this set of data, work out
  a the median   **b** the mean.
       1   2   2   3   3   3   4   4   4   4   100

2 Why are the mean and the median so far apart?
3 Which average describes the data better?
  The set of data without the final value is
       1   2   2   3   3   3   4   4   4   4

4 For this set of data, work out
  a the median   **b** the mean.
5 Produce your own set of data where the value of the mean is 10 times the value of the median.
Discussion The value 100 in the first set of data is called an 'extreme value' or an 'outlier'.
When do you think it's good to include extreme values in the mean calculation?
When do you think you shouldn't include extreme values?

---

7 **Reasoning / Problem-solving** Two go-karts race around a circuit.
Here are their times in seconds.

Go-kart X   45   55   65   55   60
Go-kart Y   40   45   125   40   50

  a Calculate the mean, median and mode for go-kart X.
  b Calculate the mean, median and mode for go-kart Y.
  c One of the go-karts got a puncture on one of its circuits.
     Which go-kart do you think this was? Explain your answer.
  d How is the range affected for the go-kart with the puncture?
  e Which average best represents the data for go-kart Y? Explain.

8 **Explore** What averages are used in car racing?
Is it easier to explore this question now you have completed the lesson? What further information do you need to be able to answer this?

9 **Reflect** In the investigation, you met the term 'outlier'. How would you explain what this means to a classmate who missed this lesson? Help your explanation by giving an example.

Explore

Reflect

3.4 Tables

You will learn to:
- Use two-way tables
- Group discrete and continuous data.

Why learn this?
A café owner needs to know how popular different foods are so that they can be sure to buy in enough of each.

Fluency
Which of these numbers are in the group 20–29?
 21 19 20 14 30
Write < or > between each pair of numbers.
- 29.5 and 30
- 15.02 and 15.1

Explore
How long does it take people in your school to travel to school?

CONFIDENCE

Warm up

Exercise 3.4

1 Copy and complete this grouped frequency table, using these values.
15 17 8 9 10 2 5 3 4 7 18 20 13 14

Class	Tally	Frequency
1–5		
6–10		
11–15		
16–20		

2 Julie recorded how many songs students in her class downloaded last month.

Number of songs	Frequency
0–4	5
5–9	6
10–14	6
15–19	3

  a How many students downloaded between 10 and 14 songs?
  b How many students downloaded more than 14 songs?
  c How many students downloaded more than 9 songs?

3 This **two-way table** shows the types of drinks bought by adults and children at a café.

	Hot drinks	Cold drinks	Total
Adults	20	15	35
Children	25	12	
Total	45		

  a Work out the total number of children who bought a drink.
  b How many cold drinks were bought altogether?
  c How many drinks were bought altogether?

Key point
A **two-way table** divides data into two different types of groups.

Q3a hint
Add together the number of hot and cold drinks bought by children.

4 **Problem-solving** The table shows the favourite subjects of girls and boys in class 9R.

	Maths	English	Science	Total
Boys	7	4		15
Girls			4	15
Total	13			

a How many girls chose maths?

b Copy and complete the two-way table.

c How many girls chose English?

d How many students were there altogether?

5 The table shows the hair and eye colour of people in Suzie's family.

		Hair colour			
		Black	**Brown**	**Blond**	**Total**
	Blue		5		18
Eye colour	**Brown**	4		1	
	Total	7			30

a Copy and complete the table.

b How many people had blond hair and blue eyes?

Q5a hint

Look for a row or column that is missing only one value.

6 For these sets of data

a list the **discrete data**   b list the **continuous data**.

Length of a pencil   Time taken to run 100 m
    Mass of a car   Favourite colour
Type of vegetable   Number of students in a class
   Number of siblings
         Price of an MP3 player
Shoe sizes   Heights of students in your class

Key point

Discrete data can only take values you can count, for example shoe size, number of people in a classroom.

Continuous data is measured and could be a decimal number, for example height, length, mass, time.

7 The handicaps of 20 members of a golf club are

12	15	19	7	25	10	24	8	14	21
16	16	12	25	17	15	6	13	15	29

a Is this data discrete or continuous?

b What is the lowest value and the highest value?

c Construct a grouped frequency table with five equal class intervals.

d Which is the modal group?

Key point

Continuous data has to be grouped so that there are no gaps in the groups. For the group $10 \leqslant h < 20$, 10 is included, but 20 is not included.

8 A lumberjack can only cut down trees that satisfy the condition $5\,\text{m} \leqslant h < 10\,\text{m}$, where h is the height of a tree.
Which of these trees can he cut down?

4.5 m   5 m   6.2 m   9.6 m   10 m   10.3 m

9 A farmer recorded the mass m of lambs when they were born.

3.8	5.2	4.3	3.8	3.1	4.5	4.2
5.4	3.9	4.0	4.1	3.7	3.5	4.1

a Copy and complete the grouped frequency table.

b What is the modal class?

Mass, m (kg)	Tally	Frequency
$3.0 \leqslant m < 3.5$		
$3.5 \leqslant m < 4.0$		
$4.0 \leqslant m < 4.5$		
$4.5 \leqslant m < 5.0$		
$5.0 \leqslant m < 5.5$		

10 STEM A scientist measured the length *l* of some embryos after
8 weeks.

15.3	19.8	11.1	14.0	18.9	16.5	18.0
15.3	14.9	10.7	19.4	16.0	14.8	15.4

Length, *l* (mm)	Tally	Frequency
$10 \leqslant l < 14$		
$14 \leqslant l < \square$		
$\square \leqslant l < \square$		

a Copy and complete the table by completing all three columns.
All the classes are the same width.
b What is the modal class?

Investigation   Reasoning / Problem-solving

The data shows the times, in seconds, that some students took to type 60 words.

72.5	83.9	59.7	62.5	95.3	85.0	69.0	82.4	99.9	78.9
83.6	87.7	93.8	90.0	69.7	75.0	70.1	84.2	60.0	69.9

1 Is this data discrete or continuous?
2 For this data, create
   a a frequency table with three equal class intervals
   b a frequency table with five equal class intervals
   c a frequency table with ten equal class intervals.
3 Which frequency table do you think shows the data best? Explain.
4 Use what you learned in lesson 3.3 to compare this data with how long students in your
   class take to type 60 words.

---

11 The table shows the frequency of heights of students in a class.
   a Copy and complete the frequency diagram.
   b What is the modal class?
   c How many students were taller than 149 cm?

Height, *h* (cm)	Frequency
$120 \leqslant h < 130$	3
$130 \leqslant h < 140$	4
$140 \leqslant h < 150$	6
$150 \leqslant h < 160$	8
$160 \leqslant h < 170$	5

> **Q11 hint**
>
> For continuous data there are no
> spaces between the bars.
> The zig-zag shows where there is a
> break in the axis scale.

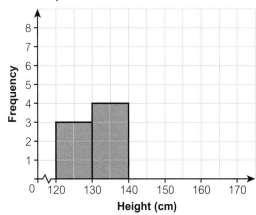

12 Explore How long does it take people in your school to travel to
school?
What have you learned in this lesson to help you answer this
question? What other information do you need?

13 Reflect Q10 described some measurements that a scientist made.
Who else might record statistics in this way?

3.5 Pie charts and scatter graphs

You will learn to:
- Construct pie charts
- Interpret and construct scatter graphs.

Why learn this?
Graphs and charts help you see patterns in data.

Fluency
How many degrees are there in a full turn?
Work out
- 360 ÷ 20
- 360 ÷ 18
- 5 × 18
- 9 × 30

Explore
How can the Government show how much it spends in different parts of the country?

Exercise 3.5

1 Use a ruler and protractor to draw these angles.

  a 60°   **b** 120°   **c** 165°

2 The pie chart shows the favourite musical instuments of some Year 9 students.

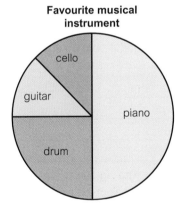

Favourite musical instrument

  a Which is the most popular instrument?
      How do you know?

  b What fraction of students prefer
     i piano
     ii drum
     iii guitar?

  c There are 24 students altogether.
      How many students preferred the guitar?

3 Draw a grid with x- and y-axes from 0 to 6. Plot these coordinates.
  a (1, 5)   **b** (5, 2)
  c (0, 3)   **d** (4, 0)

Warm up

Worked example

Draw a pie chart to show this data about the types of cars in a car park.

Type of car	Frequency
Diesel	6
Petrol	2
Hybrid electric	4

Total number of cars = 6 + 2 + 4 = 12 ———— Work out the total number of cars.

÷12 (12 cars is 360° / 1 car is 30°) ÷12 ———— The whole pie chart (360°) represents 12 cars. Work out what angle represents 1 car.

Type of car	Frequency	Angle
Diesel	6	6 × 30° = 180°
Petrol	2	2 × 30° = 60°
Hybrid electric	4	4 × 30° = 120°

Add a new column to the table with the heading 'Angle'. Multiply the number of each type of car by 30° to work out the angle for each sector.

Check: 180 + 60 + 120 = 360 ———— Check that the angles add up to 360°.

Types of cars in a car park

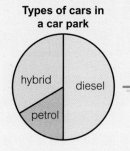

Draw a circle, and split it into each of the angles. Label each sector and give your pie chart a title.

---

4 The table shows the number of boys, girls and adults in a table tennis club.
  a Work out the total number of people in the club.
  b Copy and complete: Angle for 1 person: 360° ÷ ☐ = ☐°
  c Work out the angle for boys, girls and adults.
  d Draw a pie chart to show the data.

Members	Frequency	Angle
Boys	12	
Girls	3	
Adults	9	

5 The table shows the favourite type of films of students in class 9W.
  a Draw a pie chart to show this information.
  b What fraction of the students chose animation?

Favourite type of film	Frequency	Angle
Action	8	
Animation	6	
Comedy	6	
Drama	4	

6 The table shows the favourite sport of some students.

Favourite sport	Frequency
Hockey	10
Tennis	18
Swimming	4
Football	4

Draw a pie chart to show this information.

Subject links: Science (Q8)

7 This **scatter graph** shows the maths test marks of 10 students and the number of maths lessons they missed.

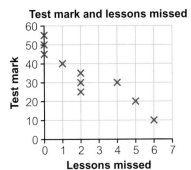

Key point

A **scatter graph** shows two sets of data on the same graph.
The shape of a scatter graph shows if there is a relationship between two sets of data.

a How many students missed 2 maths lessons?
b One student missed 5 maths lessons. What was their mark?
c 2 students scored 30 on their test. How many maths lessons did each person miss?

Discussion Describe the relationship between test mark and lessons missed.

8 **STEM / Reasoning** The table shows the size of engine and top speed of some cars.

Engine size (litres)	1.2	1.4	2	1.6	1.4	1	2	1.2	2
Top speed (km/h)	182	202	226	211	219	158	50	178	214

Key point

An **outlier** is a value that doesn't follow the trend or pattern of the rest of the data.

a Copy these axes on to graph paper and draw a scatter graph to show the information.
b Copy and complete:
   The larger the engine size, the _____ the top speed.
c One of the speeds was measured in the wrong units and is an **outlier**.
   Write down the coordinates of this point.

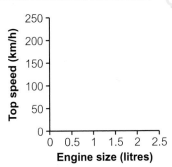

9 **Explore** How can the Government show how much it spends in different parts of the country?
   Is it easier to explore this question now you have completed the lesson?
   What further information do you need to be able to answer this?

10 **Reflect** How would you decide whether to use a pie chart or a scatter graph to show a set of data? Give examples to help your explanation.

Explore

Reflect

3.6 FINANCE: Misleading graphs

You will learn to:
- Understand what makes graphs and charts misleading.

CONFIDENCE

Why learn this?
Advertisers may use misleading graphs to try to persuade us to buy their products.

Fluency
How many of each flavour ice cream were sold?

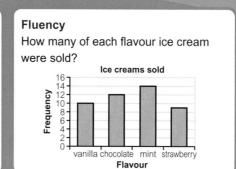

Explore
How do political parties use graphs in an election campaign?

Exercise 3.6: Misleading graphs

Warm up

1 This frequency diagram shows the scores when a dice is rolled.
   a How many times was a score of 3 rolled?
   b How many times was a score greater than 5 rolled?
   c How many times was the dice rolled altogether?

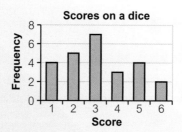

2 Use the frequency diagram to complete the table.
   Show the number of emails sent by a class in one month.

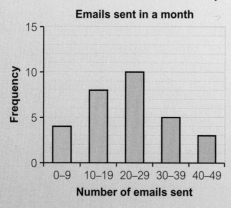

Number of emails sent	Frequency
0–9	
10–19	
20–29	
30–39	
40–49	

3 What information is missing from this frequency diagram?

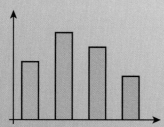

Key point

Before you read values from a graph or chart look at
- the title
- the axis labels
- the scales.

You cannot draw accurate conclusions from an inaccurate or incomplete graph.

Subject links: History (Q4)

4 Finance / Real The table and the graph show the average price of a pint of milk, in pence, from 1916 to 1991.

1916	1947	1965	1975	1979	1991
1	2	4	7	15	32

a What is unusual about the vertical scale on the graph?
b What do you think the graph would look like with a vertical scale of 0, 10, 20, …?
Draw the graph to check your prediction.
c Which graph shows the increase in price more clearly?
Discussion How does using a scale with unequal steps affect the graph?

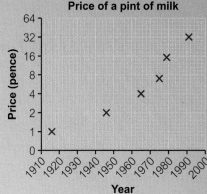

Price of a pint of milk

5 Finance These graphs show average house prices in 2005 and 2006.

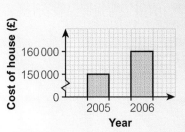 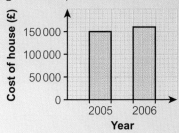

> **Key point**
> Changing the scale can make a graph look very different.

a An estate agent says, 'The average cost of a house doubled from 2005 to 2006.' Which graph has the estate agent used?
b Why is she incorrect?
c What is the actual increase in average house price?

6 Real / STEM These two graphs show the launch prices of three mobile phones since 1985.

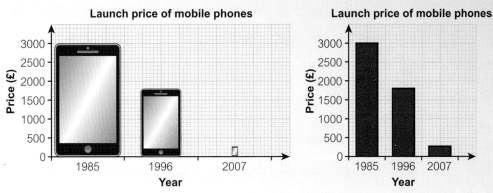

a Which graph shows the decrease in mobile phone prices more clearly?
b Which graph appears to show the bigger decrease in price?
Discussion How does the graph make the decrease look bigger?

7 Explore How do political parties use graphs in an election campaign? Is it easier to explore this question now you have completed the lesson? What further information do you need to be able to answer this?

8 Reflect Marcus says, 'If a graph or chart is showing data that's correct, it can't be misleading.' Do you agree with Marcus? Explain.

3.7 Writing a report

You will learn to:
- Write a report to show survey results.

Why learn this?
Data is used to find out about the population. The data is then used to produce a report, for example a council report showing how people recycle waste.

Fluency
Find the mean, median, mode and range of this set of data.
2, 4, 6, 10, 12, 12, 15

Explore
What type of chart would be best to compare sales figures?

CONFIDENCE

Warm up

Exercise 3.7

1 The frequency diagram shows the ages of people who visited an art gallery during an exhibition.
  a How many visitors were between 21 and 40 years old?
  b How many visitors were older than 40?
  c What was the modal age group?

Visitors to art gallery

(Bar chart: x-axis "Age" with categories 1–20, 21–40, 41–60, 61–80; y-axis "Frequency" from 0 to 40. Bars: 1–20 ≈ 18, 21–40 = 30, 41–60 = 25, 61–80 ≈ 12.)

2 The table shows the hot drinks bought in a café.

Drinks	Number sold
Coffee	15
Tea	30
Hot chocolate	15

Draw a pie chart to show this data. You could use a spreadsheet.

3 **Real** The table shows the number of gold medals won by UK countries in a sports contest.
  a Draw a frequency diagram to show this information.
  b Write two sentences explaining what your diagram shows.
  Discussion The competition involved only these countries. What other type of chart could you use to show this information?

Country	Total number of medals
England	17
Northern Ireland	15
Scotland	17
Wales	18

4 **Reasoning** Two students recorded how many emails they sent in 10 days.

Michael	3	5	8	8	8	10	15	16	17	20
Theresa	5	6	6	9	9	9	10	12	13	16

  a Work out the median, mean and range for
    i Michael's data   **ii** Theresa's data.
  b Write two sentences comparing the number of emails they sent.
  c Theresa says, 'I send more emails than Michael.'
     Do you think this is true? Use your data to explain.
  d Draw graphs to show the number of emails for each person.

Topic links: Estimation

5 Reasoning / STEM Petra is investigating how environmentally friendly different modes of transport are.
Petra says 'Travelling by plane is much more environmentally friendly than travelling by car.'
The table shows the carbon emissions for each method of transport for travelling 100 km.

Vehicle	Carbon dioxide emissions per traveller (kg)
Small car	20
Large car	40
Train only	10
Coach only	5
Plane only	25

a Draw a graph to show this information.
b Write two sentences comparing the carbon dioxide emissions.
c Do you think Petra's statement is true?
d What other data could Petra gather for this investigation?

6 Real / Reasoning Kevin is investigating the **hypothesis**
'Older students are better at estimating angles.'
He asks 50 Year 7 students and 50 Year 11 students to draw an angle of 65° without using a protractor. His results are shown in the tables.

Year 7

Actual angle, a (°)	Frequency
$50 \leq a < 55$	3
$55 \leq a < 60$	6
$60 \leq a < 65$	10
$65 \leq a < 70$	17
$70 \leq a < 75$	8
$75 \leq a < 80$	5
$80 \leq a < 85$	0
$85 \leq a < 90$	1

Year 11

Actual angle, a (°)	Frequency
$50 \leq a < 55$	0
$55 \leq a < 60$	6
$60 \leq a < 65$	23
$65 \leq a < 70$	18
$70 \leq a < 75$	3
$75 \leq a < 80$	0
$80 \leq a < 85$	0
$85 \leq a < 90$	0

Kevin also used a spreadsheet to work out the mean, median and range for each set of data.

	Mean	Median	Range
Year 7	66.9°	65.4°	37.3°
Year 11	64.5°	66.8°	17.7°

Use ICT to write a report on the data he has collected.
Discussion Are there any outliers? Why might they have occured?

7 Explore What type of chart would be best to compare sales figures?
Look back at the maths you have learned in this lesson.
How can you use it to answer this question?

8 Reflect Write a set of data that gives a mode of 10 minutes, a median of 13 minutes and a mean of your choice. Write a question about your data and swap with a classmate. How easy or hard was it to make up the question?

Key point
Choose the type of chart according to what your data shows:
• **pie chart** for dividing up a total or showing proportions
• **line graph** for data that varies over time
• **frequency diagram** for comparing frequencies
• **grouped frequency diagram** when you have lots of data items
• **scatter graph** to see how two variables are related.

Q5d hint
How does the number of people in the vehicle affect the emissions per traveller?
How do people get to and from the airport or station?

Q6 Literacy hint
A **hypothesis** is a statement you can test by collecting data.

Key point
A report should include:
• the hypothesis you are investigating
• data shown in a graph or chart
• averages and range
• a conclusion
• what else you could investigate.

3 Check up

Log how you did on your Student Progression Chart.

Planning a survey

1 Which of these sets of data would you collect to help you find out whether boys listen to music more than girls?
   A Age of students
   B Gender of students
   C Time they spend listening to music each day
   D Distance they live from school
   E Type of music they like

2 Claire wants to find out the favourite sport of all the students in her class. She only asks girls. Will her survey be biased? Explain your answer.

3 A library has 2500 members. The manager wants to find out how long people spend in the library each week.
   a How many members should she ask?
   b What unit should she use to measure the length of time?

4 The data shows the number of days people spent on holiday in a year.
   12 5 15 23 32 23 45 30 21 23
   13 1 7 8 10 13 12 11 15 23 2
   a Is this data discrete or continuous?
   b Design a grouped frequency table with five equal class intervals.
   c Complete your grouped frequency table.
   d What is the modal group?

5 The distances d, in metres, achieved in a welly-throwing competition were
   15.8 21.9 39.5 28.3 19.7 30.0 42.1 35.0 19.9 27.5
   39.9 29.7 17.3 24.1 46.2 27.3 37.3 27.4 38.8 32.0
   a Copy and complete the grouped frequency table.
   b What is the modal group?

Distance, d (m)	Frequency
$10 \leq d < 20$	
$20 \leq d < 30$	
$30 \leq d < 40$	
$40 \leq d < 50$	

6 The table shows the audience at the cinema one evening.
   a Copy and complete the two-way table.
   b How many people attended the cinema in total?

	Male	Female	Total
Adults	10		22
Children		16	
Total	22		

Averages and range

7 Janice plays football. She recorded the number of goals she scored per match in her last 20 matches.
   Work out
   a the range
   b the mean.

Goals	Frequency
1	1
2	4
3	3
4	3
5	4
6	5

8 The finishing times in a three-legged race, in seconds, were

69   52   159   47   61   74   43   52

   a One pair of runners fell over during the race. What was their time?

   b Work out

   i the mean   **ii** the median.

   c Which average represents the times of the pairs better?

Display and analyse data

9 These are the vegetables Jane dug from her allotment one day. Draw a pie chart to show this information.

Potatoes	20
Carrots	30
Beetroot	10

10 The scatter graph shows the mass of a black bear cub at different ages.

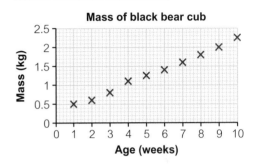

   a How much did the bear cub weigh when it was 2 weeks old?

   b How old was it when it weighed 1.8 kg?

   c Describe the relationship between the mass of the cub and its age.

11 The two graphs show the annual rainfall during 2 years.

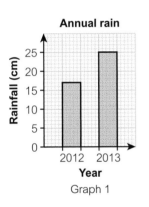

Graph 1

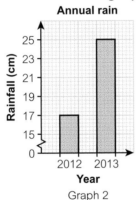

Graph 2

One of the graphs is misleading. Which one? Explain your answer.

12 How sure are you of your answers? Were you mostly

   😞 **Just guessing**   😐 **Feeling doubtful**   😊 **Confident**

   What next? Use your results to decide whether to strengthen or extend your learning.

Challenge

13 a Think of the characters in your favourite book and identify a characteristic to sort them by. Copy and complete this blank two-way table for your characters.

Q13a hint

The characteristics could be heroes and villians, or adults and children.

			Total
Total			

   b What is the smallest number of values you can write in your table so that someone else could work out the rest?

   c Give your table to someone else to see if they can fill in the gaps.

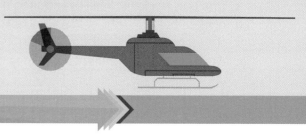

3 Strengthen

You will:
• Strengthen your understanding with practice.

Planning a survey

1 A student wants to find out whether boys spend longer getting to school than girls.
Which of these sets of data does she need to collect?
A Gender of students
B Type of transport used
C Time taken to travel to school each day
D Age
E Distance travelled to get to school

Q1 hint

What is the information that you need to answer the question?

2 There are 500 students in Nisha's school. She wants to do a survey to find out what people do at break time. What sample size should she use?
A 5   **B** 50   **C** 500

Q2 hint

A good sample size to use is about 10% of the population.

3 A village has 800 residents. The council wants to find out what people think of the local bus service. How many people should they sample?

4 STEM A biologist wants to measure the length of snails in a nature reserve. What unit should she use?

Q4 hint

How accurate does she need to be? m, cm or mm?

5 The number of adverts shown during different television programmes were
14   3   12   25   19   9   23   6   17   13
2   11   7   14   14   13   7   24   12   8
a Is this data discrete or continuous?
b Design a grouped frequency table with five equal class intervals.
c Which group has the highest frequency?

Q5 hint

Look for the smallest and largest values and then choose multiples of 5 or 10 for the class intervals. Make sure the groups don't overlap.

6 A sports coach measured the time t, in seconds, it took his team to do 50 push-ups.
25.3   36.7   42.1   28.5   43.9   38.0   23.7   19.1   32.3   30.0
20.4   34.8   40.0   38.6   29.9   35.0   26.4   37.4   34.5   48.9

Time, t (seconds)	Tally	Frequency
$0 \leqslant t < 10$		
$10 \leqslant t < 20$		
$20 \leqslant t < 30$		
$\square \leqslant t < \square$		
$\square \leqslant t < \square$		

a What does $20 \leqslant t < 30$ mean?
b Is this data discrete or continuous?
c Copy and complete the table and fill in the frequency column.
d What is the modal class?

Q6a hint

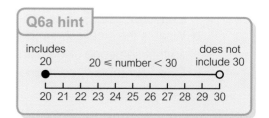

includes 20 $20 \leqslant$ number < 30 does not include 30

20 21 22 23 24 25 26 27 28 29 30

7 This two-way table shows the number of people who had skiing or snowboarding lessons at a winter sports resort one day.

	Skiing	Snowboarding	Total
Adults	25		37
Children		23	
Total		35	80

a Work out the number of adults who went snowboarding.
b Work out the total number of children.
c Work out the number of children who went skiing.
d Work out the total number of people who went skiing.

Q7a hint

Look at the rest of the row.

8 Fred did a survey of the teachers' cars. The table shows the types of cars and the fuel they use.

	Saloon	Hatchback	Estate	Total
Petrol			9	27
Diesel	1	13	4	
Total		25		

a Copy and complete the table.
b How many teachers drove diesel cars?

Averages and range

1 Mark did a sponsored swim for charity. The frequency table shows the different amounts of money he was sponsored.

Money (£)	Frequency
1	4
2	6
3	6
4	4
5	5

a How many people sponsored Mark £5?
b How many people sponsored Mark £4 or more?
c How many people sponsored Mark altogether?
d Work out the range of the amount sponsored.
e Copy and complete this table.

Money (£)	Frequency	Money × Frequency
1	4	1 × 4 = 4
2	6	2 × 6 = ☐
3	6	3 × ☐ = ☐
4	4	☐ × ☐ = ☐
5	5	☐ × ☐ = ☐
	Total number of people ☐	Total amount sponsored ☐

f Calculate the mean amount of money sponsored.

Q1f hint

Mean = total amount of money ÷ total number of people

2 Claire rolled a dice and recorded her results in this table.

Calculate her mean score.

Score	Frequency
1	2
2	3
3	5
4	5
5	3
6	2

3 Reasoning The table shows the median mark and the range of the marks two classes scored in a test.

	Median	Range
9R	42	3
9W	43	10

Choose the words in the box to complete these sentences comparing the marks of the two classes.

9W had a _____ median than 9R.

9R had a _____ range than 9W, so their results were _____ consistent.

> larger
> less   more
>   smaller

4 Reasoning Here are the number of junk emails Simon and Miriam received one week.

Simon	4	5	6	7	8	9	10
Miriam	5	5	5	6	8	8	12

  a Foe each person, calculate
    i the mean
    ii the median
    iii the range.
  b Copy and complete these sentences to compare the median emails for Simon and Miriam.
    Simon had a _____ median than Miriam.
    Miriam had a _____ range than Simon, so the number of emails was _____ consistent.

> **Q4a hint**
>
> Mean = $\dfrac{\text{total number of emails}}{\text{number of days}}$

5 Cameron recorded the time, in minutes, it took him to get to school each morning for 2 weeks.
  25 21 24 27 19 59 24 23 24 27
  a There was an accident on the road one morning. How long did it take him to get to school on that morning?
  b Work out
    i the median
    ii the mean
    iii the range.
  c Which average best represents the time it takes Cameron to get to school?

> **Q5a hint**
>
> Which day did it take him much longer?

> **Q5c hint**
>
> If you were Cameron, how long would you allow to get to school?

Display and analyse data

1 A café sold 3 different types of cake one day.

Cake	Frequency	Degrees
Chocolate	20	☐ × 20
Lemon	30	☐ × 30
Fruit	10	☐ × 10

  a How many cakes did the café sell altogether?
  b Copy and complete this sentence.
    Size of angle for one cake = 360° ÷ ☐° = ☐°
  c Copy and complete the table.
  d Draw a pie chart to show the information.

> **Q1c hint**
>
> Multiply each frequency by the angle for one cake.

2 This scatter graph shows the ages of children and the time it took them to complete a puzzle.

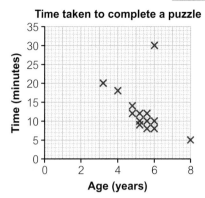

Time taken to complete a puzzle

  a How long did it take the 8-year-old to complete the puzzle?
  b Copy and complete this sentence:
    As the children got older, it took _____ time to complete the puzzle.
  c There is one outlier. How old is this child and how long did it take them to complete the puzzle?

3 Reasoning / Real / Finance An estate agent produces a bar chart to show how house prices changed in his area between 1990 and 2010.

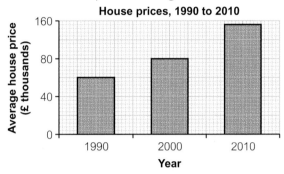

House prices, 1990 to 2010

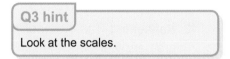

Q3 hint

Look at the scales.

Explain why the graph is misleading.

4 Reasoning / Finance These bar charts show a shop's motorbike sales over 2 years.

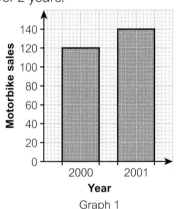

Graph 1

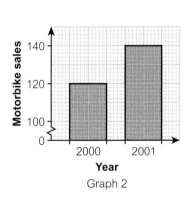

Graph 2

The shop owner says, 'My sales doubled in 2001.'
  a Is this correct?
  b Which graph is misleading? Explain why.

Enrichment

1 a Design a data collection sheet to record the shoe size and hand span of people in your class.
  b Collect the information from 10 people.
  c Draw a scatter graph of the shoe size and hand span.
  d Describe any patterns that you notice.

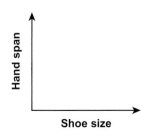

2 Reflect Look at Q7 and 8 in the *Planning a survey* section. These questions are about two-way tables. Choose one of these and write a set of steps for a classmate who is struggling with this type of question. Did you find there was more than one way you could describe what to do?

Reflect

3 Extend

You will:
• Extend your understanding with problem-solving.

1 **Reasoning** Amanda wants to find out the ages of people who use her local supermarket.
   She asks some students in her school if they use the local supermarket.
   a Will her survey give fair information? Explain.
   b Write down one way Amanda could collect unbiased information.

2 **Reasoning** The owner of a business wants to find out if his employees are happy at work. He considers two methods.
   Method 1: Ask the questions to a random selection of people individually.
   Method 2: Do an anonymous survey.
   a Which method should he use? Explain your reasons.
   b There are 1500 people in his company. What is a suitable sample size?

3 The table shows the lunch choices of boys and girls in Year 9.
   a Draw a pie chart showing the information for the boys and a pie chart showing the information for the girls.
   b Write a sentence comparing the proportion of boys who have sandwiches to the proportion of girls who have sandwiches.

	Boys	Girls
Hot lunch	26	27
Sandwiches	25	42
Go home	9	21

4 The frequency diagram shows the scores on a dice.
   a Copy and complete this frequency table.

Score	Frequency
1	
2	
3	
4	
5	
6	

Score on a dice

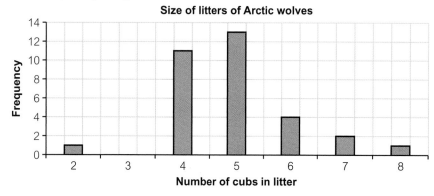

   b Calculate the mean score.

5 This frequency diagram shows the numbers of cubs in litters of Arctic wolves.

Size of litters of Arctic wolves

   Work out the mean number of cubs per litter.

Topic links: Imperial units

Subject links: Science (Q5), PE (Q7, Q9, Q11), Geography (Q12)

6 A midwife records the mass, in pounds, of 15 babies.

7.2 7.0 8.2 7.1 6.5 7.3 6.4 7.8
7.5 8.0 6.5 8.4 7.5 7.4 8.9

a Design a grouped frequency table with five equal class intervals to record the masses in pounds of the babies.

b What is the modal group?

c What is the range?

Q6a Strategy hint

Choose enough groups to divide the data, but not so many groups that there are very few data items in each group.

7 **Reasoning / Problem-solving** Here are some records from a running club's 100 m sprint.

Name	Gender	Time, t (seconds)
Jones	F	11.9
Peters	F	12.2
Clarke	M	12.0
Scott	M	12.5
Lee	F	12.0
Smith	F	12.8
Akbar	M	13.6
Ford	M	11.4

Name	Gender	Time, t (seconds)
Pitt	F	12.9
Wang	M	12.5
Henry	M	11.8
Moss	F	13.0
Campbell	F	12.8
Khalid	F	13.1
Lott	M	13.2

a Copy and complete this two-way table to record the times.

	$11 < t \leqslant 12$	$12 < t \leqslant 13$	$13 < t \leqslant 14$	Total
Male				
Female				
Total				

b How many female runners were there?

c How many male runners had a time of more than 13 seconds?

d How many female runners had a time of $11 < t \leqslant 13$ seconds?

Discussion Are male runners faster than female runners? How else could you use this data to investigate this hypothesis?

8 **Reasoning** The tables show the number of wins by Joanne and Nathaniel in 10 chess tournaments.

Joanne	
Wins	Frequency
1	1
2	2
3	3
4	1
5	3

Nathaniel	
Wins	Frequency
1	0
2	1
3	4
4	4
5	1

a Calculate the mean and range for each player.

b Which player did better? Justify your answer.

9 **Real / Reasoning** Here are the women's and men's times, in seconds, in a swimming race.

Men   47.52   47.53   47.80   47.84   47.88   47.92   48.04   48.44

Women 53.00   53.38   53.44   53.47   53.64   53.66   53.75   53.02

Compare the men's and women's times.

10 Problem-solving This table shows the numbers of members of a hockey club.

	Beginner	Intermediate	Advanced	Total
Girls	6	20		38
Boys			10	34
Women	2		13	25
Men		6		23
Total	21	50		

a Copy and complete the table.

b How many members does the hockey club have?

c Draw pie charts to show
   i the proportions of members that are boys, girls, women and men
   ii the levels of the members.

11 Reasoning Here are the results of two 100 m sprinters in a season.

	Mean (seconds)	Range (seconds)
Competitor A	12.6	0.4
Competitor B	12.4	5.2

One of the athletes sprained their ankle in one of the races.
Which athlete do you think this was? Explain your reasoning.

Key point

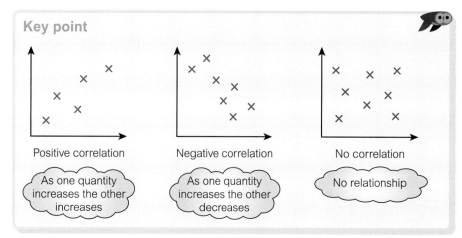

Positive correlation — As one quantity increases the other increases

Negative correlation — As one quantity increases the other decreases

No correlation — No relationship

12 Reasoning The scatter graph shows height above sea level and temperature in the west of Scotland on one day.
   a Describe what happens to the temperature as the height increases.
   b Describe the correlation shown on the graph.
   c Carole is going to climb a mountain that is 1100 m high. She says that she will be warm enough in her T-shirt. Is she correct? Explain your reasoning.

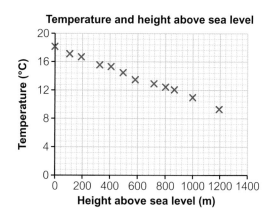

Temperature and height above sea level

13 The table gives the prices of cars with different-sized engines for one manufacturer.

Engine size (litres)	1	1.5	1.25	1.6	1.2	1.6	2	1.5	1.6	2	1.6	2.2
Price (£ thousands)	13.5	15.5	13.5	17.3	11.5	18.5	22.3	18	20	23.5	8.8	27.9

a Plot a scatter graph using this data.

b Describe the correlation shown on the graph.

c Identify an outlier. Suggest a reason for this data item.

Investigation   Reasoning / Problem-solving

The frequency diagram shows the ages of people who visit a theatre one Saturday.

1 Which is the largest age group that visits the theatre?

Here is the original theatre visitor data.

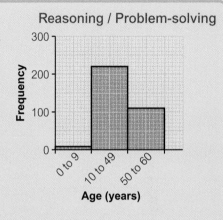

Age, a (years)	Frequency
$0 \leq a < 10$	10
$10 \leq a < 20$	30
$20 \leq a < 30$	40
$30 \leq a < 40$	50
$40 \leq a < 50$	100
$50 \leq a < 60$	110

2 a Draw a frequency diagram using the original data. Use a horizontal scale like this.

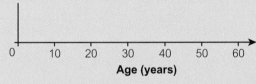

b From your frequency diagram, which age group visited the theatre the most?

c Why was the first frequency diagram misleading?

3 How else can graphs be misleading?

---

14 Reflect Q5 is about the numbers of cubs born to Arctic wolves. This sort of data might be collected by biologists or environmental scientists. Why do you think they would be interested in this type of information? What other data might they collect?

3 Unit test

Log how you did on your Student Progression Chart.

1 Caitlin wants to find out if people like using the local park. She asks people in the park what they like about it.
Will her survey provide fair information? Explain.

2 A city has 500 000 people in it. The mayor wants to find out if people are pleased with their local facilities.
How many people should she sample?
A 5   **B** 500   **C** 50 000

3 A school has 2000 students. The headteacher wants to find out students' views on the canteen.
Give an approximate sample size that he should use.

4 Peter recorded the number of moves it took him to win a board game.
He played 20 times.
  a Work out
    i the range
    ii the mode
    iii the mean.
  b Why is the mode not the best average to use? Explain your answer.

Number of moves	Frequency
5	1
6	4
7	3
8	3
9	4
10	5

5 The data shows the number of people using the local swimming pool at different times.
11   15   5   22   23   33   42   20   21   25
12   3   35   46   51   23   42   49   28   35
  a Is this data discrete or continuous?
  b Design a grouped frequency table with five equal class intervals.
  c Complete your grouped frequency table.
  d What is the modal group?

6 The data shows the amount of carbon dioxide, in grams, produced by 20 cars travelling one kilometre.
100.4   143.9   149.5   130.0   125.5   115.0   137.2   126.3   128.7   120.0
116.2   135.1   131.8   147.3   101.1   119.3   124.4   140.9   131.0   109.9
  a Design and complete a grouped frequency table.
  b What is the modal group?

7 The table shows the students who play tennis, hockey and badminton in a school.
  a Copy and complete the two-way table.
  b How many boys play tennis?
  c How many students play hockey?

	Tennis	Hockey	Badminton
Girls	20		15
Boys		26	
Total	44		35

8 The table shows the type of pets that visited a vet during one week.

Pet	Frequency
Dog	35
Cat	25
Rabbit	30

a Draw a pie chart to show this information.

b What fraction of the animals were rabbits?

9 The scatter graph shows the time it took children to complete a puzzle compared to their ages.

Time to complete a puzzle

a How long did it take the 10-year old child to complete the puzzle?

b How many children took 16 seconds to complete the puzzle?

c Describe the relationship between a child's age and the time it takes to complete the puzzle.

d One child took a break while doing the puzzle. How old was she?

10 The table shows the number of visitors to a café during 2 weeks.

	Mon	Tue	Wed	Thu	Fri	Sat	Sun
Week 1	10	11	12	12	15	15	16
Week 2	9	10	10	11	15	18	25

a On one day the café offered all its food at half price. Which day do you think this was?

b For each week, work out
  i the median
  ii the mean
  iii the range.

c Which average would be the best one to use to compare the 2 weeks?

Challenge

11 The table shows the weekly wage for one grade of worker in a company for 3 years.

	2012	2013	2014
Weekly wage (£)	410	418	422

a Draw an example of a misleading graph that the management could use to show that they had given a good pay rise.

b Draw an example of a misleading graph that employees could use to show that their pay rises have been very small.

Q11 hint

You could use the y-axis to make the graphs look different.

12 **Reflect** Give each of these statements a score from 1 to 5, where 1 means 'disagree strongly' and 5 means 'agree strongly'.

A I learned lots of new things in this unit.

B I used other maths topics in answering questions in this unit.

C The skills I learned in these lessons will be useful in everyday life.

D I need more help in answering questions about statistics.

E I am fairly confident in answering questions about statistics.

(You can just write down the letter for each statement.)

4.1 Equivalent proportions

You will learn to:
- Convert between fractions, decimals and percentages
- Compare fractions, decimals and percentages
- Write a fraction as a decimal.

CONFIDENCE

Why learn this?
Information about proportions can be given as fractions, decimals or percentages. You need to be able to convert between different types.

Fluency
What is the decimal equivalent of
- $\frac{1}{2}$
- $\frac{3}{4}$
- $\frac{1}{10}$
- $\frac{7}{10}$

Explore
Can you write the number π as a fraction?

Exercise 4.1

Warm up

1 Write as a percentage.
  a 72 out of 100   **b** 25 out of 50   **c** 0.73   **d** 1.29

2 Work out
  a $34 \div 10$ **b** $286 \div 1000$ **c** $9021 \div 100$

3 Write each decimal as a fraction.
  a 0.75   **b** 0.3   **c** 0.9

4 Write < or > between each pair of decimals.
  a 0.15 ☐ 0.172   **b** 0.62 ☐ 0.603   **c** 4.049 ☐ 4.5

5 Sort these into five sets of equivalent proportions.

$\frac{17}{100}$	$\frac{7}{10}$	$\frac{3}{4}$	$\frac{4}{5}$	$\frac{1}{20}$

0.75	0.05	0.17	0.7	0.8

5%	80%	17%	70%	75%

> **Key point**
> You can write a fraction as a decimal by dividing the numerator by the denominator.
> $\frac{2}{4} = 2 \div 4 = 0.5$

> **Q5 hint**
> Rewrite fractions so they have denominator 100 to work out the percentage.

 6 Write each fraction as a decimal and as a percentage.
  a $\frac{1}{20} = 0.\square = \square\%$ **b** $\frac{3}{10} = 0.\square = \square\%$
  c $\frac{3}{8} = 0.\square = \square\%$ **d** $\frac{7}{20} = 0.\square = \square\%$
  e $\frac{7}{8} = 0.\square = \square\%$ **f** $\frac{11}{20} = 0.\square = \square\%$

> **Q6 hint**
> Use the $\boxed{S \Leftrightarrow D}$ key on your calculator to change the fraction into a decimal.

7 Write each fraction as a decimal and as a percentage.

a $\frac{32}{40} = 0.\square = \square\%$

b $\frac{71}{80} = 0.\square = \square\%$

c $\frac{90}{120} = 0.\square = \square\%$

d $\frac{105}{150} = 0.\square = \square\%$

e $\frac{11}{16} = 0.\square = \square\%$

f $\frac{18}{125} = 0.\square = \square\%$

8 **Problem-solving** Which shape has the longer perimeter?

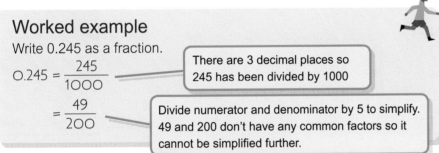

A

0.3 m   0.1 m

0.1 m

0.4 m

B

$\frac{3}{20}$ m

$\frac{7}{20}$ m

$\frac{8}{20}$ m

$\frac{1}{20}$ m

9 Use the decimal equivalent of each fraction to write the sets in order, smallest to largest.

a $\frac{13}{20}$ $\frac{3}{5}$ $\frac{5}{8}$

b $\frac{3}{8}$ $\frac{7}{20}$ $\frac{16}{40}$

10 Put these values in order, smallest to largest.

$\frac{13}{20}$ 0.62   64.5%   9 out of 16

Worked example

Write 0.245 as a fraction.

$0.245 = \dfrac{245}{1000}$

> There are 3 decimal places so 245 has been divided by 1000

$= \dfrac{49}{200}$

> Divide numerator and denominator by 5 to simplify. 49 and 200 don't have any common factors so it cannot be simplified further.

Key point

A terminating decimal ends after a definite number of digits, for example 0.39 and 1.042.
You can write any terminating decimal as a fraction.

11 Write each decimal as a fraction. Simplify where possible.

a $0.85 = \dfrac{85}{100} =$

b $0.375 = \dfrac{\square}{1000} =$

c 0.84

d 0.125

e 0.23

f 0.875

g 0.19

h 0.444

Q11 hint

Use the number of decimal places to decide whether the denominator should be 100 or 1000.

12 Write each percentage as a fraction. Simplify where possible.

a $35\% = 0.35 = \dfrac{\square}{100} = \dfrac{\square}{20}$

b $6\% = \dfrac{\square}{100} = \dfrac{\square}{\square}$

c 88%

d 5%

e $12.5\% = 0.125 = \dfrac{125}{1000} =$

f 37.5%

g 45.8%

h 1.2%

13 **Explore** Can you write π as a fraction?
Choose some sensible numbers to help you explore this situation. Then use what you've learned in this lesson to help you answer the question.

14 **Reflect** This lesson uses a lot of mathematical terms, such as
- terminating
- equivalent
- percentage
- common factor.

Write down what each of these terms means, in your own words.
Which terms are new, and which ones have you met before?

Explore

Reflect

4.2 Recurring decimals

You will learn to:
* Write recurring decimals as fractions.

Why learn this?
Lots of calculations in real life have an answer that is a recurring decimal.

Fluency
Round each number to 2 decimal places.
* 1.454
* 6.087
* 3.3642
* 10.4985

Explore
How can you tell if a fraction will be a terminating or a non-terminating decimal?

Exercise 4.2

1 Work out
   a 726 ÷ 6 **b** 7125 ÷ 5 **c** 345 ÷ 4 **d** 842 ÷ 8

2 **a** **i** Jarred thinks of a number. Half of it is 240. What is $\frac{1}{4}$ of his number?
    ii What number did Jarred think of?
   b **i** Sophie thinks of a number. $\frac{1}{6}$ of it is 12. What is $\frac{1}{3}$ of her number?
    ii What number did Sophie think of?
   c **i** Amee thinks of a number. $\frac{1}{10}$ of it is 250. What is $\frac{1}{5}$ of her number?
    ii What number did Amee think of?

Q2b hint

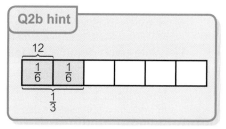

3 **Reasoning** **a** Use your calculator to match each fraction to its equivalent decimal.

$$\boxed{\frac{3}{5}} \quad \boxed{\frac{5}{8}} \quad \boxed{\frac{7}{12}} \quad \boxed{\frac{5}{9}} \quad \boxed{\frac{7}{11}} \quad \boxed{\frac{2}{3}}$$

$$\boxed{0.625} \quad \boxed{0.\dot{5}} \quad \boxed{0.6} \quad \boxed{0.\dot{6}} \quad \boxed{0.\dot{6}\dot{3}} \quad \boxed{0.58\dot{3}}$$

b Use the decimals to order the fractions in part **a**, smallest to largest.

Key point

A recurring decimal contains a digit, or sequence of digits, which repeats itself forever. A dot over the digit shows it recurs. For example, 0.111 11.... = 0.$\dot{1}$

Worked example

Write $\frac{1}{9}$ as a decimal.

$$\begin{array}{r} 0 \\ 9\overline{)1.\,000} \end{array}$$

9 doesn't go into 1 so write a 0 in the units column.

$$\begin{array}{r} 0.1111... \\ 9\overline{)1.\,0\,0\,0\,0\,0} \end{array}$$

There are now 10 tenths.

$$\frac{1}{9} = 0.\dot{1}$$

9 goes into 10 once with remainder 1. There are now 10 hundredths. Continue like this and the decimal recurs.

4 Write each fraction as a decimal.
   a $\frac{1}{8}$ **b** $\frac{1}{12}$ **c** $\frac{5}{12}$ **d** $\frac{7}{8}$
   e $\frac{1}{6}$ **f** $\frac{5}{6}$ **g** $\frac{2}{9}$ **h** $\frac{8}{9}$

5 **Problem-solving / Reasoning** Nira works out 12 ÷ 18 and gets

an answer of on her calculator.

What is the equivalent fraction?

Discussion What has the calculator done?

6 Use a written method to work out each division. Write your answers as recurring decimals using dot notation.

    a 823 ÷ 3   **b** 375 ÷ 9   **c** 37 564 ÷ 3

    d 6385 ÷ 9   **e** 97 ÷ 12   **f** 1756 ÷ 12

Investigation   **Reasoning / Problem-solving**

 Caroline says, 'Some fractions can be written as terminating decimals but some are recurring decimals'.

  1 Write each fraction as a decimal.

    $\frac{1}{2}$ $\frac{1}{3}$ $\frac{1}{4}$ $\frac{1}{5}$ $\frac{1}{6}$ $\frac{1}{7}$ $\frac{1}{8}$ $\frac{1}{9}$ $\frac{1}{10}$ $\frac{1}{11}$ $\frac{1}{12}$

  2 Sort them into terminating decimals and recurring decimals.

  3 Jack says, 'If the denominator of a fraction is even, it will be a recurring decimal'.

  Find an example to show that Jack is wrong.

  4 Which denominators give terminating decimals?

  Discussion Caroline says, 'I think it's to do with the fact that 2 × 5 = 10.' What do you think she means?

  5 Investigate what happens if the numerator is not 1.

---

7 **a** Which bag has the greater proportion of red counters?

  b What is the proportion of blue counters in each bag?

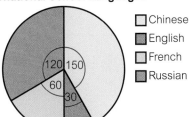

8 The pie chart shows the first language of people working in a summer school.

Write the proportion of each language as a fraction and as a percentage.

International School Languages

☐ Chinese
☐ English
☐ French
☐ Russian

Q8 hint

How many degrees represent the whole pie chart?

9 **Explore** How can you tell if a fraction will be a terminating or a non-terminating decimal?

Is it easier to explore this question now you have completed the lesson?

What further information do you need to be able to answer this?

10 **Reflect** A shorthand way of writing a recurring decimal is to use a dot, or dots, over the numbers that repeat. For example, 0.222 2… is written as 0.2̇

Write down five other short forms that you use in maths. Do you think these short forms are useful or not?

Explore

Reflect

4.3 Adding and subtracting fractions

You will learn to:

- Add and subtract fractions
- Add and subtract mixed numbers.

CONFIDENCE

Why learn this?
Statisticians add and subtract fractions to work out the probably of different events happening (or not happening).

Fluency
What is
- $\frac{1}{2} + \frac{1}{4}$
- $\frac{1}{2} - \frac{1}{4}$
- $\frac{3}{5} - \frac{3}{10}$
- $\frac{3}{8} + \frac{1}{2}$

Explore
How many years ago did people start writing fractions?

Exercise 4.3

Warm up

1 Write each improper fraction as a mixed number.

  a $\frac{14}{5}$ **b** $\frac{20}{8}$ **c** $\frac{12}{7}$ **d** $\frac{23}{3}$

2 Write each mixed number as an improper fraction.

  a $2\frac{1}{4}$ **b** $1\frac{2}{3}$ **c** $5\frac{3}{8}$ **c** $4\frac{3}{10}$

3 Work out

  a $\frac{5}{12} + \frac{1}{3}$ **b** $\frac{5}{6} - \frac{1}{3}$ **c** $\frac{3}{4} - \frac{3}{8}$ **d** $\frac{1}{3} + \frac{2}{5}$

4 Work out each calculation. Give your answer as a mixed number where necessary.

  a $\frac{5}{8} + \frac{3}{8} + \frac{1}{8}$ **b** $\frac{7}{12} + \frac{1}{12} + \frac{11}{12}$ **c** $\frac{5}{9} - \frac{2}{9} + \frac{7}{9}$

  d $\frac{1}{2} - \frac{1}{3} + \frac{1}{4}$ **e** $\frac{4}{5} + \frac{3}{10} - \frac{3}{4}$ **f** $\frac{2}{3} - \frac{4}{9} + \frac{1}{6}$

5 Work out

  a $\frac{1}{2} + \frac{1}{3} + \frac{1}{4}$ **b** $\frac{1}{3} + \frac{1}{4} + \frac{1}{5}$ **c** $\frac{1}{4} + \frac{1}{5} + \frac{1}{6}$

6 **Problem-solving** Work out the missing number.

  a $\frac{4}{5} + \frac{3}{4} + \square = 2$ **b** $\frac{5}{6} + \frac{3}{5} - \square = 1$

7 **Problem-solving** In a clothes shop, $\frac{1}{5}$ of clothes are suits, $\frac{2}{3}$ are trousers and the rest are tops. What fraction of the clothes are tops?

Q4a hint

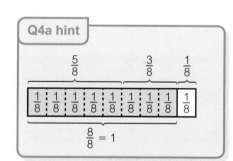

Worked example

a Work out $3\frac{5}{6} + 1\frac{3}{4}$

$3\frac{5}{6} + 1\frac{3}{4} = (3 + 1) + \left(\frac{5}{6} + \frac{3}{4}\right)$ Add the whole number parts and add the fraction parts separately.

$= 4 + \left(\frac{10}{12} + \frac{9}{12}\right)$ Convert the fractions to equivalent fractions with a common denominator.

$= 4 + \frac{19}{12}$

$= 4 + 1\frac{7}{12}$ Change the improper fraction to a mixed number

$= 5\frac{7}{12}$ so you can add the whole number parts.

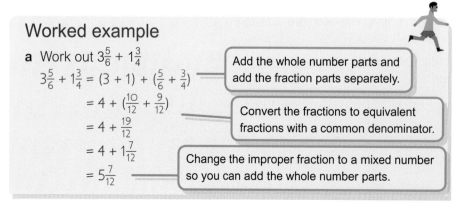

b Work out $2\frac{1}{2} - 1\frac{5}{6}$

$$2\frac{1}{2} - 1\frac{5}{6} = (2 - 1) + (\frac{1}{2} - \frac{5}{6})$$

> Subtract the whole number parts and the fraction parts separately.

$$= 1 + (\frac{3}{6} - \frac{5}{6})$$
$$= 1 + (-\frac{2}{6})$$
$$= 1 - \frac{1}{3}$$
$$= \frac{2}{3}$$

8 Work out

  a $1\frac{1}{5} + 2\frac{3}{10}$ **b** $2\frac{1}{4} + 3\frac{2}{5}$ **c** $2\frac{1}{3} + 2\frac{2}{5}$

  d $3\frac{4}{5} + 1\frac{1}{3}$ **e** $4\frac{2}{3} + 2\frac{5}{6}$ **f** $2\frac{7}{10} + 3\frac{4}{5}$

  g $1\frac{11}{12} + 1\frac{5}{6}$ **h** $3\frac{3}{4} + 1\frac{4}{5}$ **i** $2\frac{5}{9} + 3\frac{5}{6}$

9 Work out

  a $2\frac{7}{10} - 1\frac{2}{5}$ **b** $2\frac{3}{4} - 1\frac{3}{8}$ **c** $4\frac{5}{6} - 3\frac{2}{3}$

  d $3\frac{4}{5} - 1\frac{1}{3}$ **e** $4\frac{2}{3} - 2\frac{1}{6}$ **f** $3\frac{7}{10} - 3\frac{3}{5}$

  g $4\frac{11}{12} - 2\frac{5}{6}$ **h** $3\frac{3}{4} - 1\frac{3}{5}$ **i** $3\frac{5}{6} - 2\frac{5}{9}$

10 Yazdi uses $2\frac{1}{4}$ litres of white paint and $2\frac{3}{5}$ litres of blue paint. How many litres of paint did he use in total? Give your answer as a mixed number.

11 Peter walked $4\frac{5}{6}$ km, Brenda walked $3\frac{4}{5}$ km. How much further did Peter walk?

12 A farmer needs $3\frac{2}{5}$ metres of netting for his chickens. He already has $1\frac{11}{20}$ metres. How much more does he need?

13 A box of apples weighs $3\frac{5}{7}$ kg and a box of pears weighs $2\frac{3}{5}$ kg. How much do they weigh altogether?

Investigation   **Reasoning**

1 Write down six fractions that are between

  a 0 and 1   **b** 0 and $\frac{1}{2}$ **c** $\frac{1}{2}$ and 1

           0                         $\frac{1}{2}$ 1

2 Write down two fractions that are between

  a $\frac{1}{4}$ and $\frac{3}{4}$ **b** $\frac{2}{8}$ and $\frac{3}{8}$ **c** $\frac{7}{10}$ and $\frac{8}{10}$ **d** $\frac{3}{5}$ and $\frac{4}{5}$

Discussion In how many different ways can you answer the questions in this investigation?

---

14 Explore How many years ago did people start writing fractions? What information do you need to start answering this question?

15 Reflect Choose one of the parts of Q9 that you felt confident in answering. How would you explain the method you used to a classmate who had missed this lesson?

Explore

Reflect

4.4 Multiplying fractions

You will learn to:
- Use strategies for multiplying fractions.

Why learn this
You multiply fractions when working out the distance you can travel with half a tank of fuel.

Fluency
What is
- $\frac{3}{7}$ of 21
- $\frac{2}{5}$ of 15
- $\frac{2}{9}$ of 36
- $\frac{5}{6}$ of 72

Explore
How many times can you cut a piece of paper in half?

Exercise 4.4

1 Work out
  a $3 \times \frac{1}{4}$
  b $2 \times \frac{3}{7}$
  c $\frac{2}{5} \times 2$
  d $4 \times \frac{2}{9}$
  e $\frac{5}{6} \times 4$
  f $\frac{1}{3} \times 6$

2 Write each improper fraction as a mixed number in its simplest form.
  a $\frac{32}{10}$
  b $\frac{22}{4}$
  c $\frac{35}{5}$
  d $\frac{34}{6}$

3 What is the **inverse operation** of
  a multiplying by 10
  b dividing by 8?

> **Q3 Literacy hint**
> An **inverse operation** is the opposite operation.

4 Simone says, 'I'm thinking of a number. I multiply it by 8 and then divide the answer by 8, and get 5.' What number was she thinking of?

5 Reasoning Work out
  a $8 \times 1 \div 4$
  b $8 \times \frac{1}{4}$
  c $8 \div 4 \times 1$
  d Explain why the answer is the same in parts **a**, **b** and **c**.

6 Work out
  a $6 \times \frac{1}{3}$
  b $5 \times \frac{4}{5}$
  c $\frac{2}{3} \times 3$
  d $\frac{5}{7} \times 7$

> **Q6b hint**
> Work out one-fifth of 5, then multiply it by 4.

7 Work out
  a $\frac{2}{5} \times 250$
  b $\frac{2}{3} \times 360$
  c $\frac{2}{3}$ of 360

> **Q7a hint**
> Work out one-fifth of 250, then multiply by 2.

8 Real / Problem-solving A car has 45 litres of fuel in the tank. The driver uses $\frac{3}{5}$ of the fuel. How many litres of fuel are left?

9 Reasoning Which of these products will have an answer less than 1?
  a $5 \times \frac{2}{3}$
  b $\frac{1}{9} \times 7$
  c $2 \times \frac{4}{15}$
  d $\frac{3}{4} \times 6$

Worked example

Work out $\frac{1}{4} \times \frac{2}{3}$

$$\frac{1}{4} \times \frac{2}{3} = \frac{1 \times 2}{4 \times 3}$$

$$= \frac{2}{12}$$

$$= \frac{1}{6}$$

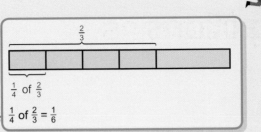

$\frac{1}{4}$ of $\frac{2}{3}$

$\frac{1}{4}$ of $\frac{2}{3} = \frac{1}{6}$

Key point

To multiply two fractions, multiply their numerators and multiply their denominators.

10 Work out each calculation. Simplify your answer where needed.

a $\frac{2}{3} \times \frac{3}{4} = \frac{2 \times 3}{3 \times 4} = \frac{\square}{\square} = \frac{\square}{\square}$ 　　　**b** $\frac{1}{4} \times \frac{4}{5}$ 　　　**c** $\frac{2}{3} \times \frac{2}{5}$

d $\frac{3}{4} \times \frac{3}{4}$ 　　　**e** $\frac{3}{4} \times \frac{6}{11}$ 　　　**f** $\frac{4}{9} \times \frac{3}{7}$ 　　　**g** $\frac{3}{5} \times \frac{7}{12}$

11 Work out

a $\frac{1}{2} \times \frac{1}{4}$ 　　　**b** $\frac{1}{2} \times \frac{1}{3}$ 　　　**c** $\frac{1}{2} \times \frac{1}{5}$ 　　　**d** $\frac{1}{2} \times \frac{1}{2}$

Discussion What happens to the denominator when you multiply a fraction by $\frac{1}{2}$?

12 Work out

a $\left(\frac{1}{4}\right)^2 = \frac{1}{4} \times \frac{1}{4} =$ 　　**b** $\left(\frac{1}{3}\right)^2$ 　　　**c** $\left(\frac{1}{5}\right)^2$

d $\left(\frac{1}{6}\right)^2$ 　　　**e** $\left(\frac{2}{3}\right)^2$ 　　　**f** $\left(\frac{3}{8}\right)^2$

Worked example

Work out $\frac{3}{8} \times \frac{2}{9}$

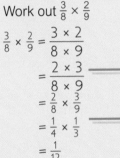

$$\frac{3}{8} \times \frac{2}{9} = \frac{3 \times 2}{8 \times 9}$$

$$= \frac{2 \times 3}{8 \times 9}$$

Rewrite the calculation with a fraction that can be simplified. 2 is a factor of 8 and 3 is a factor of 9.

$$= \frac{2}{8} \times \frac{3}{9}$$

$$= \frac{1}{4} \times \frac{1}{3}$$

Simplify the fractions before multiplying.

$$= \frac{1}{12}$$

Key point

Sometimes you can rearrange fractions so they can be simplified before multiplying.

Discussion How could you work out the multiplication using fewer steps?

13 Work out

a $\frac{5}{8} \times \frac{3}{5}$ 　　　**b** $\frac{3}{4} \times \frac{2}{7}$ 　　　**c** $\frac{3}{4} \times \frac{8}{15}$

d $\frac{4}{9} \times \frac{3}{8}$ 　　　**e** $\frac{9}{15} \times \frac{5}{6}$ 　　　**c** $\frac{5}{6} \times \frac{3}{20}$

14 Holly drank $\frac{2}{3}$ of a $\frac{1}{2}$ litre bottle of juice. How much did she drink?

15 **Explore** How many times can you cut a piece of paper in half? Choose some sensible numbers to help you explore this situation. Then use what you've learned in this lesson to help you answer the question.

16 **Reflect** Look again at Q8. Write down the steps you took to work out the answer. Work out the answer again using a different method. Did you get the same answer? If not, check your working.

4.5 Dividing fractions

You will learn to:
- Divide by fractions.

Why learn this
Real-life measurements are not usually whole numbers. You need to be able to calculate with fractions too.

Fluency
How many
- 2s are in 8
- 4s are in 20
- 1s are in 3
- 5s are in 100?

Explore
Does division always make something smaller?

Exercise 4.5

1 Write down the common factors of each pair of numbers.
a 20 and 35   **b** 16 and 40   **c** 27 and 36   **d** 25 and 55

2 Work out
a $\frac{1}{4} \times 8$ **b** $\frac{2}{3} \times 10$ **c** $\frac{4}{5} \times \frac{2}{3}$ **d** $\frac{9}{10} \times \frac{1}{3}$

3 Write each improper fraction as a mixed number.
a $\frac{8}{3}$ **b** $\frac{35}{6}$ **c** $\frac{28}{3}$

4 Complete these calculations for each diagram.

a
$$1$$
| $\frac{1}{4}$ | $\frac{1}{4}$ | $\frac{1}{4}$ | $\frac{1}{4}$ |

$1 \div 4 = \square$ $1 \div \square = 4$ $4 \times \square = 1$

b
$$2$$
| $\frac{1}{3}$ | $\frac{1}{3}$ | $\frac{1}{3}$ | $\frac{1}{3}$ | $\frac{1}{3}$ | $\frac{1}{3}$ |

$2 \div 6 = \frac{1}{3}$ $2 \div \square = \square$ $\square \times \square = \square$

c
$$3$$
| $\frac{1}{2}$ | $\frac{1}{2}$ | $\frac{1}{2}$ | $\frac{1}{2}$ | $\frac{1}{2}$ | $\frac{1}{2}$ |

$3 \div \square = \square$ $3 \div \square = \square$ $\square \times \square = \square$

5 Use your answers to Q4 to work out
a how many quarters are in 1
b how many thirds are in 2
c how many halves are in 3
d how many quarters are in 3.

6 Copy and complete.
a $4 \div \frac{1}{2}$ **b** $3 \div \frac{1}{5}$ **c** $2 \div \frac{1}{6}$ **d** $6 \div \frac{1}{4}$

> **Q6a hint**
> How many halves are in 4?

7 How many $\frac{1}{4}$ litre bottles can be filled from a 3 litre container?

8 Katie cuts 4 chocolate cakes into eighths. How many slices are there?

9 **Reasoning** Chris cuts 3 carrot cakes into equal slices. He has 30 slices. What fraction did he cut each cake into?

10 Write the **reciprocal** of each fraction or number.

a $\frac{2}{3} = \frac{3}{\square}$　　b $\frac{3}{4}$　　c $\frac{11}{4}$　　d $\frac{15}{2}$

e 2　　f 4　　g $\frac{1}{3}$　　h $\frac{1}{10}$

Q10 Literacy hint

The **reciprocal** of a fraction is the 'upside down' fraction.

Q10e hint

The number 2 can be written as $\frac{2}{1}$.

Key point

Dividing by a fraction is the same as multiplying by its reciprocal. The reciprocal of a fraction is the 'upside down' fraction.

Worked example

Work out $5 \div \frac{2}{3}$

$5 \div \frac{2}{3} = \frac{5}{1} \times \frac{3}{2}$ ── Multiply by the reciprocal of $\frac{2}{3}$. $5 = \frac{5}{1}$.

　　　$= \frac{15}{2}$

　　　$= 7\frac{1}{2}$ ── Write as a mixed number in its simplest form.

11 Work out

a $6 \div \frac{2}{3}$　　b $4 \div \frac{3}{4}$　　c $10 \div \frac{5}{9}$　　d $12 \div \frac{3}{10}$

e $18 \div \frac{2}{9}$　　f $21 \div \frac{7}{10}$　　g $15 \div \frac{1}{3}$　　h $26 \div \frac{2}{5}$

12 How many $\frac{3}{4}$ kg bags of potatoes can be filled from a 12 kg sack?

13 **STEM** An electrician needs to cut a 10 m roll of cable into lengths $\frac{5}{6}$ of a metre. How many lengths can she cut from the roll?

14 Decide if these statements are true or false. Give examples to help explain your answers.
   a The reciprocal of a proper fraction is another proper fraction.
   b The reciprocal of an improper fraction is a proper fraction.
   c When you multiply two fractions the answer is always less than 1.
   d When you multiply two proper fractions the answer is always less than 1.
   e When you multiply an integer by a proper fraction the answer is more than that integer.
   f When you divide an integer by a proper fraction the answer is greater than the integer.

15 **Explore** Does division always make something smaller?
   Choose some sensible numbers to help you explore this situation. Then use what you've learned in this lesson to help you answer the question.

16 **Reflect** Fraction calculations can often be shown using bar models as in Q4. Do these diagrams help you understand how to divide by fractions? Explain.

Explore

Reflect

4.6 Comparing proportions

You will learn to:
- Use a calculator to work out percentages
- Compare proportions.

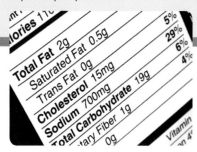

Why learn this?
Nutritional information on food packets can be given as a fraction, a percentage or as a decimal.

Fluency
Work out 20% and 5% of
- 500
- 360
- 1800

Explore
How do calculators show 150%?

Exercise 4.6

1 Work out
- **a** 25% of £1200
- **b** 15% of £1200
- **c** 30% of £1200
- **d** 75% of £1200

2 Write these scores in order, from lowest to highest.

6 out of 10   13 out of 20   14 out of 25   29 out of 50

3 Write down 6 sets of equivalent fractions, decimals and percentages from these.

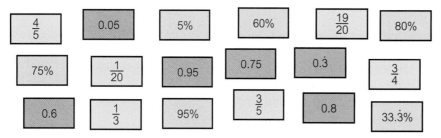

$\frac{4}{5}$ 0.05   5%   60% $\frac{19}{20}$ 80%

75% $\frac{1}{20}$ 0.95   0.75 $0.\dot{3}$ $\frac{3}{4}$

0.6 $\frac{1}{3}$ 95% $\frac{3}{5}$ 0.8 $33.\dot{3}\%$

4 Write these amounts in order, from smallest to largest.
- **a** 0.409 $\frac{4}{9}$ 41%   11 out of 20
- **b** 0.67   66%   34 out of 50 $\frac{2}{3}$

5 Reasoning Which is better value?
- **a** $\frac{1}{3}$ off or a discount of 30%
- **b** A reduction of 15% or a saving of $\frac{1}{10}$
- **c** 20% off or pay $\frac{4}{5}$ of the cost

6 Problem-solving A swimming team has 20 members. 11 members are girls. What percentage of the swimming team are boys?

Topic links: Statistics, Proportion, Pie charts

Subject links: Cookery (Q7), Geography (Q13)

7 Reasoning / Problem-solving Here is some nutritional information for two similar products.
  a Write the proportion of fat in Brand A as a percentage
  b Which brand has a higher proportion of fat?
  c Write the proportion of protein in Brand A as a percentage.
  d Which brand has a higher proportion of protein?
  e Which brand has a higher proportion of carbohydrate?

Brand A	
Per 100 g	
Protein	12.5 g
Carbohydrate	23 g
Fat	4.5 g

Brand B	
Percentage content	
Protein	15%
Carbohydrate	22.5%
Fat	5%

8 Problem-solving The ratio of boys to girls in a class is 11 : 14. What percentage of the class are girls?

9 Problem-solving / Reasoning This pie chart shows the languages studied by students at a school.

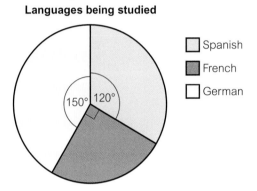

Languages being studied

- Spanish
- French
- German

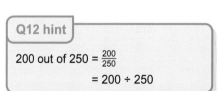

Q9 Strategy hint
Use the pie chart to work out the fraction of students who study French.

  a 15 people study French. How many people were surveyed?
  b How many people study
    i German
    ii Spanish?

10 Problem-solving / Reasoning Dave's driving theory test had 20 questions in it. He scored 70%.
How many questions did he get wrong?

11 Problem-solving / Reasoning 120 students voted in a school council election. 56 people voted for Matt, the rest voted for Hassan. What percentage of votes did Hassan win, to the nearest 1%?

12 Max scored 200 out of a possible 250 in his maths test. What was his score as a percentage?

Q12 hint
200 out of 250 = $\frac{200}{250}$
= 200 ÷ 250

13 Real There are 50 states in the USA. 27 of them have no coast. What percentage of the states have no coast?

14 Explore How do calculators show 150%?
Look back at the maths you have learned in this lesson. How can you use it to answer this question?

15 Reflect Q10 and Q11 are tagged as problem-solving questions. This means that there are alternative ways of finding the answer. Which method or methods did you choose? Explain why.

MASTER

Check
P93

Strengthen
P95

Extend
P99

Test
P103

4.7 FINANCE: Percentage change

You will learn to:
- Work out a percentage increase or decrease.

Why learn this?
Understanding percentage change means you can make sure you don't get overcharged or short-changed.

Fluency
Write 8 as a percentage of
- 10
- 16
- 100
- 200

Explore
What does 'Up to 100% less sugar' actually mean?

Exercise 4.7: Percentage change

1 Work out 30% of
 a 70 **b** 25 **c** 10 **d** 44 **e** 90

2 Write each improper fraction as
 i a mixed number
 ii a decimal
 iii a percentage.
 a $\frac{150}{100}$ **b** $\frac{375}{150}$ **c** $\frac{60}{50}$ **d** $\frac{225}{50}$

3 Increase each amount by 20%.
 a £160

$$\times 2 \left(\begin{array}{l} 10\% = \square \\ 20\% = \square \end{array} \right) \times 2$$

$$£160 + \square = \square$$

 b £3400

$$\times 2 \left(\begin{array}{l} 10\% = \square \\ 20\% = \square \end{array} \right) \times 2$$

$$£3400 + \square = \square$$

 c £25 000

> **Key point**
> An increase of 20% means original amount (100%)
> + 20% of that amount
> = 120% of the amount.

4 Work out
 a £180 increased by 20% **b** $2600 increased by 15%
 c €2500 increased by 30% **d** £4200 increased by 25%
 e $3500 increased by 5% **f** €4250 increased by 50%

5 Decrease each amount by 25%.
 a £240 ÷ 4 = $\square$
  25% of £240 = $\square$
  £240 − $\square$ = $\square$
 b £3200 **c** £24 000

> **Q5a hint**
> 25% = $\frac{1}{4}$ so divide by 4.

6 Work out

  a £80 decreased by 5%   **b** $1200 decreased by 20%
  c £680 decreased by 10%   **d** €910 decreased by 1%
  e £8050 decreased by 15%   **f** $3400 decreased by 30%

7 **Finance** A travel company advertises these holidays in June.

  Albania   £650
  Bulgaria   £725
  Croatia   £856

  All the prices go up by 12% in July. How much is each holiday in July?

8 **Real / Finance** **a** A newspaper headline reads, 'House prices rise by 100% in the last decade'. What does that mean?

  b May's house has increased in value by 100% since she bought it. It cost her £125 000. How much is it worth now?

> **Q8 hint**
>
> An increase of 100% means add on 100%.

9 **Finance** **a** A coat costs £180. It is reduced by 30% in a sale. What is its sale price?

  b A pair of jeans cost £70. They are reduced by 45% in a sale. What is the sale price?

10 **Finance** Work out the cost of each item when 20% **VAT** is added.

  a A computer that costs £720

  b A meal that costs £55

  c A haircut that costs £18

> **Q10 Literacy hint**
>
> **VAT** (Value Added Tax) is a tax that is added to some goods and services before you buy them.

11 **Finance / Problem-solving** Janet needs a new sofa. Which shop has the cheaper price?

Shop A	**Shop B**
Sofa: £350	Sofa: £340
20% off!	15% off!

12 **Reasoning** Eli saves £10, which is 20% of his allowance. How much is his allowance?

13 **Finance** A savings account advertises:

> *Earn 2% on your investment each year*

  Sue invests £2000.

  a How much interest will Sue receive each year?

  b Sue doesn't put any more money into the account. How much money will Sue have in the account in total after 5 years?

> **Q13 hint**
>
> The interest is only paid on the original investment.

14 **Reasoning** Jamie's savings account pays 5% interest each year. He receives £10 after 1 year.
  How much money was in the account?

> **Q14 hint**
>
> £10 is 5%
> How much is 10%?
> How much is 100%?

15 **Explore** What does 'Up to 100% less sugar' actually mean? Look back at the maths you have learned in this lesson. How can you use it to answer this question?

16 **Reflect** In this lesson some questions are about 'interest'. Explain in your own words what is meant by 'interest' and why it might be useful to understand its meaning.

Reflect **Explore**

4 Check up

Log how you did on your Student Progression Chart.

Equivalent proportions

1 Copy and complete the table showing equivalent fractions, decimals and percentages.
Write fractions in their simplest form.

Fraction	Decimal	Percentage
	0.45	
$\frac{2}{25}$		
		5%
$1\frac{1}{2}$		
	$0.\dot{3}$	

2 Write 0.82 as a fraction in its simplest form.

3 Write each fraction as a decimal.

a $\frac{3}{8}$　　　　b $\frac{1}{9}$

4 Write < or > between each pair of fractions.

a $\frac{19}{25} \square \frac{11}{15}$　　　b $\frac{2}{3} \square \frac{7}{10}$

5 Write these values in order, smallest to largest.

$\frac{11}{20}$　　　0.51　　　54.5%　　　8 out of 15

Fraction calculations

6 Work out

a $\frac{5}{9} + \frac{1}{6}$　　　　b $\frac{9}{10} - \frac{3}{4}$

7 Work out the sum of $\frac{1}{4}$, $\frac{5}{6}$, and $\frac{2}{3}$. Write your answer as a mixed number.

8 Work out each calculation. Write your answers in their simplest form.

a $\frac{3}{4} \times \frac{3}{5}$　　　b $\frac{2}{9} \times \frac{3}{7}$　　　c $\left(\frac{2}{5}\right)^2$

9 Work out

a $4\frac{1}{5} + 1\frac{7}{10}$　　b $1\frac{3}{4} + 2\frac{3}{5}$　　c $3\frac{9}{10} - 1\frac{4}{5}$　　d $2\frac{2}{3} - 1\frac{3}{10}$

10 Chantel needs 5 lengths of ribbon. Each length is $\frac{3}{4}$ metres.
She says, 'I know I will need less than 5 metres altogether'.
How does she know?

11 Work out $\frac{6}{13} \times \frac{2}{3}$

12 Work out

a $7 \div \frac{1}{2}$　　　b $4 \div \frac{1}{5}$　　　c $8 \div \frac{2}{3}$

13 Write the reciprocal of

a $\frac{6}{7}$　　　　b 7　　　　c $\frac{2}{3}$

Percentages

14 The ratio of boys to girls in a class is 9 : 11. What percentage of the class are boys?

15 A football club has 10 male players and 15 female players.
What percentage of the club are
a male
b female?

16 Work out
a £460 increased by 25%
b $4500 increased by 15%.

17 Anna has to pay 20% tax on a laptop. The laptop costs £450 before tax. How much does Anna pay in total?

18 Brian invests £5000 with yearly interest paid at 1%. How much interest will he earn after 1 year?

19 A flat increased in value by 150%. It was worth £200 000. What is its new value?

20 Work out
a £30 reduced by 25%
b £200 reduced by 5%

21 Steve's car has gone down in value by 15%. He paid £8600. What is it worth now?

22 20% of an amount is $25. What is the amount?

23 **How sure are you of your answers? Were you mostly**
😞 **Just guessing**   😐 **Feeling doubtful**   🙂 **Confident**
What next? Use your results to decide whether to strengthen or extend your learning.

Reflect

Challenge

24 Jarred draws a square.
He colours in half red. He colours in half of the rest orange.

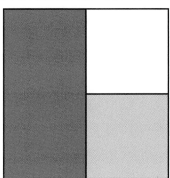

He continues like this, colouring in half of what's left using the colours of the rainbow: red, orange, yellow, green, blue, indigo, violet.
a What fraction of the square will be coloured indigo?
b What fraction will be coloured violet?
c Freya tries a similar experiment, colouring in $\frac{1}{3}$ of the shape each time. Explore the different fractions in Freya's shape.

4 Strengthen

You will:
- Strengthen your understanding with practice.

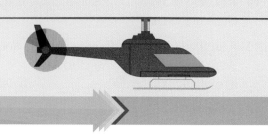

Equivalent proportions

1 Write each of these as a decimal number.
- **a** $43 \div 100$
- **b** $17 \div 100$
- **c** $32 \div 100$
- **d** $98 \div 100$
- **e** 52%
- **f** 65%

Q1e hint

52% is the same as 52 out of $100 = 52 \div 100$

2 Write each decimal as a
  i percentage
  ii fraction in its simplest form.
- **a** 0.13
- **b** 0.32
- **c** 0.68

Q2b hint

$0.32 = \frac{32}{100}$

Simplify the fraction.

3 Write each fraction as a percentage.
- **a** $\frac{3}{4}$
- **b** $\frac{3}{50}$
- **c** $\frac{7}{20}$
- **d** $\frac{17}{20}$
- **e** $\frac{19}{25}$

Q3 hint

Write an equivalent fraction with denominator 100.

4 Match up equivalent fractions, decimals and percentages.

1.4	220%	$2\frac{1}{5}$	$\frac{4}{5}$	140%	$1\frac{2}{5}$

125%	1.25	80%	0.8	$1\frac{1}{4}$	2.2

5 Write each decimal as a fraction. Simplify where possible.
- **a** $0.123 = \dfrac{123}{\square}$
- **b** 0.763
- **c** 0.442
- **d** 0.125
- **e** 0.988
- **f** 0.375
- **g** 0.128

6 Rewrite each recurring decimal using dot notation.
- **a** $0.6666\ldots$
- **b** $1.3333\ldots$
- **c** $2.151515\ldots$
- **d** $3.567567567\ldots$

Q6 Literacy hint

A dot above a digit shows it recurs.
$6.\dot{4} = 6.4444\ldots$
A dot above the beginning and end of a sequence shows the whole sequence recurs.
$9.\dot{3}9\dot{4} = 9.394394394394\ldots$

7 Write these decimals in order, from smallest to largest.
- **a** $0.3 \quad 0.\dot{3} \quad 0.329 \quad 0.32$
- **b** $0.\dot{4} \quad 0.45 \quad 0.439 \quad 0.4$
- **c** $0.\dot{5} \quad 0.549 \quad 0.5 \quad 0.56$
- **d** $0.665 \quad 0.68 \quad 0.\dot{6} \quad 0.6$

Q7a hint

Which is larger: 0.3 or 0.3333....?

8 Use a written method to work out each division.
- **a** $235 \div 5$
- **b** $135 \div 9$
- **c** $856 \div 8$

Q8a hint

$5\overline{)235}$

9 Use a written method to write each fraction as a decimal.
- **a** $\frac{7}{8}$
- **b** $\frac{3}{8}$
- **c** $\frac{5}{16}$
- **d** $\frac{3}{16}$

Q9a hint

$\begin{array}{r} 0.\square\square\square \\ 8\overline{)7.^{7}0\,0\,0} \end{array}$

10 Which of these fractions will give a recurring decimal?

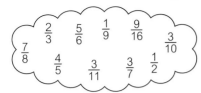

$\frac{7}{8}$ $\frac{2}{3}$ $\frac{5}{6}$ $\frac{1}{9}$ $\frac{9}{16}$ $\frac{3}{10}$ $\frac{4}{5}$ $\frac{3}{11}$ $\frac{3}{7}$ $\frac{1}{2}$

11 Write < or > between each pair of fractions.

a $\frac{1}{3} \square \frac{3}{10}$ **b** $\frac{3}{5} \square \frac{2}{3}$ **c** $\frac{4}{7} \square \frac{5}{9}$ **d** $\frac{8}{9} \square \frac{9}{11}$

Q11 hint

Write each fraction as a decimal.

12 Match each proportion to a bar. Use them to write the proportions in order, from smallest to largest.

A 0.7   **B** 0.5   **C** 60%   **D** $\frac{2}{3}$ **E** $\frac{3}{4}$

i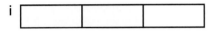

ii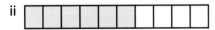

iii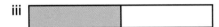

iv

v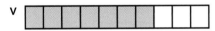

13 Write these proportions in **ascending** order.

a $\frac{4}{5}$ 0.4 30% 0.6 $\frac{2}{3}$ **b** 95% $\frac{5}{6}$ 0.9 $\frac{3}{4}$ 0.85

Q13 Literacy hint

Ascending means getting larger.

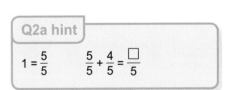

Fraction calculations

1 Write each improper fraction as a mixed number.

a $\frac{11}{3}$ **b** $\frac{22}{5}$

c $\frac{15}{4}$ **d** $\frac{24}{9}$

Q1a hint

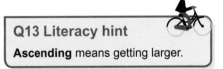

$\frac{11}{3}$

$\frac{3}{3} = 1$ $\frac{3}{3} = 1$ $\frac{3}{3} = 1$ $\frac{2}{3}$

2 Write each mixed number as an improper fraction.

a $1\frac{4}{5}$ **b** $2\frac{3}{4}$

c $2\frac{8}{9}$ **d** $3\frac{4}{7}$

Q2a hint

$1 = \frac{5}{5}$ $\frac{5}{5} + \frac{4}{5} = \frac{\square}{5}$

3 Work out each calculation. Write your answer as a mixed number.

a $\frac{2}{8} + \frac{5}{8} + \frac{7}{8} = \frac{\square}{8} = 1\frac{\square}{8}$ **b** $\frac{4}{9} + \frac{7}{9} + \frac{8}{9}$

c $\frac{4}{5} + \frac{2}{5} + \frac{3}{5}$ **d** $\frac{5}{12} + \frac{7}{12} + \frac{11}{12}$

4 Work out the missing number.

a $\frac{5}{9} + \frac{3}{9} + \square = 1$ **b** $1 - \frac{2}{9} - \frac{4}{9} = \square$

c $\frac{1}{12} + \frac{5}{12} + \square = 1$ **d** $1 - \frac{3}{7} - \frac{2}{7} = \square$

e $\frac{3}{5} + \frac{1}{10} + \square = 1$ **f** $\frac{7}{12} + \frac{1}{6} + \square = 1$

g $1 - \frac{1}{5} - \frac{3}{10} = \square$ **h** $1 - \frac{5}{8} - \frac{1}{4} = \square$

Q4a hint

How many ninths equal 1?

5 Problem-solving What fraction should the third sector on this pie chart be labelled?

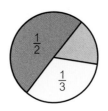

Q5 Strategy hint

Write the question as a subtraction calculation.

6 Work out

a $2\frac{1}{3} + 1\frac{4}{5} = 2 + 1 + \frac{1}{3} + \frac{4}{5}$

$= \square + \frac{\square}{\square}$

b $4\frac{5}{6} + 1\frac{2}{5}$

c $3\frac{4}{5} - 1\frac{3}{4} = (3 - 1) + \left(\frac{4}{5} - \frac{3}{4}\right)$

$= \square + \frac{\square}{\square}$

d $5\frac{2}{3} - 3\frac{1}{4}$

7 Work out

a $\frac{2}{3}$ of $\frac{1}{2} = \frac{2 \times 1}{3 \times 2} = \frac{\square}{\square}$

b $\frac{1}{4}$ of $\frac{4}{5}$

c $\frac{1}{3} \times \frac{3}{7}$

d $\frac{1}{4} \times \frac{3}{4}$

Q7a hint

Finding a fraction of an amount is the same as multiplying by the fraction.

$\frac{2}{3}$ of $\frac{1}{2}$

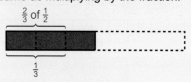

$\frac{1}{3}$

8 Work out

a $\frac{3}{4} \times \frac{5}{9}$ **b** $\frac{3}{5} \times \frac{3}{8}$ **c** $\frac{5}{9} \times \frac{2}{5}$

9 Work out

a $3 \div \frac{1}{4} = \frac{3}{1} \times \frac{4}{1} = \square$

b $3 \div \frac{3}{4} = \frac{3}{1} \times \frac{4}{3} = \square$

c $6 \div \frac{2}{3}$

d $6 \div \frac{3}{5}$

Q9a hint

How many quarters in 3?

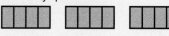

Percentages

1 The price of a computer has increased by 15%. It was originally £450. What is the new price?

Q1 hint

10% of 450 = $\square$
5% of 450 = $\square$
15% of 450 = $\square$ + $\square$ = $\square$
450 + $\square$ = $\square$

2 Reasoning Frankie works out £520 reduced by 20% like this:

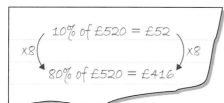

×8 (10% of £520 = £52) ×8
80% of £520 = £416

Rob works it out like this:

×2 (10% of £520 = £52) ×2
20% of £520 = £104
£520 − £104 = £416

Q2 hint

100% − 20% = 80%

Whose method do you prefer? Why?

3 The value of a car has gone down by 25%. It was originally worth £8000. What is the new value?

4 A holiday costs £1200. Booking before the end of the month saves 15%. How much is the holiday with the saving?

5 Reasoning / Problem-solving
    a 10% of a number is 25. What is the number?
    b 25% of a number is 50. What is the number?
    c 30% of a number is 24. What is the number?
    d 40% of a number is 320. What is the number?

Q5c Strategy hint

30% = 24
÷3   10% = ☐   ÷3
×10   100% = ☐   ×10

Enrichment

1 Draw a pie chart to show how you spent the 24 hours in a weekday during term-time.
What fraction or percentage of your time is spent
    a sleeping
    b in lessons
    c eating/washing/getting ready
    d socialising/entertainment/TV
    e homework?

Q1 hint

Number of degrees for each hour = 360° ÷ 24 hours.

2 How would your pie chart from Q1 be different for a Saturday in school holidays?

3 **Reflect** List these tasks in order from easiest to hardest.
    A Adding and subtracting fractions
    B Multiplying fractions
    C Dividing fractions
    D Adding and subtracting mixed numbers
    E Multiplying mixed numbers
    F Dividing mixed numbers
Look at the first task in your list (easiest). What made it easiest?
Look at the two tasks at the bottom of your list (hardest). What made them hardest?
Write a hint to help you with the two tasks you found hardest.

Q3 hint

List the letters of the tasks in order. You don't need to write out the descriptions.

Reflect

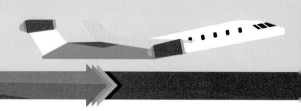

4 Extend

You will:
- Extend your understanding with problem-solving.

1 Write each percentage as a decimal.
  a 12.5% **b** 58.3% **c** 5.4%
  d 2.9% **e** 14.75% **f** 3.25%

2 Write each decimal as a percentage.
  a 0.185 **b** 0.529 **c** 0.095
  d 0.1234 **e** 0.0987 **f** 0.0037

3 Write each terminating decimal as a fraction in the simplest form.
  a 0.18 **b** 0.99 **c** 0.175 **d** 0.025
  e 1.65 **f** 4.848 **g** 3.05 **h** 6.02

4 Work out the first amount as a percentage of the second amount.
  a 80p out of £2 **b** 750 ml out of 3 litres
  c 40 minutes out of 2 hours **d** 250 cm out of 4 metres
  e 3.5 kg out of 5 kg **f** 2.4 km out of 6 km

> **Q4 hint**
> Make sure the units are the same.

5 98 out of 180 members of a tennis club are male.
  a What fraction of the club are female?
  b What percentage of the club are male, to the nearest 1%?

6 **Real** 20 out of 196 countries in the world have Spanish as their official language. What percentage of countries is that, to the nearest 1%?

7 **Reasoning** Sort these fractions into terminating or non-terminating decimals.
$$\frac{1}{2} \quad \frac{1}{3} \quad \frac{1}{4} \quad \frac{1}{5} \quad \frac{1}{6} \quad \frac{1}{7} \quad \frac{1}{8} \quad \frac{1}{9} \quad \frac{1}{10} \quad \frac{1}{11} \quad \frac{1}{12}$$

> **Q7 Strategy hint**
> Use division if you are not sure.

8 Write these fractions in order from largest to smallest.
  a $\frac{3}{4} \quad \frac{17}{20} \quad \frac{2}{3} \quad \frac{3}{5}$ **b** $\frac{2}{5} \quad \frac{3}{10} \quad \frac{7}{20} \quad \frac{11}{25}$

> **Q8 Strategy hint**
> Write each fraction as a decimal to compare them.

9 **Reasoning** Write each fraction as a decimal to show why each statement is true.
  a $\frac{1}{3} > \frac{3}{10}$ **b** $\frac{2}{3} > \frac{3}{5}$ **c** $\frac{4}{9} < \frac{1}{2}$ **d** $\frac{3}{4} < \frac{7}{9}$

10 Write each time as a mixed number.
  a 1 hour 45 minutes = $1\frac{\square}{\square}$ hours **b** 1 hour 10 minutes
  c 5 hours 40 minutes **d** 2 hours 15 minutes
  e 3 hours 55 minutes **f** 2 hours 5 minutes
  g 1 hour 25 minutes **h** 20 minutes
  i 35 minutes **j** 50 minutes

> **Q10a hint**
> 45 minutes = $\frac{45}{60}$ of an hour
> Simplify the fraction.

11 Write each of the times in Q10 as a decimal number of hours.

12 Work out each calculation. Give your answer in hours and minutes.

   a 2 hours 30 minutes × 5 = $\frac{\square}{\square}$ hours × 5 = ____ hours ____ minutes

   b 4 × 1 hour 45 minutes   **c** 3 hours ÷ 30 minutes

13 Modelling / Problem-solving A film lasts 2 hours 15 minutes. A cinema plays it continuously from 13:00 to 22:00. How many times is it played?

14 A bus journey to the city lasts 1 hour 15 minutes each way. Raghev travels by bus into the city and back three times a week. What is the total time Raghev spends travelling by bus to the city each week?

15 Match pairs of times.

   A 1 hour 6 minutes   **i** 2.9 hours

   B 2 hours 3 minutes   **ii** 1.35 hours

   C 2 hours 54 minutes   **iii** 1.1 hours

   D 1 hour 12 minutes   **iv** 2.8 hours

   E 2 hours 48 minutes   **v** 2.05 hours

   F 1 hour 21 minutes   **vi** 1.2 hours

16 Real 53 million people were recorded in the 2011 census for England. Of these, approximately 6 million people were under 10 years old. What percentage were under 10?

17 A restaurant bill costs £100 plus taxes. The final bill including tax is £110. What percentage of the restaurant bill is tax?

18 Work out the percentage increase. The first one has been started for you.

> **Q18 hint**
>
> Percentage = amount of ÷ original
> change   increase   amount

   a £80 increased to £100

      Difference: 100 − 80 = 20

$$\frac{\text{Difference}}{\text{Original amount}} = \frac{20}{80}$$
$$= \frac{1}{4} = \square\%$$

             Increase of $\square$%

        Check: £80 + 25% = $\square$

   b £120 increased to £144

      Difference: 144 − 120 = $\square$

   c £1500 to £1650   **d** £360 to £405   **e** $420 to $453.60

19 Before tax a bike costs £490. With tax it is £578.20. What percentage was the tax?

20 A school has increased in size from 2200 pupils to 2464 pupils. By what percentage has the school size increased?

21 The cost a bag of bananas has risen from £1.40 to £1.47. What percentage increase is this?

22 Work out the percentage decrease. The first one has been started for you.

   a £80 decreased to £68

      Difference: $80 - 68 = 12$

$$\frac{\text{Difference}}{\text{Original amount}} = \frac{12}{80} = 0.15$$

$$= \square\%$$

      Decrease of $\square\%$

   b £120 decreased to £96

      Difference: $120 - 96 = \square$

   c £1500 to £1125

   d £360 to £342

   e $250 to $218.75

Q22 Strategy hint

Check your answer by working out the decrease.

23 Real A ski helmet is reduced from £150 to £97.50. What percentage is it reduced by?

24 Real A jacket costs £120. There is £15 off. What percentage reduction is this?

25 Work out

   a $3\frac{2}{5} + 2\frac{1}{3} + 2\frac{7}{10}$ **b** $4\frac{5}{6} - 2\frac{2}{3} - 1\frac{2}{9}$ **c** $\frac{1}{2} \times \frac{3}{4} \times \frac{5}{6}$

   d $\frac{2}{3} \times \frac{6}{7} \times \frac{3}{4}$ **e** $(3 \div \frac{3}{4}) \times \frac{1}{3}$ **f** $3 \div (\frac{3}{4} \times \frac{1}{3})$

   g $(6 \div \frac{2}{3}) \times \frac{1}{4}$ **h** $6 \div (\frac{2}{3} \times \frac{1}{4})$

26 Use division to write each fraction as a decimal.

   a $\frac{7}{11}$ **b** $\frac{4}{15}$ **c** $\frac{17}{24}$

27 Write the reciprocals of each number. Give your answers in their simplest form.

   a $\frac{7}{11}$ **b** $\frac{4}{15}$ **c** $3\frac{5}{6}$

Q27c hint

Write mixed numbers as improper fractions first.

28 Work out the sum of $3\frac{2}{9}$, 1.8 and $4\frac{2}{3}$

29 How many $\frac{3}{4}$ litres bottles can be filled from a 9-litre container?

30 Problem-solving Graham, Andrea and Carly are playing a missing-number game.

Graham says, '35% of my number is 70'.

Andrea says, '15% of my number 75'.

Carly says, '30% of my number is 60'.

What is the sum of all three of their numbers?

Investigation   Reasoning / Modelling / Problem-solving

1 Write the next four terms in each of these fraction sequences.

   a $\frac{1}{2}, \frac{1}{3}, \frac{1}{4}, \frac{1}{5}, \dots$ **b** $\frac{1}{2}, \frac{2}{3}, \frac{3}{4}, \frac{4}{5}, \dots$ **c** $\frac{9}{10}, \frac{8}{9}, \frac{7}{8}, \dots$

2 Write each term in the sequence as a decimal number.

3 Bhavika says, 'Each sequence is getting closer and closer to a number'.

   For each sequence, write down which number it is getting closer to.

Discussion Do you think the sequence will reach that number? Explain

31 a Match each statement to the percentage it gives of the original amount.

A An increase of 30%	**i** 70%
B A decrease of 10%	**ii** 82%
C Interest of 18%	**iii** 130%
D Interest gain of 1%	**iv** 99%
E Saving of 30%	**v** 90%
F 18% reduction	**vi** 118%
G 1% less	**vii** 101%

b Write each percentage in part **a** as a decimal.

 32 Work out these percentages of amounts using a **decimal multiplier**.
  a 80% of 2756 = 0.8 × 2756 = ☐   **b** 5% of 650 = 0.05 × ☐ =
  c 72% of 3675   **d** 90% of £148
  e 7% of £1240   **f** 125% of £32000

 33 Use a decimal multiplier to work out
  a £120 increased by 30%   **b** £1500 increased by 15%
  c $4800 increased by 5%   **d** €2240 increased by 12.5%.

34 Use a decimal multiplier to work out
  a £1240 decreased by 10%   **b** £3500 decreased by 15%
  c $2800 decreased by 30%   **d** $7200 decreased by 22%
  e €1242 decreased by 5%   **f** €1250 decreased by 7.5%.

35 Problem-solving / Finance An insurance company offers two ways of paying.

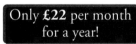

Only **£22** per month for a year!

ONE-OFF PAYMENT OF £240.

  a How much more expensive, overall, is the pay monthly option?
  b What percentage of the yearly payment is added to the monthly option?

36 Reflect Write down three new skills you have learned in this unit. For each one of these, choose a question that used this new skill.

Key point
You can multiply an amount by a **decimal multiplier** to work out percentage change.

Q33a hint
An increase of 30% = 100% + 30%
                   = 130%
                   = ☐.☐

Q34a hint
A decrease of 10% = 100% − 10%
                  = 90%
                  = ☐.☐

Reflect

4 Unit test

Log how you did on your Student Progression Chart.

1 Write each decimal number as a percentage.
  a 0.15   **b** 0.2
  c 0.01   **d** 3.4

2 Write each decimal number as a fraction or mixed number in its simplest form.
  a 0.08   **b** 1.25

3 Write $\frac{13}{20}$ as
  a a percentage   **b** a decimal.

4 Write these fractions in order, smallest to largest.
  $$\frac{7}{10} \quad \frac{6}{5} \quad \frac{11}{20} \quad \frac{12}{25} \quad \frac{7}{10} \quad \frac{6}{5} \quad \frac{11}{20} \quad \frac{12}{25}$$

5 Write $\frac{4}{15}$ as a decimal.

6 Work out
  a $\frac{3}{5} + \frac{1}{6}$ **b** $\frac{8}{9} - \frac{2}{3}$

7 Work out $\frac{4}{7} + \frac{5}{7} + \frac{6}{7}$. Give your answer as a mixed number in its simplest form.

8 Work out
  a $4\frac{4}{5} - 1\frac{3}{10}$ **b** $2\frac{2}{3} + 1\frac{4}{5}$

9 In a triathlon, Rich swims $1\frac{3}{4}$ km, cycles $15\frac{7}{10}$ km and runs $8\frac{4}{5}$ km. What is the total distance covered by the triathlon?

10 The ratio of boys to girls in a class is $13:12$.
  a What fraction of the class are girls?
  b What percentage of the class are girls?

11 Increase $2640 by 5%.

12 Work out $4 \div \frac{1}{6}$

13 Work out each calculation. Give your answers in their simplest form.
  a $\frac{4}{15} \times \frac{3}{8}$ **b** $\frac{1}{2} \times \frac{3}{5} \times \frac{5}{9}$
  c $3 \div \frac{3}{4}$

14 Write the reciprocal of
  a $\frac{11}{12}$ **b** 3
  c $\frac{1}{10}$ **d** $\frac{12}{5}$

15 A house increased in value by 200%. It was originally worth £215 000. What is its new value?

16 Reduce £470 by 6%.

17 A restaurant bill says £60.50 + 14% service charge. How much is the total bill, with service charge?

18 25% of a number is 14. What is the number?

19 A truck has gone down in value from £50 000 to £42 500. By what percentage has the value reduced?

20 Write 2 hours 15 minutes as
  a a fraction of an hour
  b a decimal proportion of an hour.

21 Copy and complete, writing < or >. $\frac{4}{5} \square \frac{7}{9}$.

22 Write the decimal multiplier for working out a
  a 90% increase   **b** 3% increase
  c 40% decrease   **d** 2% decrease

Challenge

23 **Reasoning** Use these number cards to make 2 different proper fractions, for example $\frac{2}{5}$ and $\frac{1}{3}$.

  a Work out the sum of your two fractions
  b Work out the difference between your two fractions.
  c Do you think the sum is as large as possible? If not, make two different fractions using the numbers.
  d Do you think the difference is as small as possible? If not, make two different fractions using the numbers.
  e How can you make sure the sum is as large as possible?
  f How can you make sure the difference is as small as possible?
  g Try with 4 different numbers.

24 **Reflect** Look back at this test. Which questions took the shortest time to answer and which took the longest? Why do you think you could answer some questions more quickly than others?

5.1 Angles

You will learn to:
* Identify alternate and corresponding angles
* Work with angles in polygons.

Why learn this?
Lots of sports techniques are based on angle properties.

Fluency
What are the missing numbers?
* $20 + \square = 90$
* $45 + \square = 90$
* $120 + \square = 180$
* $40 + \square = 180$

Explore
What are the interior angles of the hexagons and pentagons on a football?

Exercise 5.1

1 a How many degrees are there in a right angle?
   b How many degrees are there in a quarter turn?

2 Work out the size of each angle marked with a letter.

a

b

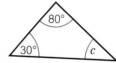

c

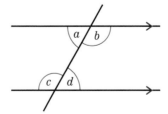

3 Reasoning The diagram shows a line crossing two **parallel** lines.
   a Measure angles a, b, c and d.
   b Write down two pairs of equal angles.

> **Q3 Literacy hint**
> **Parallel** lines are marked with an arrowhead.
>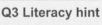
>

4 Reasoning The diagram show two lines crossing two parallel lines.

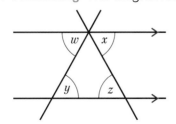

Copy and complete these statements.
   a Angle w and angle $\square$ are equal because they are **alternate angles**.
   b Angle x and angle $\square$ are equal because they are _____ angles.

> **Key point**
> When a line crosses two parallel lines it creates a 'Z' shape.
> Inside the Z shape are **alternate angles**. Alternate angles are equal.
>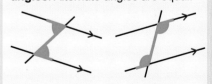
> Alternate angles are on different (alternate) sides of the diagonal line.

5 Reasoning Write down the sizes of the angles marked with letters.

a
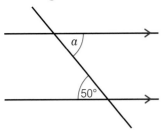

b
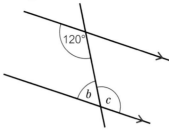

Give reasons for your answers.

Q5 hint

Angles b and c are on a straight line.

6 Reasoning The diagram shows a line crossing two parallel lines.

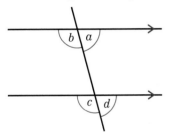

a Measure angles a, b and c.
b Which angles are equal?
c Which angles add to 180°?

Key point

When a line crosses two parallel lines it creates an 'F' shape. There are **corresponding angles** on an F shape. Corresponding angles are equal.

Corresponding angles are on the same (corresponding) side of the diagonal line.

7 Reasoning The diagram shows a line crossing two parallel lines.

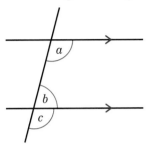

Copy and complete these statements.
a Angle a and angle ☐ are equal because they are _____ angles.
b Angle b and angle ☐ are equal because they are _____ angles.
c Angles ☐ and ☐ add up to 180° because _____.

8 Reasoning Write down the sizes of the angles marked with letters.

a
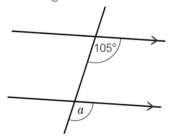

b
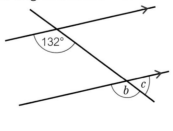

Give reasons for your answers.

9 a Measure each
exterior angle of
this pentagon.
b Work out the
sum of the
exterior angles.

Discussion
What do you
notice about the
sum of the exterior
angles?

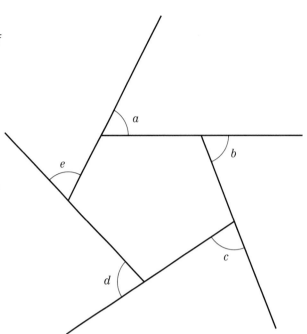

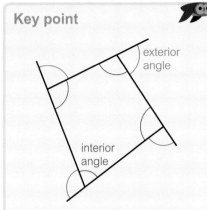
Investigation   Reasoning

You can work out the sum of the **interior angles** in a polygon by splitting the polygon into triangles.

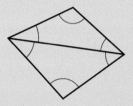 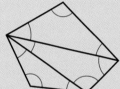

A quadrilateral can be split into two triangles. A pentagon can be split into three triangles.

1 Copy and complete this table.

Shape	Number of sides	Number of triangles	Sum of interior angles
Triangle	3	1	180°
Quadrilateral	4	2	360°
Pentagon	5	3	□°
Hexagon	6	□	□°

2 Describe in your own words how to work out the number of triangles from the number of sides.
3 Describe in your own words how to work out the sum of the interior angles from the number of sides.

10 Reasoning
a What is the sum of the interior angles of a hexagon?
b Work out the size of one interior angle in a **regular** hexagon.

11 Explore What are the interior angles of the hexagons and the pentagons on a football?
Is it easier to explore this question now you have completed the lesson?
What further information do you need to be able to answer this?

12 Reflect In this lesson you used alternate and corresponding angles to work out the size of unknown angles. Do you find it easy to remember which is which? Think of a hint that would help you or a classmate to remember the difference.

*Active*Learn   Pi 3, Section 5.1

Explore

Reflect

5.2 Maps and scales

You will learn to:
- Use scales in maps and plans
- Draw diagrams to scale.

Why learn this?
Scales on maps help you work out real distances between places.

Fluency
How much of each ingredient do you need to make 12 pancakes?

Makes 4 pancakes:

1 egg

50 g flour

150 ml milk

Explore
How big would a scale model of your school be?

Exercise 5.2

1 Measure the length of each line.

a ———————————

b ———————————

2 Draw a line AB 4.5 cm long.

3 In this diagram, 1 cm represents 2 m in real life.

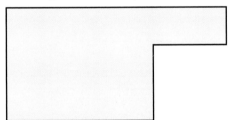

a Measure each side.

b Write the real-life lengths on a copy of the drawing.

> **Q3b hint**
>
> Diagram   Real life
>
> ×3 (1 cm   is   2 m) ×3
>   3 cm   is   ☐ m

4 On a scale drawing, 1 cm represents 5 cm. Work out the real-life distance of

   a 5 cm   b 4 cm   c 3 cm   d 2.5 cm

5 Jonah makes a scale drawing of this flowerbed, using a **scale** of 1 cm for every 5 m.
What are the **dimensions** of Jonah's drawing?

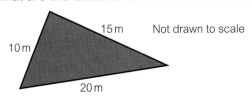

15 m   Not drawn to scale

10 m

20 m

> **Q5 Literacy hint**
>
> The **scale** shows the ratio of the measurements on the drawing to the measurements in real life.
> **Dimensions** is another way of saying lengths or widths.

Warm up

6 A map uses a scale where 1 cm represents 10 m. What is the measurement on the map for each real-life distance?

   a 20 m   **b** 50 m   **c** 60 m   **d** 25 m

Q6a hint
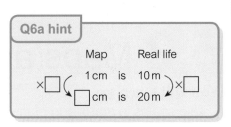

7 This map uses a scale where 1 cm represents 20 m in real life.

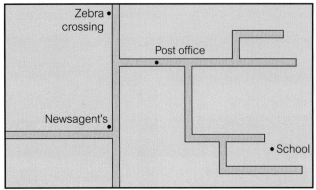

   a Use a ruler to work out the real-life distance on the roads between
      i the newsagent and the zebra crossing
      ii the school and the post office.
   b Alix walks from the newsagent's to the post office.
     How far does she walk?

8 **Real** The diagram shows a sketch of a skateboard ramp.

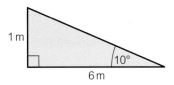

Use a scale of 1 cm for every 1 m to make an **accurate drawing** of the ramp.

> **Key point**
> **Accurate drawings** are drawn to scale, with accurate angles.
> Use a ruler and protractor to make accurate drawings.

9 **Real / Problem-solving** The diagram shows a sketch of a playground.

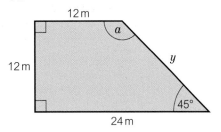

   a Work out the size of the angle marked a.
   b Use a scale of 1 cm for every 4 m to make an accurate drawing of the playground.
   c Measure the length of the side marked y on your diagram.
   d Work out the real length of y.

10 **Explore** How big would a scale model of your school be?
Is it easier to explore this question now you have completed the lesson?
What further information do you need to be able to answer this?

11 **Reflect** Look again at Q5. Write a Worked example for a question like this that will help you when you come to revise this topic.

Topic links: Ratio, Measure   *Active* Learn   Pi 3, Section 5.2

Explore

Reflect

5.3 Constructions

You will learn to:
- Use a ruler and compasses to bisect a line segment
- Use a ruler and compasses to bisect an angle.

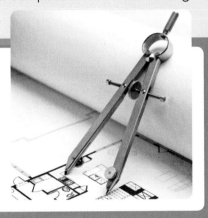

Why learn this?
Architects bisect lines and angles when drawing plans of buildings.

Fluency
Copy and complete
- A right angle is ☐°
- Half of 360° is ☐°
- $\frac{1}{2}$ of 30 is ☐
- $\frac{1}{2}$ of 60 is ☐

Explore
What is the shortest distance across a river?

Exercise 5.3

1 Use compasses to draw three different sized circles.

2 Draw an angle of 35°.

Worked example

Construct the **perpendicular bisector** of a line 8 cm long.

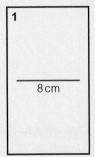 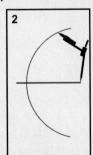 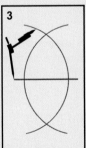 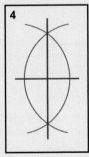

| 1 | 2 | 3 | 4 |

8 cm

1 Use a ruler to draw a line 8 cm long.
2 Open your compasses greater than half the length of the line. Place the point on one end of the line and draw an arc above and below.
3 Keeping the compasses the same, put the point on the other end of the line and draw another arc.
4 Use a ruler to join the point where the arcs intersect. The vertical line divides the horizontal line exactly in half and is perpendicular to it.
Do not rub out the construction lines (arcs).

Key point
Construct means draw accurately using a ruler and compasses.
Perpendicular means 'at right angles'.
Bisect means 'to cut in half'.
A **perpendicular bisector** is the line that cuts another line in half at right angles.

3 a Draw a line 10 cm long. Construct the perpendicular bisector of the line.
  b Check by measuring that your line cuts the original line in half.
  c Check the angle where the lines cross.

4 Problem-solving Two rescue boats, P and Q are 24 m apart.

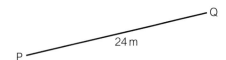

a Using a scale where 1 cm represents 4 m, draw an accurate scale drawing of the rescue boats.

b An injured dolphin is exactly the same distance from both boats. Mark two points where the dolphin could be.

c Draw a line to show all the points where the dolphin could be.

Worked example

Construct the **bisector** of a 60° angle.

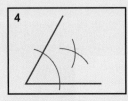
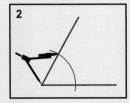
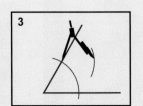

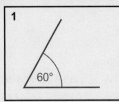
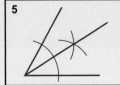

1 Draw the angle using a protractor.
2 Open your compasses and place the point at the vertex of the angle. Draw an arc that cuts both arms of the angle.
3 Keep the compasses the same. Move them to a point where the arc crosses one of the arms. Make an arc in the middle of the angle.
4 Do the same from the point where the arc crosses the other arm.
5 Join the point where the arcs cross to the vertex of the angle. The line joins the point where the two small arcs intersect to the point of the angle; it divides the angle exactly in half. Measure the two halves of the angle to check that they are equal.

5 a Draw a right angle using a protractor.
  b Construct the angle bisector using compasses and a ruler.

6 a Draw an angle of 45° using a protractor.
  b Using only compasses and a ruler, bisect the angle.

7 Explore What is the shortest distance across a river? Is it easier to explore this question now you have completed the lesson? What further information do you need to be able to answer this?

8 Reflect Put these in order, depending on how important you think they are for this lesson. (You can just write the letters for each statement.)
  A I know how to use a protractor.
  B I know number complements to 180.
  C I always have a sharp pencil when constructing diagrams.
  D I use a ruler when drawing straight lines.
  E I know what is meant by the words 'arc' and' bisector'.

Explore

Reflect

5.4 3D solids

You will learn to:
- Use 2D representations of 3D solids
- Work out the volume of shapes made from cuboids.

Why learn this?
Designers use 2D representations to instruct a 3D printer.

Fluency
Write the names of these 3D solids.

Explore
Which 3D objects will look like a square when viewed from above?

Exercise 5.4

1 On a scale drawing, 1 cm represents 25 cm. Calculate the real-life length of a line on the drawing which is

   a 2 cm   **b** 4 cm   **c** 10 cm   **d** 12 cm

2 Work out the volume of each solid.

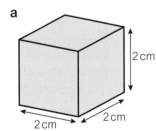

a 2 cm, 2 cm, 2 cm   **b** 10 m, 6 m, 2 m   **c** 3 m, 2 m, 50 cm

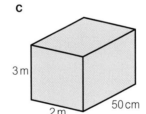

Q2c hint
Write 50 cm as 0.5 m so the units are the same.

Key point
You can use isometric paper to draw 2D representations of 3D objects.

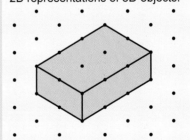

3 Draw each cuboid on isometric paper.

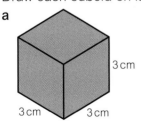

a 3 cm, 3 cm, 3 cm   **b** 3 cm, 4 cm, 6 cm

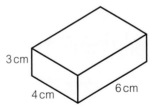

4 Using isometric paper, make an accurate drawing of this solid.

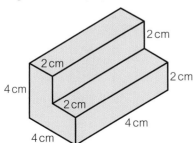

2 cm, 2 cm, 2 cm, 4 cm, 2 cm, 4 cm, 4 cm

Q4 hint
Draw the front face first.

Warm up

5 A gym is in the shape of a cuboid. Use a scale where 1 cm represents 4 m to draw an accurate scale drawing of the gym on isometric paper.

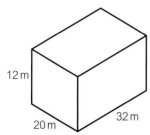

12 m
20 m
32 m

6 The diagram shows an L-shaped prism made from six cubes.
Write down
  a the number of faces
  b the number of edges
  c the number of vertices.

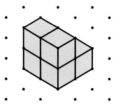

Q6 hint

Remember to include the faces, edges and vertices that you can't see.

7 Reasoning Jordan has a cube made of clay. He cuts off one of the vertices. How many faces does the solid have now?

Worked example

Draw the **plan**, the **front elevation** and the **side elevation** of this cuboid on squared paper.

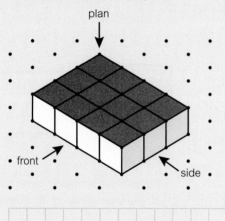

plan

front
side

Key point

Plans and **elevations** show you different views of 3D objects.

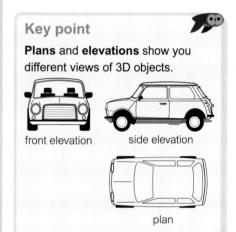

front elevation   side elevation

plan

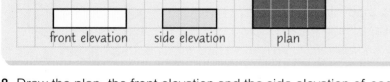

front elevation   side elevation   plan

---

8 Draw the plan, the front elevation and the side elevation of each 3D solid on squared paper.

a 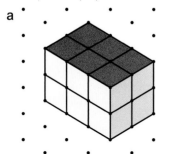   **b** 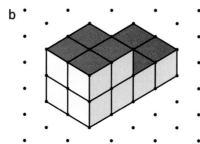   **c**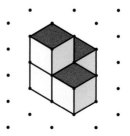

9 Draw the plan, the front elevation and the side elevation of a cube of length 4 cm.

10 Problem-solving / Reasoning L-shaped prisms can be split into two cuboids.
  a Work out the missing length on cuboid A.
  b Calculate the volume of cuboid A.
  c Calculate the volume of cuboid B.
  d Calculate the volume of the L-shaped prism.

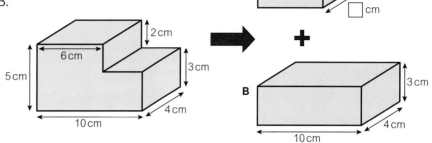

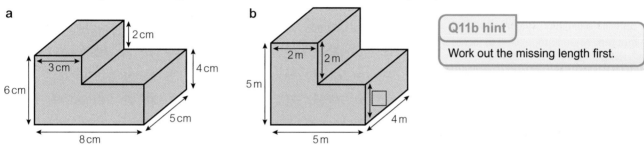

11 Problem-solving / Reasoning Calculate the volume of each L-shaped prism.

a

b

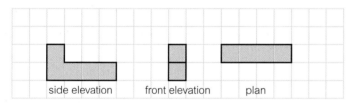

> **Q11b hint**
>
> Work out the missing length first.

12 Reasoning / Problem-solving The diagram shows the plan and elevations of a solid made from cubes.

side elevation   front elevation   plan

  a Use isometric paper to draw the solid.
  b Work out the volume of the solid.

13 **Explore** Which 3D objects will look like a square when viewed from above?
Look back at the maths you have learned in this lesson.
How can you use it to answer this question?

14 **Reflect** 3D solids can be represented by sketches, nets, isometric drawings or plans and elevations. Which representation do you find easiest to understand? Why?

Explore

Reflect

5.5 MODELLING: Pythagoras' theorem

You will learn to:

- Use Pythagoras' theorem to work out missing lengths.

Why learn this?
Satellite navigation systems use Pythagoras' theorem when triangulating to locate a vehicle.

Fluency
Work out
- 3^2
- 5^2
- 9^2
- $\sqrt{49}$
- $\sqrt{16}$
- $\sqrt{100}$

Explore
How do electronics shops advertise the size of television screens?

CONFIDENCE

Exercise 5.5: Geometry in real life

1 Work out each calculation. Give your answers to 1 decimal place where necessary.

  a $2^2 + 3^2$

  b $4^2 + 5^2$

  c $6^2 + 4^2$

  d $\sqrt{49}$

  e $\sqrt{16}$

  f $\sqrt{81}$

2 Solve each equation.

  a $x^2 = 121$

  b $c^2 = 100$

  c $y^2 = 36$

3 Substitute $s = 5$ and $t = 2$ into each equation. Solve the equations to work out the value you don't know.

  a $p = s + t$

  b $g + t = s$

  c $u - s = t$

  d $t - q = s$

4 Write down the length of the **hypotenuse** of each right-angled triangle.

Warm up

  a

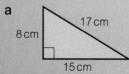
8 cm, 17 cm, 15 cm

  b

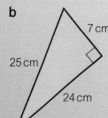
7 cm, 25 cm, 24 cm

  c

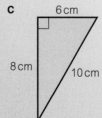
6 cm, 8 cm, 10 cm

Key point

The **hypotenuse** of a right-angled triangle is the longest side and is opposite the right angle.

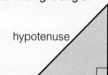
hypotenuse

Worked example

Work out the length of the hypotenuse in this right-angled triangle.

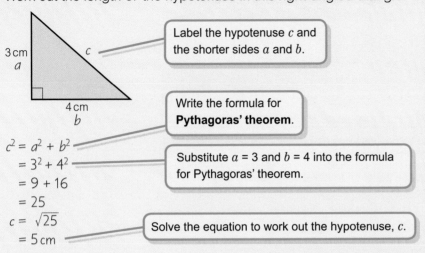

Label the hypotenuse c and the shorter sides a and b.

Write the formula for **Pythagoras' theorem**.

$c^2 = a^2 + b^2$
$= 3^2 + 4^2$
$= 9 + 16$
$= 25$
$c = \sqrt{25}$
$= 5\,\text{cm}$

Substitute $a = 3$ and $b = 4$ into the formula for Pythagoras' theorem.

Solve the equation to work out the hypotenuse, c.

Key point

Pythagoras' theorem shows the relationship between the lengths of the three sides of a right-angled triangle.

$c^2 = a^2 + b^2$

Discussion Does it matter which side you label a and which side you label b?

5 Work out the length of the hypotenuse of each right-angled triangle.

a
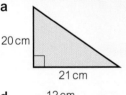
20 cm
21 cm

b

12 cm
35 cm

c

33 cm
56 cm

d

12 cm
16 cm

e

77 cm
36 cm

6 **Real / Modelling** The diagram shows a ladder leaning against the wall of a house.
  a Sketch the triangle.
  b Work out the length of the ladder, to the nearest metre.

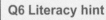
Wall
Ladder
7 m
2 m

Q6 Literacy hint

A **sketch** is a simple useful drawing. It doesn't have to be drawn to scale.

7 **Problem-solving / Modelling** A plane leaves an airport and flies 20 km east and then 45 km north.
Work out the distance of the plane from the airport.
Give your answer to the nearest km.

Q7 Strategy hint

Draw a sketch of the journey.

8 **Real / Modelling** Work out the diagonal length of this tablet screen.
Give your answer to 1 decimal place.

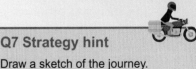
6.6 inches

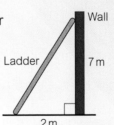

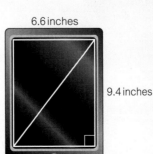
9.4 inches

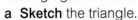

Worked example

Work out the length of the unknown side of this right-angled triangle.

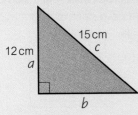

15 cm
c

12 cm
a

b

$c^2 = a^2 + b^2$
$15^2 = 12^2 + b^2$ ——— Substitute the values you know into Pythagoras' theorem.
$b^2 = 15^2 - 12^2$ ——— Rearrange the equation to make b^2 the subject.
$= 81$
$b = \sqrt{81}$
$= 9$ cm ——— Solve the equation to work out b.

9 Work out the length of the unknown side of each right-angled triangle.

a

12 cm

13 cm

b

16 cm

34 cm

c
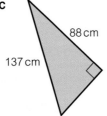
88 cm

137 cm

10 Modelling Work out the height of the flag above the ground.

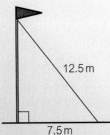
12.5 m

7.5 m

11 Explore How do electronics shops advertise the size of television screens?
Is it easier to explore this question now you have completed the lesson? What further information do you need to be able to answer this?

12 Reflect Marcia says, 'Pythagoras came up with an interesting theory, but it's not much use in real life.' How would you respond to Marcia? Is she right or wrong?

5 Check up

Log how you did on your Student Progression Chart.

Angles

1 Work out the size of the angles marked with letters in these diagrams. Give reasons for your answers.

a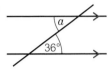
b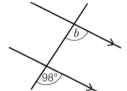
c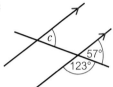
d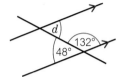

2 The diagram shows a pentagon split into triangles. Copy and complete this formula for working out the sum of the interior angles in a pentagon.

Sum of the interior angles in a pentagon = □ × 180° = □°

3 Work out the sum of the interior angles in a hexagon.

4 Which letter represents an exterior angle of this triangle?

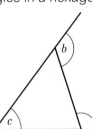

5 What is the sum of the exterior angles of a 7-sided shape?

Accurate drawings and constructions

6 A diagram uses a scale where 1 cm represents 4 cm in real life. Calculate the real-life length represented by

  a 5 cm   b 1.5 cm.

7 A map uses a scale of 1 cm to 20 m. A path is 80 m long. How long is the path on the map?

8 Draw a straight line 6 cm long. Construct the perpendicular bisector of the line.

9 a Copy this right angle.
   b Construct the angle bisector.

3D solids

10 This 3D solid is made from 8 cubes. Draw the solid on isometric paper.

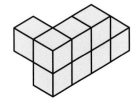

11 Draw the plan, the front elevation and the side elevation of this 3D solid on squared paper.

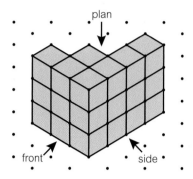

plan

front   side

12 Work out the volume of this L-shaped prism.

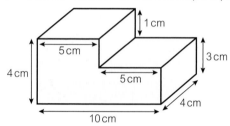

1 cm
5 cm
4 cm   5 cm   3 cm
4 cm
10 cm

Pythagoras' theorem

13 Work out the length of the hypotenuse of this triangle.

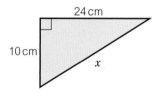

24 cm
10 cm
x

14 Calculate the length a of this triangle.

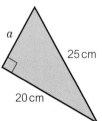

a
25 cm
20 cm

15 **How sure are you of your answers? Were you mostly**
☹ **Just guessing**   😐 **Feeling doubtful**   🙂 **Confident**
What next? Use your results to decide whether to strengthen or extend your learning.

Challenge

16 A Pythagorean triple is a group of three numbers a, b and c that satisfy Pythagoras' theorem so that
$c^2 = a^2 + b^2$
3, 4 and 5 is a Pythagorean triple because
$5^2 = 3^2 + 4^2$
Find as many other Pythagorean triples as you can.

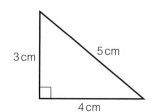

3 cm   5 cm
4 cm

> **Q16 hint**
>
> What happens if you enlarge this triangle by a scale factor of 2? What about other scale factors?

Reflect

5 Strengthen

You will:
- Strengthen your understanding with practice.

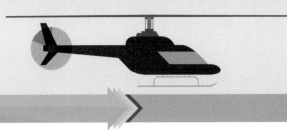

Angles

1 The diagram shows a line crossing two parallel lines.
Use the word **alternate** or **corresponding** to
complete these statements.

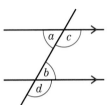

a a and b are _____ angles.

b c and d are _____ angles.

Q1 hint

Z N S

alternate (Z shape)

F E >

corresponding (F shape)

2 Write down the sizes of the angles marked with letters in these
diagrams.
Give a reason for each answer. The reason for the first one has
been done for you.

a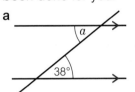

b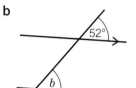

c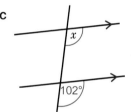

d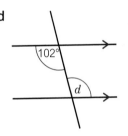

a $a = \square°$ alternate angles are equal

3 What is the sum of the interior angles of a triangle?

4 Reasoning a These two triangles have been joined
along one edge to create a quadrilateral. What is the
sum of the interior angles of the quadrilateral?

b Copy and complete
The sum of the interior angles of a quadrilateral is $\square \times 180° = \square°$

c Draw a pentagon, and split it into 3 triangles.

d Copy and complete
The sum of the interior angles of a pentagon is $\square \times 180° = \square°$

e Copy this hexagon.
Draw diagonals from the marked corner to split
the hexagon into triangles.

f Copy and complete
The sum of the interior angles of a hexagon
is $\square \times 180° = \square°$

5 Reasoning The diagram shows the exterior angles of a quadrilateral.
  a Trace the exterior angles of this polygon and cut them out.
  b Place them together so that the points are together.
  c What angle do they make?

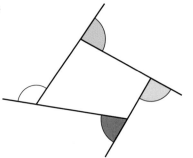

Q5b hint
Your diagram could start like this:
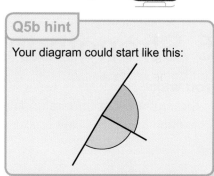

Accurate drawings and constructions

1 A diagram uses a scale where 1 cm represents 2 cm.
  Calculate the real-life value of these lengths on the diagram.
  a 4 cm   **b** 5 cm   **c** 8 cm   **d** 2.5 cm

Q1 hint
diagram   1 cm   2 cm   3 cm   4 cm
  ×2 (————+————+————+————) ÷2
real-life   2 cm   4 cm

2 A map uses a scale where 1 cm represents 3 m.
  Calculate the real-life value of these lengths on the diagram.
  a 4 cm   **b** 10 cm   **c** 12 cm   **d** 1.5 cm

Q2 hint
Draw a number line like the one in Q1 to help you.

3 A map uses a scale where 1 cm represents 5 m.
  What distance on the map represents a real-life distance of
  a 10 m   **b** 20 m   **c** 25 m   **d** 40 m?

Q3 hint
map   1 cm
  ×500 (——+——+——+——+——) ÷500
real   5 m 10 m 15 m 20 m

4 The map of a town has a scale where 1 cm represents 20 m.

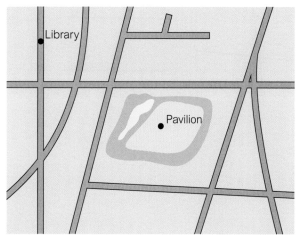

  a Measure the distance as the crow flies on the map from the library to the pavilion.
  b What is the real distance between the library and the pavilion?

5 Use this diagram to help you construct the perpendicular bisector of a line AB that is 6 cm long.

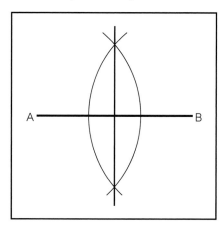

6 Draw an angle of 72° using your protractor.
Use the diagram to help you construct the angle bisector. Check your completed diagram with a protractor.

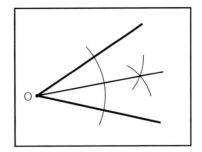

3D solids

1 Copy and complete this drawing of a cuboid that is 2 cm wide, 1 cm high and 4 cm long.

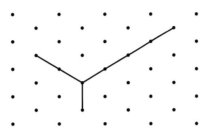

2 Draw this shape made from cubes on isometric paper.

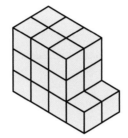

3 The diagram on the left shows a shape made from four cubes. Which of the diagrams on the right shows the

   a plan   **b** side elevation   **c** front elevation?

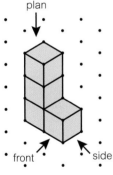

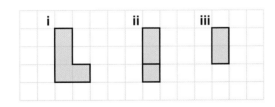

4 The diagram shows a shape made from 10 cubes.

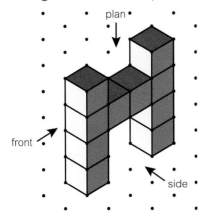

Draw the plan, the front elevation and the side elevation.

5 a Work out the volumes of cuboids A and B.

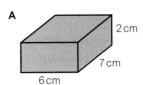

A — 2 cm, 7 cm, 6 cm

B — 3 cm, 7 cm, 10 cm

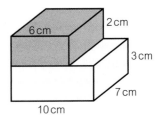

6 cm, 2 cm, 3 cm, 7 cm, 10 cm

b Use your answers to part **a** to work out the volume of this solid.

Pythagoras' theorem

1 For each triangle, which letter represents the hypotenuse?

a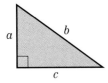

a, b, c

b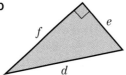

f, e, d

c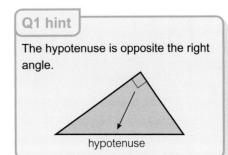

g, i, h

Q1 hint

The hypotenuse is opposite the right angle.

hypotenuse

2 Work out the length of the hypotenuse of this triangle.

$$c^2 = a^2 + b^2$$
$$c^2 = 5^2 + \square^2$$
$$c^2 = \square + \square$$
$$c = \sqrt{\square}$$
$$c = \square \text{ cm}$$

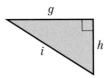

5 cm, c, 12 cm

3 Work out the length of side a in this triangle.

$$c^2 = a^2 + b^2$$
$$\square^2 = a^2 + 12^2$$
$$\square = a^2 + 144$$
$$\square - 144 = a^2$$
$$a^2 = \square$$
$$a = \sqrt{\square}$$
$$a = \square \text{ cm}$$

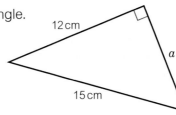

12 cm, a, 15 cm

Enrichment

1 Mariana makes this solid from four cubes.

a Draw the solid on isometric paper.

b Ben makes a different solid from four cubes.

On isometric paper, draw all the different solids that Ben could have made.

Q1b Strategy hint

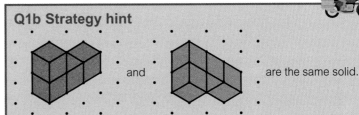

and   are the same solid.

2 Reflect Put these topics in order, starting with the one you liked doing least to the one you enjoyed most.

A Pythagoras' theorem

B Plans and elevations

C Isometric drawings

D Maps and scales

E Finding unknown angles

(You can just write the letters for each statement.)

Reflect

Master
P105

Check
P118

Strengthen
P120

EXTEND

Test
P128

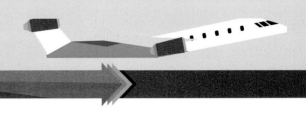

5 Extend

You will:

• Extend your understanding with problem-solving.

1 Problem-solving Copy this diagram onto squared paper.
Construct the perpendicular bisector of the line XY.

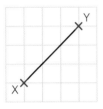

2 Problem-solving

a Draw an accurate scale drawing of this park using a scale of 1 cm for every 5 m.

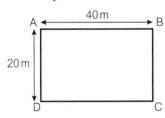

b Craig wants to make a straight path that is always the same distance from a gate at A and a gate at B. Construct the path on your scale drawing.

3 This plan of a garden uses a scale where 1 cm represents 2 m.

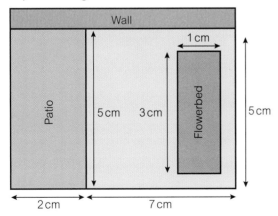

a What is the real length of the wall?

b What is the real length of the flowerbed?

c Find the area of the patio.

d The area that is not used for the patio or the flowerbed is grass. Calculate the area of grass.

Q2b Strategy hint

Draw some points in the diagram that are the same distance from A and from B. What would you get if you joined the points? Use a pair of compasses to construct this accurately.

4 Draw the plan, the front elevation and the side elevation of these shapes made of cubes.

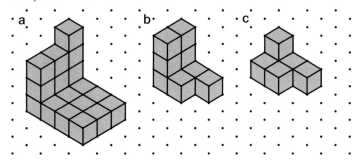

5 Write down the size of the angle x in each of these diagrams. Give reasons for your answers.

a

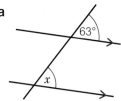

b

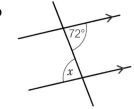

6 Problem-solving
Work out the sizes of the angles marked with letters.

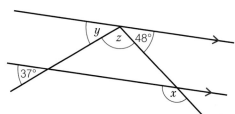

Q6 hint

Angles on a straight line add up to 180°.

7 Work out the value of y.

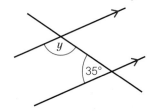

8 Work out the value of x and y. Give reasons for your answers.

a

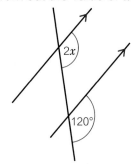

b

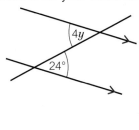

Q8 hint

Form an equation $2x = \Box$

9 Copy and complete.
The sum of the interior angles of a polygon
= (number of sides – $\Box$) × 180°

10 Problem-solving / Reasoning
  a Calculate the sum of the interior angles of an octagon.
    Show how you worked it out.
  b Use your answer from part **a** to find the size of one interior angle of a regular octagon.

Q10b Strategy hint

Draw a diagram.

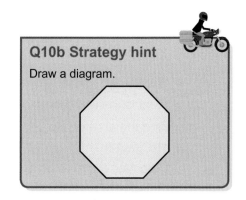

11 a What is the sum of the exterior angles of a pentagon?

b Use your answer to part **a** to work out the size of one exterior angle of a regular pentagon.

12 Problem-solving The exterior angle of a regular polygon is 36°. How many sides does the polygon have?

13 Draw an acute angle AOB.

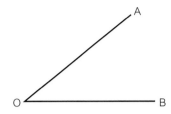

Construct the bisector of the angle.

14 Problem-solving

a Draw an accurate scale drawing of this garden using a scale of 1 cm for every 2 m.

b Sarah wants to plant a tree the same distance from the house as it is from the wall.
Construct a line on your scale drawing to show where she could plant the tree.

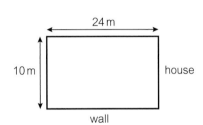

> **Q14b Strategy hint**
> Draw some points in the diagram that are the same distance from the house and from the wall. What shape do they make? Use a pair of compasses to construct the shape accurately.

15 Reasoning Here are the views of a solid made from cubes. Draw the solid on isometric paper.

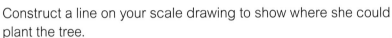

front elevation   side elevation   plan

16 Problem-solving The diagram shows an L-shaped prism.

a Calculate the length of a and b.

b Calculate the volume of the prism.

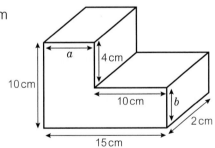

17 Problem-solving Work out the volume of this T-shaped prism.

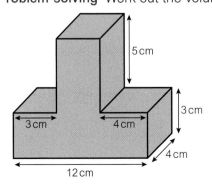

> **Q17 Strategy hint**
> Split the prism into two cuboids.

18 Problem-solving Cuboids A and B each have a volume of 50 cm³.
The area of one face is shown.
Work out the length of each cuboid.

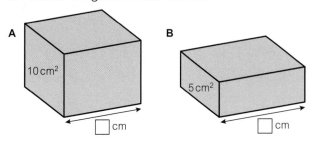

A
10 cm²
☐ cm

B
5 cm²
☐ cm

19 Problem-solving The volume of this
cuboid is 60 cm³. Work out the missing
length of the cuboid.

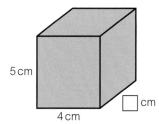

5 cm
4 cm
☐ cm

20 Real / Modelling How far does the player at the corner need to pass
the ball to reach the striker in front of the goal?

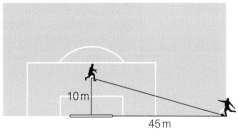

10 m
45 m

Investigation   Reasoning

Henry Perigal was an amateur mathematician.
He found this proof for Pythagoras' theorem.
Trace the diagram and cut out quadrilaterals
A, B, C, D and E.
Place the shapes so that they cover the area
of the square on the hypotenuse.
Explain how this proves Pythagoras' theorem.

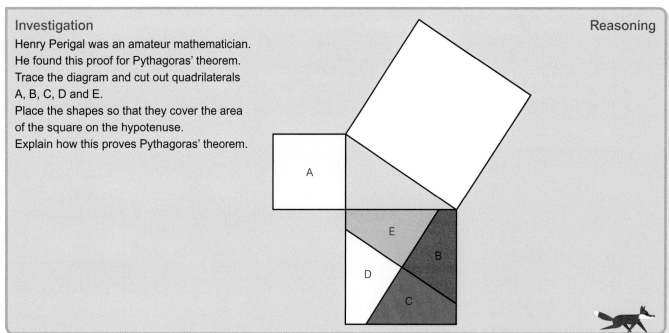

A

E

B

D

C

21 Reflect Q13 asked you to construct an angle bisector. Did you have
to look back at Lesson 5.3 to remind yourself how to do this, or did
you remember? Now write some hints that will help jog your memory
in a few weeks' time.
You could start, '1 Put the compasses point on the angle vertex.'

Reflect

5 Unit test

Log how you did on your Student Progression Chart.

1 Work out the size of the angles marked with letters. Give reasons for your answers.

a

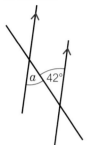

b

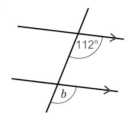

c

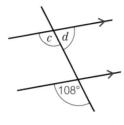

2 Draw a line 7 cm long.
Label the end points A and B.
Using a ruler and compasses, construct the perpendicular bisector of AB.

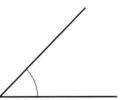

3 Draw an angle of 45° with your protractor.
Using a ruler and compasses, construct the angle bisector.

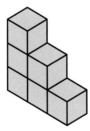

4 A map of a farm uses a scale of 1 cm to 5 cm.
What is the real-life length of
a a barn that is 4 cm long on the map
b a path that is 9 cm long on the map?

5 On a map 1 cm represents 15 cm in real life.
What distance on the map represents 75 m?

6 Draw this 3D solid on isometric paper.

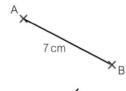

7 The diagram shows a solid made from cubes.
On squared paper, draw the plan, the side elevation and the front elevation.

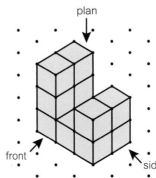

8 Work out the volume of this solid.

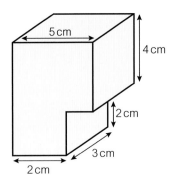

9 Calculate the length of the hypotenuse c of this triangle.

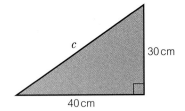

10 Calculate the unknown length in this right-angled triangle.

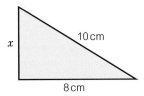

Challenge

11 Look at this 3D solid made from five cubes.

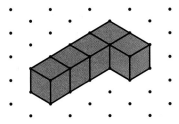

    a Draw the plan, the front elevation and
    the side elevation.
    The solid has a horizontal **plane of symmetry**.
    The horizontal plane of symmetry cuts the
    solid into two equal parts.

    b Draw a line on the front elevation and the
    side elevation to show where the plane of
    symmetry divides the solid.

    c On isometric paper, draw some more 3D solids that have planes
    of symmetry. Mark the planes of symmetry on your diagrams.
    Make each solid using linking cubes to check.

> **Q11b Literacy hint**
>
> A **plane of symmetry** divides a 3D
> solid into two equal parts.

12 **Reflect** Now you have finished this unit, copy and complete five of
these statements.
I showed I am good at _____
I need more help with _____
I got better at _____
I found _____ hard.
I can improve my _____ by _____
I was pleased with _____

6.1 Reading graphs

You will learn to:
- Read information from graphs.

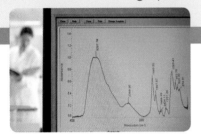

Why learn this?
Scientists use graphs to look for patterns.

Fluency
What number comes next in each sequence?
- 5, 8, 11, 14, ...
- 10, 15, 20, ...

Explore
How do scientists use graphs to help predict climate change?

Exercise 6.1

1 The graph shows the temperature in a garden over one day.
   a Look at the vertical axis. What values have been replaced by ⩘?
   b What was the maximum temperature?
   c When was the temperature 15°?
   d How often was the temperature measured?

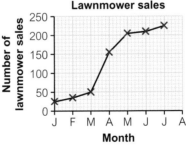

Garden temperature

2 The graph shows sales of a new lawnmower over a period of 7 months.
   a Are the sales increasing or decreasing?
   Explain how you know.
   b Between which 2 months do the sales increase the most?
   Explain how you know.

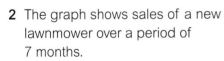

Lawnmower sales

Key point
The shape of the graph will tell you whether quantities are increasing or decreasing.

3 **Reasoning** Christine is an electrician. The graph shows how much she charges for jobs.
   a How much does Christine charge for 4 hours' work?
   b Christine charges a call-out fee. How much is this?
   c Does Christine charge the same amount for every hour?

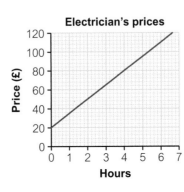

Electrician's prices

4 Bethan runs a bath. The line graph shows the depth of water in the bath over time.

Match each point on the graph, labelled 1–6, to one of the statements, labelled A–F.

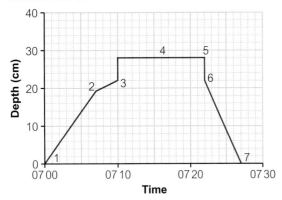

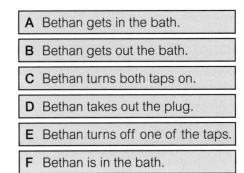

A Bethan gets in the bath.

B Bethan gets out the bath.

C Bethan turns both taps on.

D Bethan takes out the plug.

E Bethan turns off one of the taps.

F Bethan is in the bath.

5 **Reasoning** Linda measures the depth of water in her pond at the end of each day. The graph shows her measurements over 10 days.

a Between which days did the level of water increase the most?

b On which day did the level drop most quickly?

c On which two consecutive days were her measurements the same?

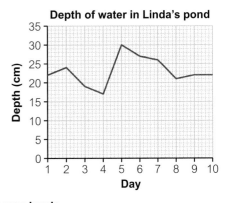

6 **Reasoning** The graph shows the depth of water in a reservoir.

a Why is the blue line horizontal?

b When was the reservoir nearly full?

c In which month did the amount of water increase fastest?

d In which month did the amount of water decrease fastest?

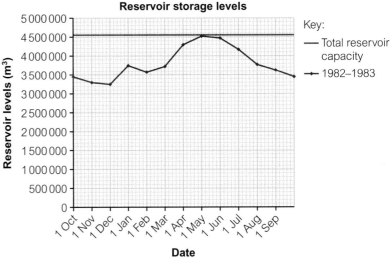

7 **Explore** How do scientists use graphs to help predict climate change? What have you learned in this lesson to help you answer this question? What other information do you need?

8 **Reflect** Look back at Q3, 5 and 6. How have you used mathematical reasoning to answer these questions? Does reasoning help you to understand a topic more clearly?

Topic links: Line graphs   **Subject links:** Geography (Q6)   *Active* Learn   Pi 3, Section 6.1

6.2 Plotting graphs

You will learn to:
- Plot graphs of simple functions.

Why learn this?
Plotting results of a science experiment helps you see any patterns in the data.

Fluency
$y = 2x$
What is the value of y when x is equal to
- 3
- 4
- 5?

Explore
What does the graph of $y = x + 3$ look like?

Exercise 6.2

1 Draw axes with x and y from 0 to 8. Plot points
   A(2, 3)   B(4, 6)   C(7, 1)   D(2, 5)

2 Write the coordinates of points A, B, C, D and E.

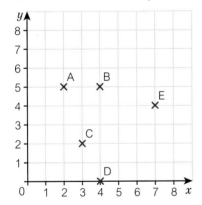

3 a Draw axes with x and y from 0 to 8. Plot points
   A(1, 3)   B(4, 3)   C(5, 3)   D(7, 3)
   b Join the points with a straight line.
   c Continue the line to the edge of the axes.
   d What do you notice about the y-coordinates?
   e Copy and complete the name for this line $y = \square$

4 Use the same axes as Q3.
   a Plot the points
      P(2, 5)   Q(2, 1)   R(2, 2)   S(2, 7)
   b Join the points in a straight line.
   c What do you notice about the x-coordinates?
   d Write the name of this line.
   Discussion What axis is the line parallel to?

Key point
The equation $y = 2$ is a line on which every point has a y-coordinate of 2.

Q4d hint

$x = \square$

5 Draw axes with x and y from −3 to 6 and plot the points from the tables of values.

Key point

A line where all the x-coordinates are equal is parallel to the y-axis.

  a Complete this table of values for $y = 2$ and plot the graph of $y = 2$.

x	−2	−1	0	1	2	3
y						

  b Complete this table of values for $y = 5$ and plot the graph of $y = 5$.

x	−2	−1	0	1	2	3
y	−3	−2	−1	O	1	2

  c Write down three points on the line $x = 3$ and plot the graph of $x = 3$.

  d Write down three points on the line $x = 4$ and plot the graph of $x = 4$.

Worked example

a Complete the table of values for $y = x - 1$

x	−2	−1	0	1	2	3
y	−3	−2	−1	O	1	2

$y = -2 - 1$
  $= -3$

$y = -1 - 1$
  $= -2$

$y = O - 1$
  $= -1$

> Substitute the different values of x into $y = x - 1$.

b Draw the graph of $y = x - 1$.

$(-2, -3), (-1, -2), (O, -1), (1, O), (2, 1), (3, 2)$

> Write the coordinates from your table.

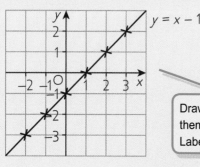

> Draw a coordinate grid. Plot the points. Join them with a straight line to the edge of the grid. Label the line $y = x - 1$.

6 a Copy and complete this table of values for $y = 2x$.

x	−2	−1	0	1	2	3
y						

Q6a hint

$y = 2x$ means $y = 2 \times x$. Multiply each x-value by 2 to work out the y-value.

  b Write the coordinates from the table.

  c Draw axes with x and y from −6 to 6. Plot the points.

  d Join the points with a straight line. Label your line $y = 2x$.

7 a Copy and complete this table of values for $y = x + 4$.

x	−2	−1	0	1	2	3
y						

Q7c hint

The y-axis goes up to your highest y-value and down to your lowest y-value.

  b Write the coordinates from the table.

  c Draw axes and plot the points.

  d Join the points with a straight line. Label your line $y = x + 4$.

Topic links: Straight-line graphs, Coordinates

8 a Copy and complete this table of values for $y = x - 2$.

x	-2	-1	0	1	2	3
y						

b Write the coordinates from the table.

c Draw axes and plot the points.

d Join the points with a straight line. Label your line $y = x - 2$.

9 Reasoning a Copy and complete this table of values using the graph.

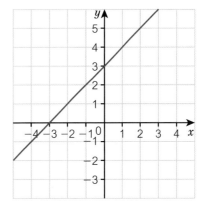

x	-2	-1	0	1	2	3
y						

b Copy and complete: $y = x + \square$.

10 Reasoning Use the graph to work out

a y when $x = 2$

b x when $y = 5$

c y when $x = -2$

d x when $y = -2$

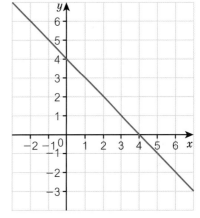

11 Explore What does the graph of $y = x + 3$ look like?
Look back at the maths you have learned in this lesson.
How can you use it to answer this question?

12 Reflect Write the letters of the statements that you feel confident about:

A I know which is the x-axis and which is the y-axis.

B I know how to complete a table of values for $y = x + 2$.

C I know how to plot points from a table of values.

D I know how to plot points from a list of coordinates.

E I know how to find a value of y from a graph if I'm given the value of x.

Ask a classmate or a teacher to explain any statements you don't feel confident about.

6.3 Distance–time graphs

You will learn to:
- Draw and interpret distance–time graphs.

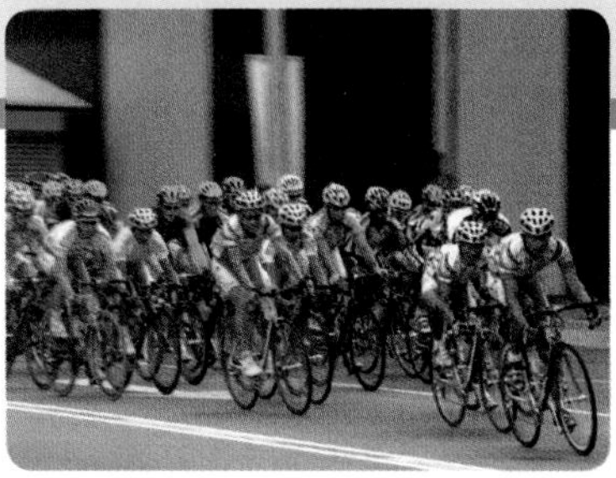

Why learn this?
Distance–time graphs can be used to analyse the performance of cyclists in races.

Fluency
A car travels 50 miles in an hour. How far does it travel in half an hour?

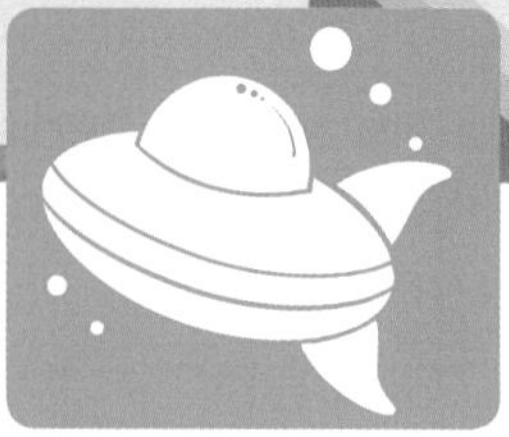

Explore
What story does this distance–time graph tell you?

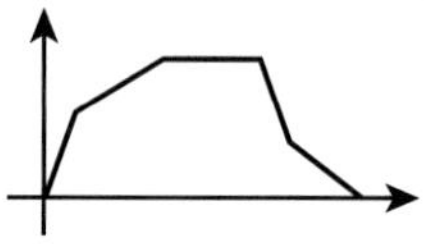

Exercise 6.3

1 Work out the value, in minutes, of one small square in each of these scales.

a 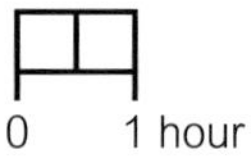

b 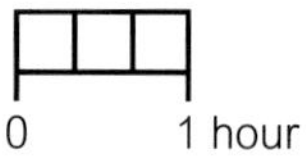

c 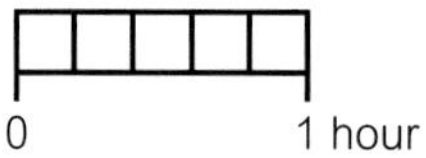

Q1a hint
÷□ 2 small squares = 60 minutes ÷□
1 small square = □ minutes

2 A train arrives in Liverpool from London at 3.10 pm.
The train journey lasts 2 hours and 30 minutes.
What time did the train leave London?

3 Reasoning Evan drives from his house to visit a friend. He stays there for a while, and then drives home. The **distance–time graph** shows his journey.

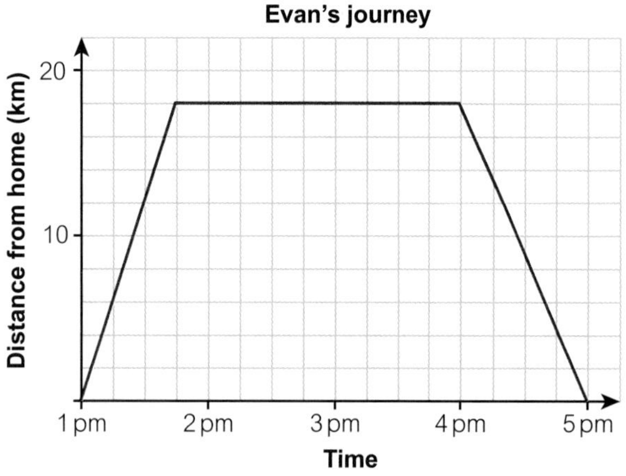

a How far is Evan's house from his friend's house?
b What time does Evan arrive at his friend's house?
c How long does he take to drive to the house?
d How long does he stay at his friend's house for?
e How long does he take to drive home?
f Was Evan driving faster on the way there or on the way back?

Key point
In a **distance–time graph**, the vertical axis represents the distance from the starting point. The horizontal axis represents the time taken.

Q3b hint
Each small square represents 15 minutes on the horizontal axis.

Topic links: Line graphs

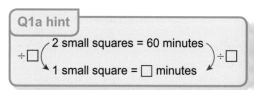

4 Nadia walks from home to the supermarket. She stops to talk to a friend on the way home. The graph shows her journey.

  a How far away is the supermarket from Nadia's house?

  b How long does it take Nadia to get to the supermarket?

  c How long does Nadia spend at the supermarket?

  d How far does Nadia walk before she stops to talk to her friend?

  e How long does it take Nadia to get from the supermarket back to her house?

  f How long was Nadia away from home?

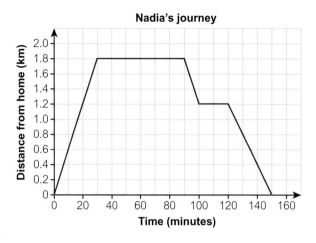

Nadia's journey

5 One evening Siobhan walks to the theatre. The graph shows her journey.

Siobhan's journey

  a How far is the theatre from Siobhan's home?

  b How far does Siobhan walk in total?

6 Michaela drives to a wedding.
She drives 150 km in 3 hours. Then she stops for a 45 minute break.
She then drives 100 km in 1.5 hours and arrives at the wedding.

  a On graph paper draw a horizontal axis from 0 to 6 hours and a vertical axis from 0 to 300 km. Draw a distance–time graph to show Michaela's journey.

  b During which part of her journey was she travelling fastest?

7 Jayden leaves home at 8.30 am and cycles 6 km to work. It takes him half an hour. He leaves work at 5 pm and cycles 4 km further away from home to see his friend. This takes him a quarter of an hour. He spends three-quarters of an hour with his friend, then cycles directly home. He arrives home at 7 pm.

  a Draw a distance–time graph to show Jayden's journey.

  b During which part of his journey is Jayden cycling the quickest?

8 The graph shows two train journeys.
One train leaves Brighton at 10 am and travels to London.
The other train leaves London at 10 am and travels to Brighton.

  a Which line shows the Brighton to London train?

  b Which line shows the London to Brighton train?

  c Which train travels more quickly?

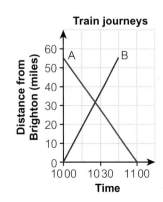

Train journeys

> **Q8c hint**
> Compare the steepness of the lines.

9 Josh and Ben take part in a 70 km sponsored bike ride.
The graph shows their journeys.

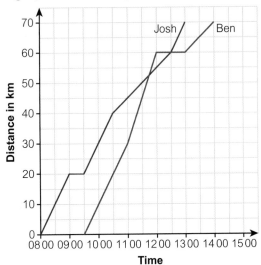

Q9 hint

Think about the steepness of the lines.

a Who completed the ride first?
b Who stopped for the longer period of time overall?
c Who had the faster speed?
d Who cycled faster overall?
e What happened to Josh's speed at 10.30?
Discussion Who completed the ride more quickly?

Investigation   Reasoning

Design a simple cycle race course, including hills, bends, fast and slow sections.
Draw a distance–time graph to represent the journey along the course.

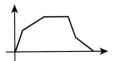

10 Explore What story does this distance–time graph tell you?
Look back at the maths you have learned in this lesson. How can you
use it to answer this question?

11 Reflect You have seen lines like this on distance-time graphs:

A ╱   B ╲   C ─────

Describe, in your own words, what each type of line tells you.
What if lines A and B were steeper? What if lines A and B were
less steep?
Would there ever be a line like this | on a distance–time graph?
Explain.

6.4 Midpoints

You will learn to:

• Find the midpoint of a line segment.

Why learn this?
Surveyors and cartographers need to know the midpoint of a slope.

Fluency
What is halfway between
• 31 and 37
• 15 and 21
• 51 and 75?

Explore
Where is halfway down the slope?

Exercise 6.4

1 Work out the difference between −4 and 6.

2 Add 8 and 10, then halve the answer.

3 **a** Draw axes with x and y from 0 to 6 and plot points A(2, 3) and B(4, 5).
 b Join the two points together.

4 The graph shows the **line segment** PQ. A red cross has been placed on the **midpoint**.
What are the coordinates of the midpoint?

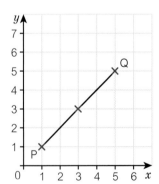

Q4 Literacy hint

A straight line between two points is called a **line segment**. These are *line segments* and not just lines because they have a definite beginning and end.

Key point

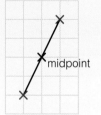

The **midpoint** of a line segment is a point exactly in the middle.

midpoint

5 Copy and complete the table to show the midpoint of each of these line segments.

Line segment	Beginning point	End point	Midpoint
AB	(−2, −2)	(3, −2)	
CD	(−3, 4)		

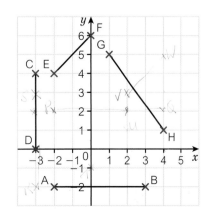

Discussion Look at your table. How can you find the midpoint of a line segment by just looking at the beginning and end coordinates?

Warm up

Worked example

Work out the midpoint of this line segment.

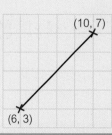

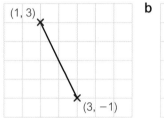

x: $(6 + 10) \div 2 = 8$ ——— Add the two x-coordinates together and divide by 2.

y: $(3 + 7) \div 2 = 5$ ——— Add the two y-coordinates together and divide by 2.

Midpoint = $(8, 5)$ ——— These are the x- and y-coordinates of the midpoint.

6 Work out the midpoint of each line segment.

a 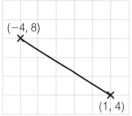   **b**   **c**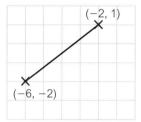

7 Problem-solving The diagram shows a square.
Make a copy of the diagram.
a Find the midpoint of each side.
b Join the midpoints together
c What shape has been formed?

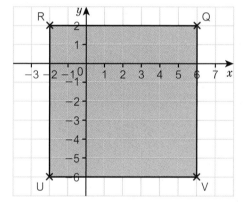

8 Explore Where is halfway down the slope?
Is it easier to explore this question now you have completed the lesson?
What further information do you need to be able to answer this?

9 Reflect In this lesson you have added up numbers and divided them by a number.
Where else in maths do you need to add and divide?
How is the maths in this lesson similar? How is it different?

Topic links: Geometry

Active Learn   Pi 3, Section 6.4

Explore

Reflect

MASTER

Check
P143

Strengthen
P145

Extend
P151

Test
P155

6.5 Intercepts and gradients

You will learn to:
- Work out the *y*-intercept of a line
- Work out the gradient of a line

Why learn this?
Engineers use graphs to help predict how heavy safe loads on bridges can be.

Fluency
x = 2   What is the value of 2*x* + 1?
x = 3   What is the value of 2*x* + 1?

Explore
Do all graphs have a gradient?

Exercise 6.5

1 a Copy and complete the table of values for $y = x + 1$.

x	−2	−1	0	1	2	3
y						

  b Write the coordinates from the table.

  c Draw axes with *x* and *y* from −5 to 5 and plot the points to draw the graph of $y = x + 1$.

> ### Worked example
> Copy and complete the table of values for $y = 2x + 1$
>
> | *x* | −2 | −1 | 0 | 1 | 2 | 3 |
> |---|---|---|---|---|---|---|
> | *y* | −3 | −1 | 1 | 3 | 5 | 7 |
>
> When $x = -2$ ———— Substitute each value of *x* into $y = 2x + 1$.
> $y = 2 \times (-2) + 1 = -3$

2 a Copy and complete the table of values for $y = 2x + 2$.

x	−2	−1	0	1	2	3
y						

  b Write the coordinates from the table.

  c Choose a suitable pair of axes and plot the graph of $y = 2x + 2$.

> **Q2c hint**
> The *y*-axis should go up to your highest *y*-value and down to your lowest *y*-value.

3 a Copy and complete the table of values for $y = 3x - 1$.

x	−2	−1	0	1	2	3
y						

  b Write the coordinates from the table.

  c Choose a suitable pair of axes and plot the graph of $y = 3x - 1$.

Warm up

4 a Copy and complete the table of values for y = 2x + 3.

x	−2	−1	0	1	2	3
y						

b Write the coordinates from the table.

c Choose a suitable pair of axes and plot the graph of $y = 2x + 3$.

Investigation   Reasoning

1 Draw axes with x and y = −5 to 5.
2 Using your answers from **Q2, 3** and **4**, plot the graphs of the lines $y = 2x + 2$, $y = 3x − 1$ and $y = 2x + 3$.
3 Which two lines are parallel?
4 Write the coordinates of the point where each line crosses the y-axis.
5 Can you tell from the equation where the graph will cross the y-axis?

---

5 The graph shows the cost of a call made on a mobile phone.

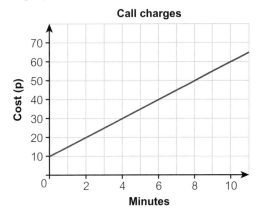

What does the **y-intercept** of this graph tell you?

Key point

The **y-intercept** of a line is where it crosses the y-axis.
The line $y = 3x + 2$ intercepts the y-axis at the point (0, 2).

Worked example

Work out the **gradient** of this line.

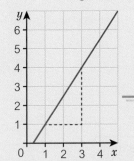

Divide the vertical distance by the horizontal distance.

The graph goes 3 units up every 2 units across.
Gradient = $\frac{3}{2}$

Key point

The steepness of the graph is called the **gradient**.
To find the gradient, work out how many units the graph goes up for every one unit across.
Lines with the same gradient are parallel.

Topic links: Interpreting graphs   *Active* Learn   Pi 3, Section 6.5

6 Work out the gradient of each line segment in the diagram.

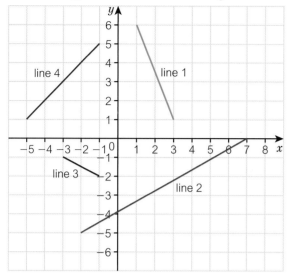

Q6 hint

A gradient can be a fraction. Write the fraction in its simplest form.
If the line slopes downwards, the gradient is negative.

7 a Copy and complete the table of values for $y = 4x - 3$.

x	−2	−1	0	1	2	3
y						

b Write the coordinates from the table.

c Choose a suitable pair of axes and plot the graph of $y = 4x - 3$.

d Find the gradient of the graph.

8 a Copy and complete the table of values for $y = 3x + 2$.

x	−2	−1	0	1	2	3
y						

b Write the coordinates from the table.

c Choose a suitable pair of axes and plot the graph of $y = 3x + 2$.

d Find the gradient of the graph.

9 a Copy and complete the table of values for $y = 2x - 5$.

x	−2	−1	0	1	2	3
y						

b Write the coordinates from the table.

c Choose a suitable pair of axes and plot the graph of $y = 2x - 5$.

d Find the gradient of the graph.

Discussion How can you tell the gradient of a line from its equation?

10 Explore Do all graphs have a gradient? Is it easier to explore
this question now you have completed the lesson? What further
information do you need to be able to answer this?

11 Reflect Write down, in your own words, as many facts about
gradients of straight lines as you can.
Think about what 'gradient' means, different types of gradients, and
how to find a gradient.
Compare your list of facts with those of your classmates.

Explore

Reflect

6 Check up

Log how you did on your Student Progression Chart.

Reading and plotting graphs

1 The graph shows the sales of skateboards over an 8-month period.

  a Are sales increasing or decreasing?

  b In which month are most skateboards sold?

  c When is the biggest increase between one month and the next?

  d Which is the smallest increase between one month and the next?

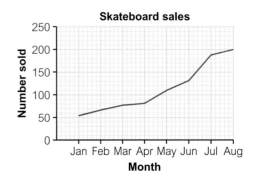

2 The graph shows how much it costs to hire a go-kart for a number of days.

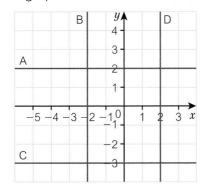

  a How much does it cost to hire the go-kart for 2 days?

  b How much does it cost to hire the go-kart for 5 days?

  c How much does each extra day cost?

3 The graph shows four lines A, B, C and D.

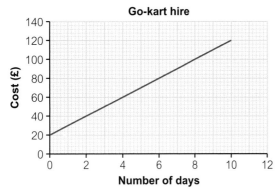

Write the equation of each line.

4 Draw axes with x and y from −5 to 5 and plot the graph $y = x + 3$.

5 Plot the graph of $y = 3x$ on your axes in Q4.

Distance–time graphs

6 Grace visits her brother. She stops to fill up her car with petrol on the way.
The graph shows her journey.

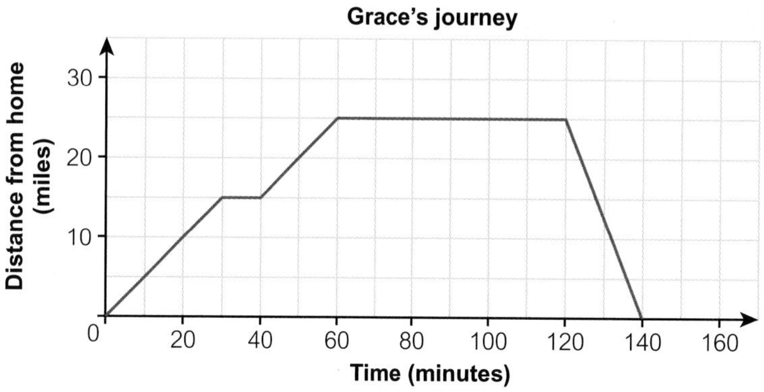

a How far away from Grace does her brother live?
b How long does Grace spend at the petrol station?
c How long does Grace spend at her brother's house?
d How long does it take Grace to get home from her brother's?
e On which part of the journey is Grace driving fastest?

Coordinate geometry

7 The graph shows the line segment AB.
What are the coordinates of the midpoint of AB?

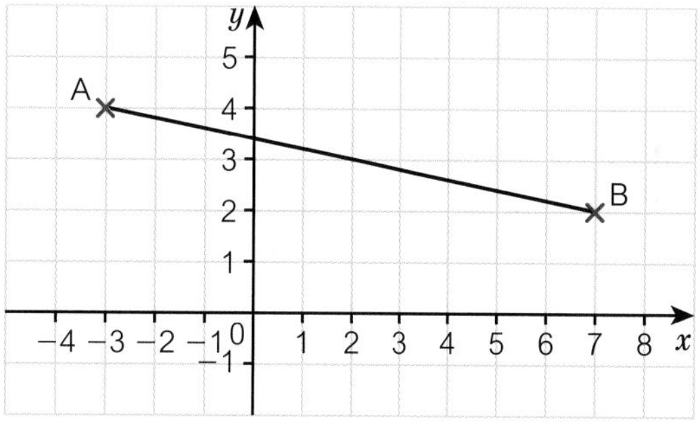

8 P is point (−1, 1) and Q is the point (7, 5).
What are the coordinates of the midpoint of PQ?

9 **a** The graph shows the line $y = 3x + 2$.

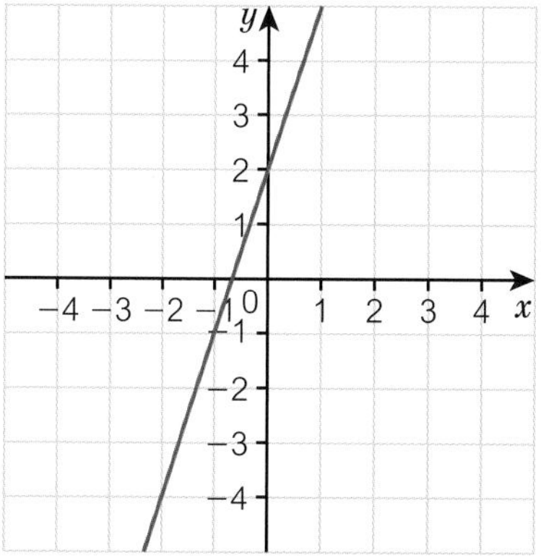

a What are the coordinates of the y-intercept?
b What is the gradient?

10 How sure are you of your answers? Were you mostly
Just guessing **Feeling doubtful** **Confident**
What next? Use your results to decide whether to strengthen or extend your learning.

Reflect

Challenge

11 The lines $x = 1$ and $y = 1$ both meet at the point (1, 1).
Write the equations of other lines which also go through this point.

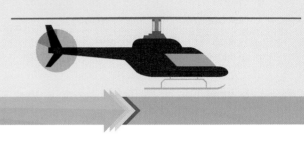

Master
P130

Check
P143

STRENGTHEN

Extend
P151

Test
P155

6 Strengthen

You will:

• Strengthen your understanding with practice.

Reading and plotting graphs

1 The graph shows the number of cars sold by a car dealer each week for 10 weeks.

a Between which two weeks is the biggest increase in sales?

b Between which two weeks is the biggest decrease in sales?

c What happened to sales in week 5?

> **Q1a hint**
>
> Look for the steepest line between two points.

2 Real The graph shows the number of cars on the road in the UK for the last 10 years.

a Look at the scale on each axis.
Copy and complete these statements.

  i One square on the vertical axis represents ☐ cars.

  ii One square on the horizontal axis represents ☐.

b How many cars were on the road in

  i 2005

  ii 2011?

c In which year were 28.4 million cars on the road?

d During which year did the number of cars on the road stay the same? How is this shown on the graph?

e What is happening to the overall number of cars on the road in the UK?

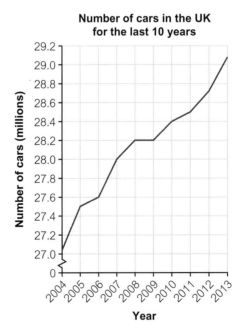

Source: DFT

3 The graph shows the amount a plumber charges his customers.

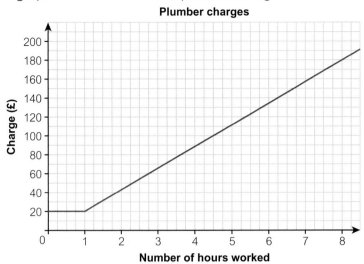

a How much does the plumber charge for
   i 1 hour's work
   ii $4\frac{3}{4}$ hours' work?
b How much does the plumber charge per hour?

Q3b hint

Look at the difference in charge for 1 hour's work and for 2 hours' work.

4 a Draw axes from x and y from −5 to 5 and plot three points with y-coordinates 5.
b Join all your points with a straight line. Where does the line cross the y-axis?
c The equation of the line is $y = 5$. Which of these points will also lie on the line?
   i (0, 5) **ii** (5, 5) **iii** (2, −5) **iv** (−5, −5) **v** (4, 5) **vi** (−3, 5)

5 Copy the grid from Q4 and draw these lines.
   a $x = 2$ **b** $x = -4$ **c** $x = 1$

6 Reasoning **a** Aruna tried to plot the line $x = 4$.
What line has she plotted instead?

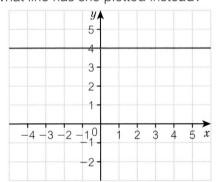

b Write Aruna a hint, explaining how to plot the graph of a line like $x = 4$.

Q6b hint

You could use these words to help.
x-coordinate   straight   axis

7 Copy and complete the table of values for $y = 5x$.

x	−2	−1	0	1	2	3
y	−10					

When $x = -2$, $y = -10$ When $x = -1$, $y = \square$

8 Use a new copy of this table for each part of the question.

x	-2	-1	0	1	2	3
y						

Copy and complete the table of values for

a $y = x + 5$ **b** $y = 3x$ **c** $y = x - 4$

d $y = 2x + 3$ **e** $y = 4x - 1$

9 **a** Use this table of values to work out the x- and y-coordinates to plot a graph.

x	-2	-1	0	1	2	3
y	-5	-4	-3	-2	-1	0

Coordinates (−2, __) (__, __) (__, __) (__, __) (__, __) (__, __)

b Copy the grid from Q4 and plot the coordinates.

c Join the points with a straight line right to the edge of the grid.

Q9a hint

(x-coordinate, y-coordinate)

10 Draw a graph for each table of values you made in Q8.

11 Copy and complete this table of values from the graph.

x	-2	-1	0	1	2	3
y						

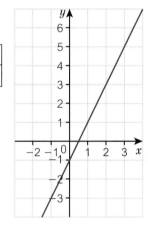

Q11 hint

Find the value of the y-coordinate when the x-coordinate is −1.

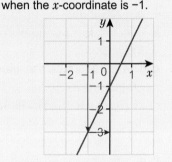

Distance–time graphs

1 Petra goes to the gym by car.
The graph shows her journey.

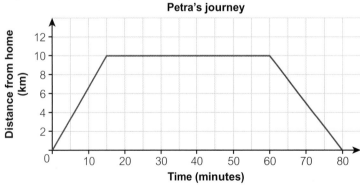

Petra's journey

a How can you tell from the graph when Petra is at the gym?

b How long does it take Petra to get to the gym?

c How long does Petra spend at the gym?

d How long does it take Petra to get home from the gym?

e Which part of Petra's journey was quicker?

f Petra leaves home at 10 am. What time does she get back home?

Q1c hint

Time spent at the gym is the difference between the arrival time and leaving time.

2 The graph shows Joe's bike ride.

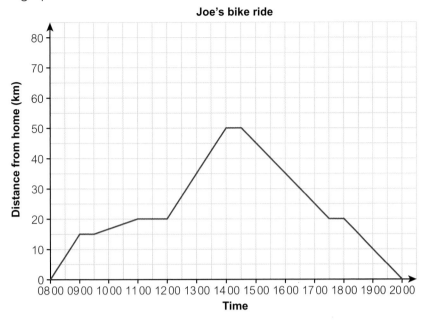

Joe's bike ride

a How long does Joe ride before he first stops?
b How long does it take Joe to get to his destination?
c When does Joe cycle slowest?
d What time does Joe get back to the start?
e When is Joe cycling fastest?

3 This is a description of Nasim's journey on Saturday.
He sets off from home at 10 am. He drives 40 miles in an hour before stopping for half an hour at a café. He then drives a further 20 miles, arriving at his destination at 12.45 pm.
He meets up with his friend, staying for 90 minutes before driving straight home in $1\frac{1}{2}$ hours.
a Draw a distance–time graph to show Nasim's journey.
Use a scale of 4 squares = 1 hour on the horizontal axis.
b How many miles did Nasim drive altogether?
c What time did he arrive home?

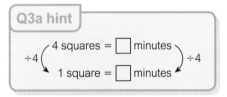

Q3a hint

$\div 4 \left(\begin{array}{l} 4 \text{ squares} = \boxed{} \text{ minutes} \\ 1 \text{ square} = \boxed{} \text{ minutes} \end{array} \right) \div 4$

Coordinate geometry

1 The graph shows the line segment AB.
What are the coordinates of the midpoint of this line segment?

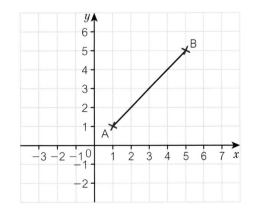

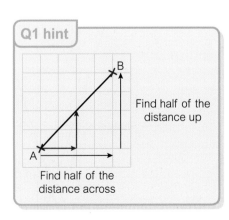

Q1 hint

Find half of the distance up

Find half of the distance across

2 The graph shows a line segment CD.

   a Label the midpoint of CD 'M'.

   b Copy and complete the calculation to work out the coordinates of M.

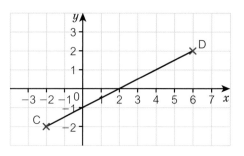

(x, y)

C(−2, −2)

D(6, 2)

M ($\square$, $\square$)

$$\frac{-2 + 6}{2} \quad \frac{-2 + 2}{2}$$

   c Check your answer matches the midpoint on the line.

3 Find the coordinates of the midpoints of these line segments.

   a The line segment joining A(2, 2) and B(2, 6)

   b The line segment joining G(3, 2) and H(8, 8)

   c The line segment joining I(−1, −2) and J(7, 9)

   d The line segment joining K(−2, 3) and L(−7, 6)

> **Q3 Strategy hint**
>
> Draw the line segments on a coordinate grid.

4 a Which hill is steepest?

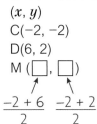

A   B   C

   b Which line is steepest?

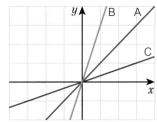

   c What is the steepness of a graph called?

5 Work out the gradients of these graphs by counting the squares up and dividing by the squares across.

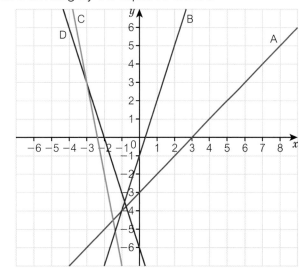

> **Q5 hint**
>
> Choose two points on the line.
> What is the vertical distance between the points?
> What is the horizontal distance between the points?
>
>

6 a Work out the gradient of these lines. What do you notice?

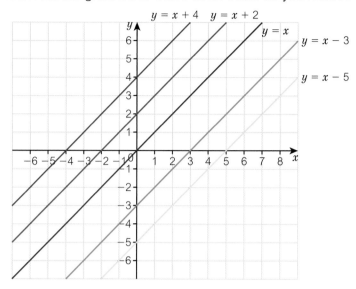

b Copy and complete this table.

Line	y-intercept
$y = x + 4$	
$y = x + 2$	
$y = x$	
$y = x - 3$	
$y = x - 5$	

Q3b hint

The y-intercept is the value where the line crosses the y-axis.

c What is the y-intercept of the line $y = x + 1$?

Enrichment

1 Plot the line $y = 3$.
Give the equations of three other lines to form a square.
Give the equations of three other lines to form a non-rectangular parallelogram.

2 Reflect For the first three questions in *Reading and plotting graphs*, you were asked to read information from a graph. Later questions asked you to plot graphs. Which type of question do you prefer? Write down one thing about reading graphs and one thing about drawing graphs you think you need more practice on.

6 Extend

You will:
• Extend your understanding with problem-solving.

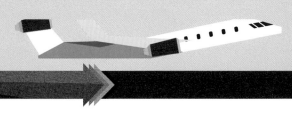

1 **Real** The graph below shows the average water level at a reservoir.

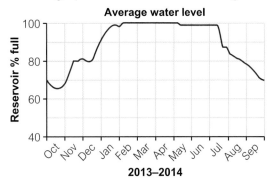

Average water level

2013–2014

a For roughly how many months was the reservoir full?
b Suggest a reason why the level fell quickly in July 2014.
c In which months was there most rainfall?

2 **Problem-solving** The graph shows the line $y = 2x - 4$.

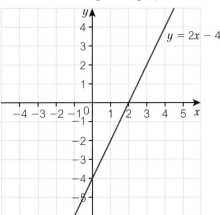

$y = 2x - 4$

a Copy the graph.
b Write the equations of four other lines which are parallel to
 $y = 2x - 4$ and plot them on the graph.
c Write the equation of two other lines with the same y-intercept as
 $y = 2x - 4$, and plot them on the graph.

3 **Problem-solving** Plot the line $y = -4$.
 Give the equation of three other lines that will form a square with an
 area of 9 squares.

> **Q3 hint**
>
> Sketch the graph of $y = -4$ to start.

4 **Problem-solving** A gym charges a £50 joining fee and a monthly fee
 of £15.
 a Choose suitable axes and draw a graph to represent the cost of
 being a member of the gym for 18 months.
 b Use your graph to find the total cost for a year's membership.

Topic links: Algebra

Subject links: Geography (Q1)

5 Use the graph to work out
  a the value of x when $y = 2$
  b the value of y when $x = -2$
  c the value of x when $y = -3$
  d the value of y when $x = 0$.

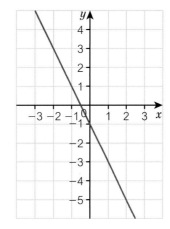

6 Reasoning / Modelling The graph shows a journey taken by Ewan in his car.

On his journey Ewan passed these road signs.

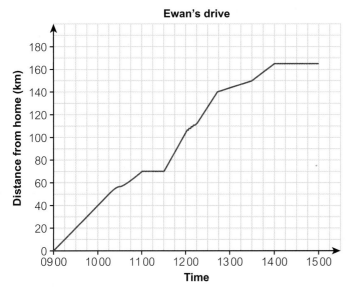

Write the times when you think Ewan passed each of the road signs.

7 Christine and Linda are competing in a triathlon thst consists of a 1.5 km swim, a 40 km cycle ride and and a 10 km run.
Christine completes her swim in 30 minutes, her cycle in 2 hours 15 minutes and her run in 45 minutes.
Linda takes 45 minutes for her swim, 105 minutes for her cycle and 35 minutes for her run.
Draw a distance–time graph to show their race.

8 Choose suitable axes and draw the triangle ABC with vertices A(−4, 4), B(6, 4) and C(8, −4).

  a Find the midpoint of each side.

  b Label these points P, Q and R.

  c Join P, Q and R. What shape is PQR?

  d What shape would be created by joining the midpoint of each side in PQR?

9 **Problem-solving** ABCD is a quadrilateral with vertices A(−3, 3), B(2, 3), C(−1, -1), D(−6, −1). What shape is formed by joining the midpoints of each side?

Q9 Strategy hint

Draw the quadrilateral if you need to.

10 a Copy and complete the table of values for $y = 2x − 2$

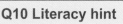

x	−4	−2	0	2	4
y					

Q10 Literacy hint

The **point of intersection** is where two lines cross.

  b Copy and complete the table of values for $y = −2x + 2$.

x	−4	−2	0	2	4
y					

  c What is the **point of intersection** for these two graphs?

11

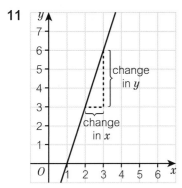

  a Work out the gradient of this line using the formula.

  $$\text{gradient} = \frac{\text{change in } y}{\text{change in } x}$$

  b What do you think the y-intercept is?

12 a Write the midpoint of the line AB where A is (1, 5) and B is (7, 1).

  b Work out the midpoint using the formula

  $$\left(\frac{x_1 + x_2}{2}, \frac{y_1 + y_2}{2}\right)$$

  Do you get the same answer?

Key point

The midpoint of a line segment is
$$\left(\frac{x_1 + x_2}{2}, \frac{y_1 + y_2}{2}\right)$$

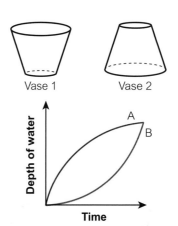

13 **Reasoning** Vase 1 and vase 2 hold the same amount of water. They are both filled with water at the same steady rate. The graph shows the depth of water in each vase over time.

Vase 1   Vase 2

  a In which vase will the water level rise faster at first?

  b Which line graph is for vase 1 and which is for vase 2?
  Explain your answers.

153

1 Follow these steps to draw the graph of $y = x + 5$ using a spreadsheet.
  a Input the x-coordinates you want to use in cells A1 to A6.
  b In cell B1, type '=A1+5', and drag the formula down to B6.
  c Select all 12 cells and use the graph-plotting function to plot a straight line.
2 What happens if you change the x-values?
3 What happens if you change the formula?

14 **Reflect** Amy says, 'When I see a question with a graph
  • I cover the question with my hand, so I can only see the graph.
  • I read the graph title
  • I read the titles of each axis
  • I make sure I know what a square on each axis represents
  • finally, I randomly pick a point on the graph and ask myself,
    'what does this point tell me?'
It is really quick and always helps me to understand and answer the
question.'
Look at the graph in Q1.
Use Amy's method to help you understand the graph.
Does this help you answer Q1 and Q2?
Is Amy's method helpful? Explain.

Reflect

Master
P130

Check
P143

Strengthen
P145

Extend
P151

TEST

6 Unit test

Log how you did on your
Student Progression Chart.

1 Write the equations of the lines A, B, C and D shown in the graph.

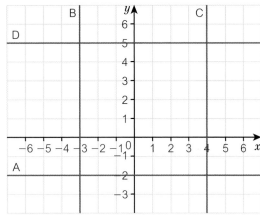

2 What is the midpoint of the line segment EF?

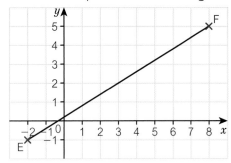

3 Draw the graph of $y = x + 1$.

4 The graph shows the number of views a video got each day.

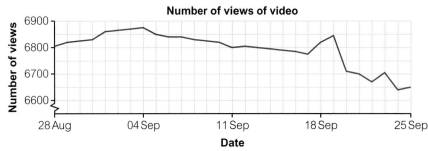

Number of views of video

a When did the video have the most views?

b When did the video have the least views?

c On which day was the greatest rise?

d On which day was the greatest fall?

e How many views did the video get on its first day?

5 It costs £5 to register at a fitness centre and £2 for every visit.
Draw a graph to show the cost of using the fitness centre. Put the cost
on the vertical axis and the number of visits on the horizontal axis.

6 a Copy and complete the table of values for the equation $y = 3x - 4$.

x	-2	-1	0	1	2	3
y						

b Write the coordinates from the table.

c Draw the graph of the line $y = 3x - 4$ on suitable axes.

7 The graph shows the average mass of a Dalmatian puppy up to 10 weeks old.

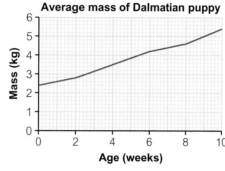

a What is the average mass of a puppy aged 5 weeks?

b At what age does an average puppy reach a mass of 3 kg?

c Samantha has a puppy that is 7 weeks old. It has a mass of 4 kg. Is its mass more or less than the average?

8 The graph shows a straight line.

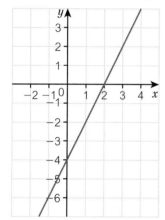

a What is the gradient of the line?

b What is the y-intercept of the line?

Challenge

9 a i On graph paper plot the points

$(-7, 5)$ $(10, 5)$ $(14, -3)$ $(-3, -3)$.

ii Join the points to make a quadrilateral.

iii Find the midpoint of each side.

iv Join the midpoints to make a new shape.

b Continue this process with each new shape.

c How many shapes can you draw?

d What do you notice about each shape?

10 Reflect Which of the questions in this test took:
- the shortest time to answer? Why?
- the longest time to answer? Why?
- the most thought to answer?

7.1 STEM: Using ratios

You will learn to:
• Share a quantity in a given ratio
• Simplify ratios with different units.

CONFIDENCE

Why learn this?
Builders often have to mix quantities in a given ratio.

Fluency
Work out these equivalences
• 4.5 cm = ☐ mm
• ☐ g = 4.05 kg
• ☐ litres = 463 ml

Explore
How much cement, sand and aggregate do you need to make 50 kg of concrete?

Exercise 7.1: Ratios in science

Warm up

1 Phil has 6 DVDs and Betty has 14. Write the ratio of Phil's DVDs to Betty's in its simplest form.

2 A jumper is made from balls of red wool and blue wool in the ratio 1 : 3. How many balls of blue wool are needed for 4 balls of red wool?

3 A recipe for pasta sauce uses tomato puree and fresh basil in the ratio 3 : 2. Antonio uses 6 tablespoons of tomato puree. How much basil does he use?

Worked example
Share £200 between Carla and David in the ratio 2 : 3.

2 + 3 = 5 parts ——— Work out how many parts there are in total.

5 parts = £200

1 part = £200 ÷ 5 = £40 ——— Work out how much one part is worth.

Carla: 2 parts = 2 × £40 = £80

David: 3 parts = 3 × £40 = £120 ——— Multiply one part by each number in the ratio.

Carla has £80 and David has £120.

Check: £80 + £120 = £200 ——— Check your answer by adding the parts.

		£200		
£40	£40	£40	£40	£40
£80			£120	

Topic links: Unit conversion

Subject links: Science (Q7, Q8), Cookery (Q11)

4 Share these amounts between Abed and Britta in the ratios given.
   a £560 in the ratio 5:3   b £121 in the ratio 7:4
   c £810 in the ratio 3:6   d £270 in the ratio 6:3

5 STEM In a science lesson Andrew and Ben have 123 ml of a solution to share in the ratio 1:2.
   How much liquid should each get?

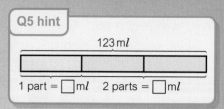

Q5 hint

123 ml

1 part = ☐ ml   2 parts = ☐ ml

6 STEM In a science lesson Sam is told to make 98 g of a substance by mixing together two powders A and B in the ratio 3:4.
   What mass of each powder does Sam use?

7 STEM The bronze used to make bells is an alloy of copper and tin. The ratio of copper to tin is 4:1.
   A bell has a mass 225 kg. How much copper is in the bell?

Q7 Literacy hint
An alloy is a metal made by combining two or more metals.

8 STEM A botanist knows that the ratio of male to female holly trees is usually 7:4.
   How many male trees should she find in a wood with 99 holly trees?

9 Problem-solving / STEM 240 ml of liquid is shared between a bottle and a jar in the ratio 5:7.
   How much more liquid will be in the jar?

10 Share these amounts between Demi and Edward in the ratios given.
   a £45 in the ratio 3:7   b £25 in the ratio 1:3
   c £64 in the ratio 17:3   d £54 in the ratio 3:5
   e £100 in the ratio 13:27   f £63 in the ratio 7:5

11 A recipe uses sugar, flour and butter in the ratio 4:5:6.
   The mixture has a mass of 900 g. How much of each ingredient is used?

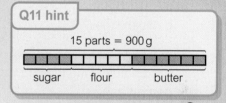

Q11 hint

15 parts = 900 g

sugar   flour   butter

12 Three children inherit £24 000 in the ratio 3:5:4.
   How much do they get each?

13 Write each ratio in its simplest form.
   a 25 g:1 kg   b 15 cm:3 m   c £5:25p
   d 40 ml:4 litres   e 12 mm:4 cm   f 350 mm:0.5 m

Q13 Strategy hint
Make both quantities the same unit before cancelling down the ratio.

14 STEM A solution is made using 150 ml of ethanol with 2 litres of water. What is the ratio of ethanol to water? Give your answer in its simplest form.

15 Problem-solving A photograph has a length of 24 cm and a width of 164 mm.
   What is the ratio of the length to the width? Give your answer in its simplest form.

16 **Explore** How much cement, sand and aggregate do you need to make 50 kg of concrete?
   Look back at the maths you have learned in this lesson. How can you use it to answer this question? What further information do you need to be able to answer this?

17 **Reflect** The hint for Q5 included a diagram to help you answer the question. Did the diagram help you? Write a sentence explaining how.

Explore

Reflect

7.2 Using proportions

You will learn to:
- Solve problems using ratio and proportion.

CONFIDENCE

Why learn this?
Pharmacists use multiplicative reasoning to make sure that medicines are mixed in the correct proportions.

Fluency
What is
- 24 × 16
- 15 × 12
- 350 ÷ 50
- 200 ÷ 8?

Explore
How much concentrated squash do you need to make a litre of diluted squash?

Exercise 7.2

Warm up

1 4 biscuits have a total mass of 120 g. What is the mass of 8 biscuits?

2 In a box of fruit the ratio of strawberries to blueberries is 3 : 2.
What fraction of the box is
a strawberries
b blueberries?

3 In a box there are 6 dark chocolates, 12 milk chocolates and 7 white chocolates. Write the proportion of each colour as a fraction and a percentage.
a dark
b milk
c white

4 In a class $\frac{1}{3}$ of the students are boys.
Write the ratio of boys to girls in the class.

> **Q4 hint**
>
> | boys | girls |
> |------|-------|

5 In a box of eggs 20% are rotten.
What is the ratio of good eggs to rotten eggs in the box?

6 Real A machine makes CDs. The proportion of corrupt CDs is 2%.
What is the ratio of clean to corrupt CDs?

7 The proportion of people aged over 60 in a village is $\frac{3}{8}$
What is the ratio of over-sixties to under-sixties?

8 Five chocolate bars cost £1.50.
How much will 15 bars cost?

> **Q8 hint**
>
>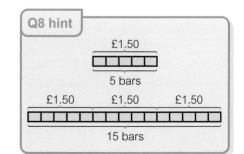

9 A recipe for 6 people needs 150 g of sugar.
How much sugar is needed for
a 18 people
b 36 people
c 48 people?

10 12 packets of nails contain 108 nails.
How many nails will there be in 18 packets?

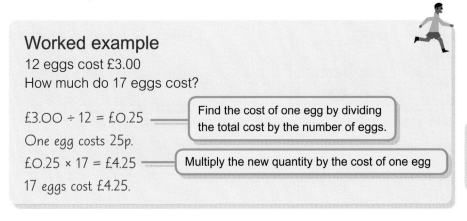

Worked example

12 eggs cost £3.00
How much do 17 eggs cost?

£3.00 ÷ 12 = £0.25 ⎯ Find the cost of one egg by dividing the total cost by the number of eggs.

One egg costs 25p.

£0.25 × 17 = £4.25 ⎯ Multiply the new quantity by the cost of one egg

17 eggs cost £4.25.

Key point

In the unitary method you find the value of one item first.

11 Real / STEM Burning 6 litres of diesel emits about 15 kg of CO_2.
How much CO_2 is emitted from burning
  a 9 litres of diesel
  b 21 litres of diesel
  c 50 litres of diesel?

12 11 identical memory sticks can hold 88 GB of data.
How many GB can be stored on
  a 25 memory sticks
  b 31 memory sticks
  c 47 memory sticks?

13 Problem-solving A factory worker can wire 24 plugs in an hour.
  a How long does she take to wire one plug?
  b How many plugs can she wire in 20 minutes?

Q13a hint

Convert 1 hour to minutes.

14 Problem-solving A manager orders official company shirts for all 27 of his staff.
The value of the order is £135.
Three new members of staff join the company.
What would the value of the order be now?

15 Problem-solving A designer earns £450 for providing 18 designs.
She is asked to provide a further 7 designs. How much will she earn in total?

16 Problem-solving 4 fruit bars weigh the same as 10 biscuits.
  a How many biscuits weigh the same as one fruit bar?
  b How many fruit bars weigh the same as 35 biscuits?

17 Problem-solving / Real Two shops are selling identical white chocolate cookies.

Q17 hint

Compare the price of one cookie in each shop.

Shop A	Shop B
£3 for 6 cookies	£4 for 9 cookies

Which shop gives better value for money?

18 Problem-solving / Real Paint is sold in 1 litre, 2.5 litre and 5 litre containers.

1 litre £4.40 2.5 litres £11 5 litres £21

Which container size is the best value for money?

 19 Problem-solving / Real A supermarket has two different offers on washing tablets.

Offer A
24 tablets for £4.32

Offer B
16 tablets for £3.20

Which offer gives better value for money?

20 This is a recipe for pastry.
   a Write the ratio of flour to pastry.
   b What fraction of the pastry is flour?

> 55 g butter
> 110 g flour

 21 Problem-solving / Real Zoe scored 35 out of 40 in paper A and 40 out of 55 in paper B.
In which paper did she get the better score?

> **Q21 hint**
> Convert both scores to a percentage.

22 Explore How much concentrated squash do you need to make a litre of diluted squash?
Is it easier to explore this question now you have completed the lesson? What further information do you need to be able to answer this?

23 Reflect List at least five mathematics skills you used to solve the problems in this lesson. For example, you might have used equivalent percentages and fractions in answering Q5.

7.3 Problem-solving with proportions

You will learn to:
• Solve problems using direct and inverse proportion
• Use graphs to solve proportion problems.

Why learn this?
Some healthcare professionals use simple proportional graphs to check, for example, height against weight.

Fluency
• What is double 42?
• What is half 42?

Explore
How many euros can you get for £100?

Exercise 7.3

1 The graph shows the price of a taxi fare as the distance increases.
Use the graph to find the price of taking a taxi for
   a 3 miles
   b 5 miles
   c 8 miles

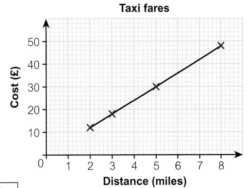

Taxi fares

2 Use a suitable pair of axes to draw a graph using the values in this table.

Length (m)	2	4	6	8	10
Price (£)	3	6	9	12	15

Investigation   **Reasoning**

Taxi Company A charges 80p per mile for all journeys.
1 Choose suitable values and draw a graph to show its prices.
2 Explain how you could use the graph to find the price of a journey of 2.2 miles.
Taxi Company B charges a 50p fee for each journey plus a rate of 60p per mile.
3 Choose suitable values and draw a graph to show their prices.
4 Compare your two graphs. What is the main difference between them?
Discussion Is the price for 20 miles double the price for 10 miles for both companies?

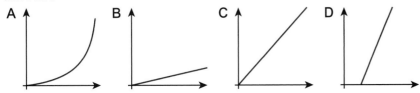

3 Which of these graphs show one variable in **direct proportion** to another?

A   B   C   D

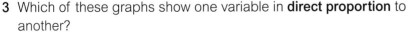

Key point

When two quantities are in **direct proportion**:
• plotting them as a graph gives a straight line through the origin
• when one variable is zero, the other variable will also be zero
• when one variable doubles, so does the other.

4 Real / Problem-solving The graph shows the price
of pick-and-mix sweets according to their mass.
   a How much do 100 g of sweets cost?
   b How many grams of sweets can you get for £5?
   c How much do 250 g of sweets cost?
   d How many grams of sweets can you get for £6.50?
   e On a trip to the cinema, Jane buys her six friends
   and herself 50 g of pick-and-mix each.
   How much does this cost her?
   f How much does the price increase for every extra
   100 g of sweets?
   g Are the two quantities in direct proportion?
   h Use the graph to work out the cost of 1 kg
   of sweets.

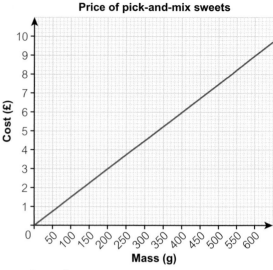

Price of pick-and-mix sweets

5 Finance The graph shows the exchange rate between pounds and
euros.

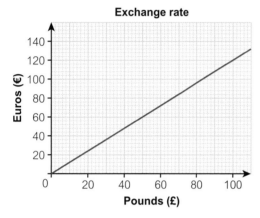

Exchange rate

   a Use the graph to complete:
      i £30 = €☐   **ii** £90 = €☐   **iii** €40 = £☐   **iv** €110 = £☐
   b Explain how you use the graph to find the value of £300.

> **Q5 hint**
>
> Are the quantities in direct
> proportion?

6 STEM In a science experiment, students measure how far a spring
extends when different masses are hung from it.
The results are shown in this graph.

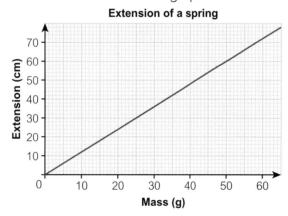

Extension of a spring

   a Are extension and mass in direct proportion?
   b How far does the spring extend if a mass of 25 g is hung from it?
   c What mass causes the spring to extend by 20 cm?
   d How far does the spring extend if a mass of 40 g is hung from it?
   e What mass causes the spring to extend by 45 cm?

Subject links: Science (Q6)

7 Real / Reasoning / Problem-solving The table shows some equivalent temperatures in degrees Celsius (C) and Fahrenheit (F).

Celsius	10°	−10°	20°	30°
Fahrenheit	50°	14°	68°	86°

a Plot a line graph for these values.

b Are temperatures in Celsius and Fahrenheit in direct proportion? Explain how you know.

c Find the value in Fahrenheit of 0°C.

Q7a hint

Plot Celsius on the horizontal axis and Fahrenheit on the vertical axis. The Celsius axis needs to go from −10 to 30 and the Fahrenheit axis from 0 to 90.

Key point

When increasing one quantity causes the other quantity to decrease, the quantities are inversely proportional.

Worked example

It takes 2 people 6 days to lay out a new garden.
How long does it take

a 4 people   b 1 person?

a Number of : Time
   people   (days)

$$×2 \left(\begin{array}{c} 2:6 \\ 4:3 \end{array} \right) ÷2$$

The more people there are, the less time it takes. Doubling the number of people halves the time.

b Number of : Time
   people   (days)

$$÷2 \left(\begin{array}{c} 2:6 \\ 1:12 \end{array} \right) ×2$$

Halving the number of people doubles the time.

8 Real / Problem-solving 4 mechanics can repair a coach in 2 hours.
How long would it take

a 2 mechanics

b 1 mechanic

c 8 mechanics?

Q8 Strategy hint

Use a table to set out your working.

Number of people	Time (hours)
4	2
2	☐

9 Real / Problem-solving It takes 60 minutes to empty a pool with 2 pumps.
How long would it take with 3 pumps?

Q9 hint

Work out how long it would take with 1 pump first.

10 Real / Problem-solving 5 workers can dig a 48 m trench in 4 days.

a How long would it take 10 workers to dig a 48 m trench?

b How long would it take 10 workers to dig a 12 m trench?

11 Explore How many euros can you get for £100?
What have you learned in this lesson to help you answer this question? What other information do you need?

12 Reflect For Q10, you could use a table or a graph to help you answer the question. Did you use either of these or another method? Explain why you chose your method.

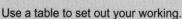

Explore   Reflect

7.4 Measures and conversions

You will learn to:
- Use units of measurement to solve problems
- Convert between metric and imperial measurements.

CONFIDENCE

Why learn this?
Surveyors have to convert between a variety of different measures accurately.

Fluency
What is
- 34 × 10
- 34 × 100
- 34 × 1000
- 456 ÷ 10
- 456 ÷ 100
- 456 ÷ 1000?

Explore
What number of goldfish have the same mass as an elephant?

Exercise 7.4

Warm up

1 Complete these conversions.
   a 3.53 cm = □ mm
   b 0.67 km = □ m
   c 7.1 *l* = □ m*l*
   d □ g = 4.08 kg

2 Harry used his calculator to work out some questions involving money in pounds (£).
His calculator display for each question is shown below.
Write out each answer correctly using £.
   a 3.06   **b** 4   **c** 8.6   **d** 57.3

3 Problem-solving Khouresh has pieces of wood that are 45 cm, 2.06 m and 456 mm long.
   a What is the total length of wood he has?
   b What is the biggest difference between any two pieces?

> **Q3a hint**
> Change all measurements to the same units.

4 Problem-solving Noreen has two rectangular pieces of carpet.
One measures 3.5 m × 2.3 m and the other is 264 cm × 325 cm.
   a Which piece of carpet has the larger area?
   b What is the total area of the two carpets together?

> **Q4 Strategy hint**
> Choose to work in either cm² or m².

5 Problem-solving A smart TV records a programme that starts at 11.55 am.
The programme lasts 95 minutes.
What time does the programme stop recording?

6 Work out these conversions.
   a 5467 kg = □ **tonnes**
   b 2262 kg = □ tonnes
   c 34.2 tonnes = □ kg
   d 0.238 tonnes = □ kg

> **Key point**
> The **tonne** is used to measure mass.
> 1 tonne (t) = 1000 kg

7 Calculate the areas of these rectangular fields. Give your answers in **hectares**.
   a 341 m × 508 m
   b 784 m × 492 m
   c 473 m × 329 m
   d 1024 m × 53 m

> **Key point**
> The **hectare** is used to measure area.
> 1 hectare (ha) = 10 000 m²

Topic links: Area

8 Write the value of these calculator displays in the units shown.

a | 4.05 | in metres and centimetres

b | 7.39 | in kilograms and grams

c | 16.008 | in litres and millilitres

9 Decide if **A**, **B** or **C** is equivalent to each measurement.

a 30 m 6 cm   **A** 30.6 m   **B** 30.06 m   **C** 30.006 m

b 9 litres 350 m*l*   **A** 9.35 litres   **B** 9.035 litres   **C** 9.0035 litres

c 880 g   **A** 8.8 kg   **B** 0.88 kg   **C** 0.088 kg

Investigation

1 Draw a square with side length 1 cm.
2 Use a sharp pencil to measure and mark mm along each side, and join up opposite marks.
3 How many small squares are in the square cm?
4 What is the area of each small square?
5 Complete this statement: $1\,cm^2 = \square\,mm^2$
6 Draw a diagram to show how many cm^2 there are in a square metre.
7 Complete this statement: $1\,m^2 = \square\,cm^2$

---

10 Complete these area conversions.

a $5\,cm^2 = 5 \times \square = \square\,mm^2$ b $3.5\,m^2 = 3.5 \times \square = \square\,cm^2$

c $800\,mm^2 = 800 \div \square = \square\,cm^2$ d $420\,mm^2 = 420 \div \square = \square\,cm^2$

e $90\,000\,cm^2 = \square \div \square = \square\,m^2$ f $170\,000\,cm^2 = \square \div \square = \square\,m^2$

> **Key point**
>
> $1\,cm^2 = 100\,mm^2$
> $1\,m^2 = 10\,000\,cm^2$

11 Complete these conversions.

a 7 feet = $\square$ cm   b 104 km = $\square$ miles

c 3 litres = $\square$ pints   d 165 lb = $\square$ kg

e 9 gallons = $\square$ litres   f 1.5 m = $\square$ feet

> **Key point**
>
> You can use these approximations between metric and imperial units.
> 1 foot (ft) ≈ 30 cm
> 1 mile ≈ 1.6 km
> 1 kg ≈ 2.2 pounds (lb)
> 1 litre ≈ 1.75 pints
> 1 gallon ≈ 4.5 litres

12 **Explore** What number of goldfish have the same mass as an elephant?
Look back at the maths you have learned in this lesson.
How can you use it to answer this question?

13 **Reflect** The photo caption for this lesson is 'Surveyors have to convert between a variety of different measures accurately.'
What other careers are likely to make use of conversions?

Master
P157

CHECK

Strengthen
P169

Extend
P173

Test
P177

7 Check up

Log how you did on your
Student Progression Chart.

Using ratios

1 Share these amounts in the given ratios.
   a £82 in the ratio 3:2   **b** £144 in the ratio 8:7

2 Express each ratio in its simplest form.
   a 32mm:12cm   **b** 75g:1kg

3 The ratio of male to female birds in a population is 5:6.
   How many female birds would you expect in a population of 231 birds?

4 Bella and her two brothers share some money in proportion to their ages.
   Bella is 12, Callum is 9 and Tony is 7.
   They share £12663 in total. How much do they each get?

5 A zoologist surveys the population of blackbirds and pigeons in a park.
   $\frac{2}{3}$ of the birds he surveys are pigeons.
   What is the ratio of blackbirds to pigeons in the park?

Proportions

6 A recipe for 4 people uses 240ml of milk.
   How much milk is required for
   a 3 people   **b** 14 people?

7 Three supermarkets sell identical dishwasher tablets in different quantities.

Supermarket A	**Supermarket B**	**Supermarket C**
24 tablets for £2.76	36 tablets for £4.32	30 tablets for £3.90

   Which supermarket offers the best value for money?

8 Dean makes muesli using 8 times as much oats as dried fruit.
   a What is the ratio of oats to fruit?
   b What fraction of the muesli is fruit?

9 The graph shows the exchange rate between
   pounds (£) and dollars ($) on one day.
   a Are pounds and dollars in direct proportion?
   b Use the graph to complete:
      i $40 = £☐
      ii £65 = $☐
   c How many pounds can you get for $200?

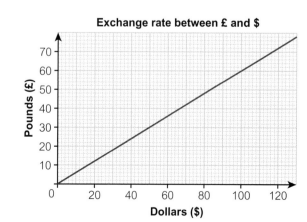

10 4 machines are digging a deep hole in a quarry.
   It will take 48 hours to dig the hole.
   How long will it take 6 machines to dig the hole?

Measures

11 A ball of string is 40 m long. Tracy cuts 75 cm off the string then Simon uses 5.3 m.
How much string is left?

12 A rectangular park is 865 m by 720 m.
What is the area of the park in
a m²
b hectares?

13 A fully loaded lorry can have a maximum total mass of 44 tonnes.
A partly loaded lorry weighs 42.15 tonnes.
How much more can the lorry carry? Give your answer in kg.

 14 Work out these conversions.
a 56 km = ☐ miles   b 4 pints = ☐ litres
c 6.5 kg = ☐ lb   d 5 feet = ☐ metres

15 Copy and complete these area conversions.
a 25 mm² = ☐ cm²   b 64 cm² = ☐ m²
c 568 cm² = ☐ mm²   d 2.5 m² = ☐ cm²

16 **How sure are you of your answers? Were you mostly**
😠 **Just guessing**   😐 **Feeling doubtful**   🙂 **Confident**
What next? Use your results to decide whether to strengthen or extend your learning.

Challenge

 17 Three princes will inherit money from a duke in proportion to their ages.
The duke left them a total of £12 000.
The princes are currently 3, 4 and 5 years old.
a How much will each prince get if they inherit this year?
b How much would each prince have got if they inherited last year?
c How much will each prince get if they inherit next year?
d When the duke dies the youngest prince's share is £3500.
How old is each prince when they inherit the money?

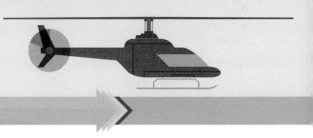

7 Strengthen

You will:
- Strengthen your understanding with practice.

Using ratios

1 Share these amounts between Rik and Sophia in the ratios given.
 a £15 in the ratio 2:3
 b £72 in the ratio 7:5
 c £450 in the ratio 4:5

Q1a hint

£15

2 A survey of people walking in a country park found that the ratio of dog owners to non-dog owners is 5:2.
 One day there are 315 visitors to the park. How many are likely to have dogs?

3 Share these quantities in the ratios given.
 a £96 in the ratio 3:2
 b 670g in the ratio 11:9
 c 236m*l* in the ratio 1:4
 d 432mm in the ratio 7:3

4 Share these amounts in the ratios given.
 a 73km in the ratio 1:3:4
 b 785kg in the ratio 6:8:11
 c £624 in the ratio 2:3:5
 d 55 litres in the ratio 2:5:1

Q4a hint

73km

5 Marion has a paint colour that she wants to reproduce precisely.
 It is made from red, white and yellow paint in the ratio 5:58:1.
 How much of each colour does she need to make 4 litres of the paint?
 Give your answer in m*l*.

6 Express each ratio in its simplest form.
 a 25cm to 1m
 b 500m*l* to 2 litres
 c 250m to 5km
 d 16g to 0.5kg

Q6a hint

25cm:1m
Both numbers need to be in the same units. 1m = ☐ cm

7 In a supermarket $\frac{3}{4}$ of the customers pay using a debit card.
 The rest pay with cash.
 What is the ratio of card payers to cash payers in the shop?

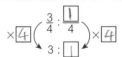

$$\times\boxed{4}\left(\frac{3}{4}:\frac{\boxed{1}}{4}\right)\times\boxed{4}$$
$$3:\boxed{}$$

Proportions

1 **Real** Dog treats are sold by a pet shop for 75p per 100g.
 How much does it cost to buy
 a 200g
 b 400g
 c 1kg?

Q1a hint

pence : grams

75 : 100

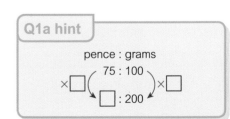

☐ : 200

2 12 breakfast bars cost £1.68. What is the cost of
  a 32 bars
  b 48 bars
  c 57 bars
  d 75 bars?

Q2 Strategy hint

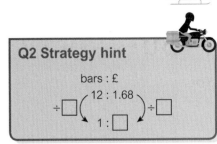

bars : £

12 : 1.68

÷☐ (↓) ÷☐

1 : ☐

3 Real Laptop A has a 3GB memory and costs £240.
Laptop B has a 4GB memory and costs £350.
Which laptop gives you more memory for your money?

4 Real Three printers are competing for business.
Printer A will print 200 leaflets for £4.50.
Printer B will print 250 leaflets for £5.50.
Printer C will print 150 leaflets for £3.75.
Which printer is the best value for money?

5 In a brownie recipe there is 3 times as much sugar as
there is flour.
  a What is the ratio of flour to sugar?
  b Write the quantity of flour as a fraction of the quantity
    of sugar.

6 a Draw a pair of axes like this:
  b Draw any straight line through the origin.
  c Label your graph 'Direct proportion'.
  d Underneath your graph, copy and
    complete this statement.
    When two quantities are in direct proportion
    the graph is a _____ _____ through the _____

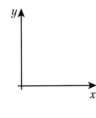

7 Reasoning The graph shows
the amount of fuel used by
an aircraft when cruising
at 30000 feet.
  a How does the graph
    show that the amount
    of fuel used is in direct
    proportion to the
    distance travelled?
  b How much fuel is
    used to travel
    i 1500km
    ii 2500km
    iii 3200km
    iv 8000km?
  c How far can the aircraft travel on
    i 8000kg
    ii 10000kg
    iii 12000kg
    iv 18000kg of fuel?

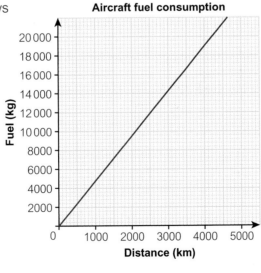

Aircraft fuel consumption

Q7b i hint

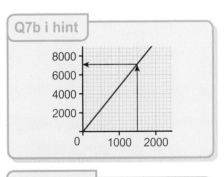

Q7b iv hint

Double the amount of fuel used to
travel 4000km.

8 Which of these graphs show variables in direct proportion?

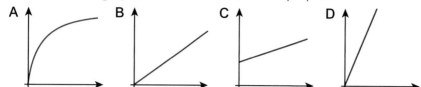

9 **Real / Problem-solving** The graph shows the conversion between speed in miles per hour (mph) and km per hour (km/h).
   a What speed in mph is equivalent to 0 km/h?
   b Are mph and km/h in direct proportion? Explain.
   c Which is the faster speed, 100 mph or 140 km/h?
   d A train is travelling at 200 mph. What is this speed in km/h?
   e French autoroutes have a speed limit of 110 km/h when it is wet. What is this in mph?

10 **STEM / Reasoning** In a science experiment, students measure the force exerted on a spring by different masses. The results are shown in this table.

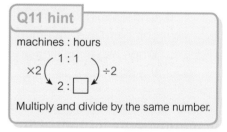

Speed conversion graph

Mass (g)	50	100	200	400
Force (N)	0.5	1	2	4

   a Plot a line graph for these values.
   b Are the force and mass in direct proportion? Explain how you know.
   c What is the force exerted by a mass of 300 g?
   d What mass would exert a force of 1.5 N?

11 **Problem-solving** A machine can make 360 items in an hour. How long would it take 2 machines to make 360 items?

12 **Problem-solving** A construction company is building a motorway. It is using 4 surfacing machines and expects to finish in 12 days' time. If one of the machines breaks down, when are they likely to finish?

4 mach → 12 days
∴ 1 mach → 48 days
⇒ 3 mach = 16 days (= 12 × 4/3)

> **Q11 hint**
>
> machines : hours
>
> ×2 (1 : 1) ÷2
>   2 : ☐
>
> Multiply and divide by the same number.

> **Q12 hint**
>
> First work out how long it would take to complete the job with one machine.

Measures

1 Work out these conversions.
   a 3 hectares = ☐ m²
   b 4.35 hectares = ☐ m²
   c 75 000 m² = ☐ hectares
   d 18 500 m² = ☐ hectares

> **Q1a hint**
>
>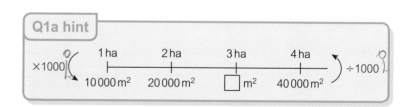

2 Work out these conversions.
   a 2 tonnes = ☐ kg
   b 13.75 tonnes = ☐ kg
   c 1500 kg = ☐ tonnes
   d 76 500 kg = ☐ tonnes

> **Q2a hint**
>
>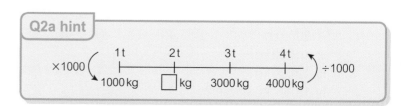

3 Work out these conversions.

a 15 miles ≈ ☐ km

b 40 km ≈ ☐ miles

c 90 cm ≈ ☐ feet

d 1.25 feet ≈ ☐ cm

e 10 gallons ≈ ☐ litres

f 27 litres ≈ ☐ gallons

g 20 pints ≈ ☐ litres

h 26.25 litres ≈ ☐ pints

i 4 kg ≈ ☐ lb

j 13.2 lb ≈ ☐ kg

Q3 hint

Draw number lines to help you.
1 foot ≈ 30 cm
1 litre ≈ 1.75 pints
1 gallon ≈ 4.5 litres
1 kg ≈ 2.2 lb
1 mile ≈ 1.6 km

Q3a hint

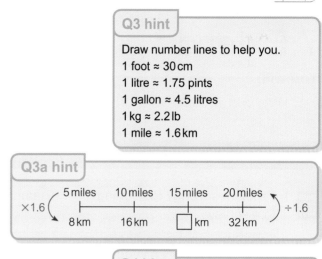

4 Work out these conversions.

a $2\,cm^2 = \square\,mm^2$

b $4.5\,m^2 = \square\,cm^2$

c $900\,mm^2 = \square\,cm^2$

d $120\,000\,cm^2 = \square\,m^2$

Q4 hint

Draw a number line to help you.
$1\,cm^2 = 100\,mm^2$ $1\,m^2 = 10\,000\,cm^2$

Enrichment

1 One person takes 45 minutes to weed a 6 metre flower bed.

a Write a question using this information.

b Swap questions with a classmate and work out the answer.

a Write a new question that has an answer of '5 people'.

2 Reflect Is finding a ratio the same as finding a proportion? Explain.

Q2 hint

Look back at Q1 and Q2 in 'Using ratios' and Q1 in 'Proportions'. Did you do the same thing?

Reflect

7 Extend

You will:
• Extend your understanding with problem-solving.

 1 Problem-solving / Reasoning Four researchers collected responses to a survey.

Researcher	Number of responses	Time taken
Eduardo	15	1 hour 40 minutes
Ferri	21	2 hours
Gretel	14	1 hour 35 minutes
Hannah	26	2 hours 24 minutes

Which of the researchers was the most efficient?
Explain.

> **Q1 hint**
>
> Find how long it takes each researcher to get one response.

 2 STEM The alloy shakudo is made by mixing 0.96 g of copper with 0.04 g of fine gold.
Copy and complete the table to show the amounts of each metal needed.

Mass of shakudo (g)	Mass of copper (g)	Mass of fine gold (g)
50		
	12	
		2.0
96		
	9	
		1.5

3 Problem-solving The table shows measurements made on some maps and their real distance.
Copy and complete the table to show the scale of the map as a ratio in its simplest form.

Distance on map	Real distance	Ratio in simplest form
2 cm	45 km	
25 mm	200 m	
3.6 cm	12 km	
12 cm	306 km	
3 mm	600 m	

4 Problem-solving In a car park, $\frac{1}{6}$ of the spaces are reserved for cars with children and $\frac{1}{12}$ of the spaces are reserved for drivers with a disability.
Write the ratio of the total number of reserved spaces to all other spaces. Write your ratio in its simplest form.

Topic links: Scale, Area

Subject links: Science (Q2, Q10, Q11, Q13, Q14), Geography (Q3)

5 Problem-solving A company sells peanuts and sultanas in small bags for £1.40.
An average small bag contains 12 peanuts and 32 sultanas.
The company wants to make a larger bag that sells for £2.45.
How many peanuts and sultanas should they put on average in each bag?

6 Problem-solving / Real Three different types of tea bags are on sale at a supermarket.

Tea Tips	**Phoo Tea**	**T'bags**
Boxes of 80 for £2.24	Boxes of 120 for £2.95	Boxes of 140 for £3.40

a Which box is the best value?

b Write your own price for a box of teabags that is better than the worst of these three prices, but not as good as the best.

7 Problem-solving / Reasoning Dilshan has been collecting data on the mass of people in his class.
Some people have supplied the data in grams, some in kg and some in pounds (lb).

a Copy and complete the table so that Dilshan has a complete record of masses in kg.

Person	Given mass	Mass in kg
A	68 kg	
B	54 683 g	
C	145 lb	
D	201 lb	
E	9458 g	
F	185 lb	

b Which person appears to have made a mistake?

8 Problem-solving The table gives the dimensions for sheets of A3 and A4 paper.

Paper size	Long side (mm)	Short side (mm)	Area (mm²)	Area (cm²)
A0				
A1				
A2				
A3	420	297		
A4	297	210		
A5				
A6				

A3 paper is larger than A4 paper. The short side of A3 is the same as the long side of A4. The long side of A3 is twice the short side of A4.
This rule is repeated for all other A series paper sizes.
Copy and complete the table.

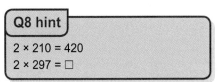

Q8 hint

2 × 210 = 420
2 × 297 = □

9 **Problem-solving / Finance** Three co-workers, Bill, Cheryl and Daisy, bought some Premium Bonds together.
Bill invested £150, Cheryl £350 and Daisy £200.
They win a jackpot of £50 000.
They divide the prize in the same ratio that they invested.
How much does each person get?

Q9 Literacy hint
A Premium Bond is an investment that enters the investor into a monthly prize draw.

10 **Problem-solving / STEM** Bronze is an alloy where the principal metal is copper. Different amounts of other metals are mixed with the copper to make an alloy.
The table shows the ratios of metals for different types of bronze.

Type of alloy	Metals	Ratio
Commercial bronze	Copper, zinc	9:1
Architectural bronze	Copper, lead, zinc	57:3:40
Bismuth bronze	Copper, nickel, zinc, lead, bismuth	52:30:12:5:1
Bell bronze	Copper, tin	4:1
Phosphor bronze	Copper, tin, phosphorus	200:20:1

Which bronze has the highest proportion of copper?

11 **STEM** The radius of the Earth is 6378 km. The table gives the radius of four other planets in miles.

Planet	Radius (miles)
Mars	2123
Mercury	1525
Neptune	15479
Venus	3783

Write the ratio of the radius of the Earth to the radius of each planet in the form $1:n$.

Q11 hint
Convert the radius of the Earth to miles so you only need to do one conversion!

12 **Problem-solving** A farmer plants wheat, barley and oats in the ratio 4:7:3. She plants 385 hectares of wheat and barley altogether.
How many hectares of oats does she plant?

Q12 hint

385 hectares

13 **STEM / Reasoning / Modelling** In a science experiment, students hang different masses from two springs and measure the extension of the springs.
The results are given in the tables.

Spring A	
Mass (g)	Extension (mm)
10	22
15	33
25	55
35	77

Spring B	
Mass (g)	Extension (mm)
10	18
15	27
25	45
35	63

a Choose suitable axes and draw a graph to show these results.
Label the line representing each spring.
b Are both relationships directly proportional? Explain.
c Which spring extends further?

Q13a hint
Plot extension on the vertical axis and mass on the horizontal axis.

14 STEM In a science experiment, students measure the current, I, flowing through a resistor for different voltages, V. The results for two resistors are shown in the tables.

Resistor A	
Voltage, V (volts)	Current, I (amps)
1	0.5
3	1.5
4	2.0
6	3.0

Resistor B	
Voltage, V (volts)	Current, I (amps)
2.0	0.4
4.5	0.9
6.0	1.2
7.5	1.5

    a Plot the graphs for these results on the same set of axes.
    b Is current flowing through a resistor directly proportional to voltage?

Q14a hint
Plot voltage on the vertical axis and current on the horizontal axis.

15 On a farm 6 workers can harvest a field of cabbages in 20 hours. How long would it take 4 workers to harvest the same field?

16 Problem-solving 10 people go on an expedition with enough supplies for 20 days.
At the last minute 2 extra people join the expedition and don't bring any extra supplies.
How long will the supplies last now?

17 Problem-solving A major cleaning job will take 4 machines 9 days. The contractor would like to finish in 6 days. How many machines should he use to make sure this happens?

18 Problem-solving A rectangle has an area of $12\,\text{cm}^2$.
The length of one side is doubled and the length of the other side is halved.
What happens to the area of the rectangle?

Q18 Strategy hint
Try a pair of factors of 12.

Investigation   **Problem-solving**
A farmer wants to create a rectangular field. He has 2 km of fencing in 50 m sections.
1 Find as many different-sized fields as you can that he can enclose with this amount of fencing.
2 Work out the area of each field in hectares.
3 What is the size of the largest field he can enclose?

19 Reflect It is often a good idea to 'sense check' your answer to a question. For example, by looking at your answers to Q7, you can quickly spot the mistake in the data. Did you sense check any other answers in this section? Explain why sense checking can be a good strategy.

7 Unit test

Log how you did on your Student Progression Chart.

1 Harry has three containers that he wants to fill with liquid.
The containers are marked 450 ml, 0.75 l and 600 cm³.
a Which container holds the most liquid?
b What is the total amount of liquid he can store?

2 Share these amounts in the ratios given.
a £63 in the ratio 2:7
b 280 kg in the ratio 1:6

3 A skip is licensed to carry 2 tonnes of waste.
Verity fills her skip with 1.4 tonnes of waste soil, an old shed that weighs 345 kg, and 30 old tiles that weigh 50 g each.
How much more can Verity put into her skip?

4 Express each ratio in its simplest form.
a 4 cm:2 m
b 45 g:0.6 kg

5 20% of the students in a class have blue eyes.
What is the ratio of blue-eyed to non-blue-eyed students in the class?

6 A printer can print 64 sheets of paper in 4 minutes.
How long will it take to print
a 32 sheets
b 112 sheets?

7 Simon is cooking chilli con carne for 8 people and buys 1.5 kg of meat for his recipe.
How much meat would he need to buy if he was cooking for
a 3 people
b 25 people?

8 A special offer in a supermarket means Myra can buy either Box A or Box B.
Which box of cereal is better value?

200 g £1.20	250 g £1.49
Box A	Box B

9 Work out these conversions.
a 8 km ≈ ☐ miles
b 75 cm ≈ ☐ feet
c 3 litres ≈ ☐ pints
d 2.5 gallons ≈ ☐ litres

10 Copy and complete these area conversions.
a 36 mm² = ☐ cm²
b 453 cm² = ☐ m²
c 45 cm² = ☐ mm²
d 1.6 m² = ☐ cm²

11 Share these amounts in the ratios given.
a 420 m in the ratio 2:3:5
b £525 in the ratio 7:5:8

12 James has 5 times as many football stickers as Miguel.
a What is the ratio of James' stickers to Miguel's?
b What fraction of the total number of stickers does Miguel have?

13 Which graph shows a relationship that is in direct proportion?

Graph A

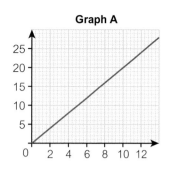

Graph B

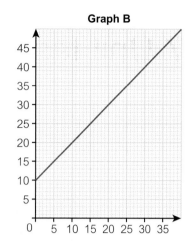

14 This graph shows the relationship between quantities measured in pints and in litres.

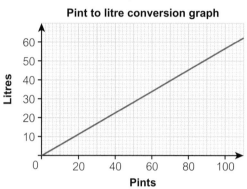

Use the graph to convert
a 30 litres to pints
b 90 pints to litres.

 15 3 painters can paint 450 m² of wall in 2 hours.
    a How long would it take 2 painters to paint the same area of wall?
    b What area of wall could 2 painters paint in 5 hours?

Challenge

16 The diagram shows a set of coloured rods.
Each rod is a multiple of the white cube, for example a red rod is 2 whites and a light green rod is 3 whites.
Using the rods, how many different ratios can you make?
Remember to simplify each one to make sure it is unique.

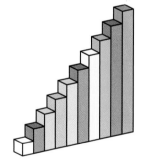

17 **Reflect** Choose the statement that best describes how you feel about this unit:
- I have a good understanding of ratio and proportion.
- I feel very confident in answering any question about ratio and proportion.
- I need more practice in answering the type of questions we have done in this unit.
- My maths skills have improved during this unit, but I occasionally need a bit of help.

If there are any areas you don't feel confident about, make an action plan to address this.

8 Algebraic and geometric formulae

MASTER

Check
P193

Strengthen
P195

Extend
P199

Test
P203

8.1 Substituting into formulae

You will learn to:
- Substitute into formulae.

CONFIDENCE

Why learn this?
Police substitute numbers into formulae to work out the speed of a car when they know the distance and time it has travelled.

Fluency
When $a = 6$ and $b = 5$, work out
- $a + b$
- $a - b$
- $2a - b$
- $3a - 2b$

Explore
Which is hotter, 100°C or 100°F?

Exercise 8.1

Warm up

1 Solve each equation.

  a $x + 10 = 22$ **b** $y - 6 = 18$

  c $5p = 30$ **d** $\dfrac{s}{4} = 5$

2 Match each equation to its description in words. Then work out the value of n.

  A When I add 6 to my number, the answer is 17.   **i** $5n = 10$

  B When I subtract 6 from my number, the answer is 17.   **ii** $2n + 1 = 20$

  C When I multiply my number by 5, the answer is 10.   **iii** $n + 6 = 17$

  D When I divide my number by 5, the answer is 10.   **iv** $\dfrac{n}{2} - 5 = 20$

  E Double my number add 1 is 20.   **v** $n - 6 = 17$

  F Half my number subtract 5 is 20.   **vi** $\dfrac{n}{5} = 10$

3 Write down the value of each expression when $a = 8$ and $b = 5$.

  a $a + b$ **b** $a - b$

  c ab **d** $6ab$

  e $\dfrac{a}{b}$ **f** $2a + 3b$

  g $a^2 + b^2$ **h** $a^2 - b^2$

Q3g hint
$a^2 = 8^2$

Topic links: Angles, Pythagoras' theorem, Perimeter, Area, Volume, Temperature

4 Substitute the given values into each expression.
  a $10(2x + 4y)$ when $x = 6$ and $y = 3$
  b $\dfrac{4y - 2}{3}$ when $y = 5$
  c $\dfrac{(5a - 2b)}{a}$ when $a = 10$ and $b = 7$
  d $(c + d)^2$ when $c = 5$ and $d = 4$
  e $\sqrt{(xy)}$ when $x = 16$ and $y = 4$
  f $\dfrac{(a - b)^2}{(a + b)^2}$ when $a = 12$ and $b = 8$

5 The perimeter of this regular pentagon is $5y$.
  a What is the perimeter when $y = 10\,$cm?
  b What is the value of y when the perimeter is $30\,$cm?

6 A square has sides of length d.
  a Write an expression for the perimeter of the square.
  b The perimeter is $40\,$cm. Write an equation involving d.
  c Solve the equation to find the length d.
  d What is the perimeter of a square with sides of length $5\,$m?

7 **Problem-solving** a Write an expression for the perimeter of a regular octagon with sides of length $x\,$cm.
  b What is the length of one side of a regular octagon that has a perimeter of $72\,$cm?

8 A rectangle is $x\,$cm long and $y\,$cm wide.
  a Write a formula for working out
    i the perimeter of a rectangle
    ii the area of a rectangle.
  b Use your formula to work out the perimeter and area when
    i $x = 4$, $y = 6$
    ii $x = 10$, $y = 12$
    iii $x = 2.4$, $y = 10$

9 Match each expression to a description.

A	s^2	i	Volume of a cube with sides length s
B	$6s$	ii	Perimeter of square with sides length s
C	s^3	iii	Perimeter of regular hexagon with sides length s
D	$3s$	iv	The total area of 3 squares, each with side length s
E	$3s^2$	v	Area of a square with sides length s
F	$4s$	vi	Perimeter of an equilateral triangle with sides length s

10 The formula for the surface area, S, of a cube with side length a, is $S = 6a^2$.
  What is the surface area of a cube with sides of length
  a $10\,$cm
  b $5\,$cm?

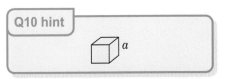

Q10 hint

11 A square has sides of length s cm.

  a Write an expression for the area of the square.

  b Write an equation involving s when the area is 64 cm^2.

  c Solve the equation to find the length, s.

  d What is the area of a square with sides of length 15 cm?

12 Construct formulae to convert these units of time.

  a The number of days, d, in w weeks $d = \square \times w$

  b The number of days, d, in y years

  c The number of months, m, in y years

  d The number of hours, h, in d in days

Q12b hint

1 year = 365 days

13 **Problem-solving** The formula for working out the surface area, A, of this rectangular prism is

$$A = 2ab + 2bc + 2ac$$

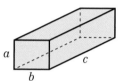

Work out the surface area, A, when

  a $a = 4$ cm, $b = 5$ cm and $c = 6$ cm

  b $a = 4.5$ cm, $b = 9$ cm and $c = 6.4$ cm

  c What is the value of c when $a = 6$ cm, $b = 2$ cm and the surface area is 88 cm^2?

Q13c hint

$2ab + 2bc + 2ac = 88$
Substitute $a = 6$ and $b = 2$, then solve the equation.

14 **Explore** Which is hotter, 100°C or 100°F?
What have you learned in this lesson to help you answer this question? What other information do you need?

15 **Reflect** Meg writes:
'When substituting into formulae or expressions, look out for:
• Brackets – work out whatever is in the brackets first.'
Look back at the questions you answered in this lesson.
Write your own 'look out for' list. Write a short hint for each point in your list.

Q15 hint

You could begin with the same point as Meg.

Explore

Reflect

8.2 More complex formulae

You will learn to:

- Substitute into more complex formulae and solve equations
- Construct more complex formulae.

Why learn this?
You can use formulae as instructions for computers to carry out different calculations.

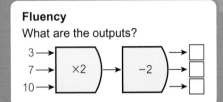

Fluency
What are the outputs?

3 →
7 → ×2 → −2 →
10 →

Explore
What does the formula
=(B1)^2–5*B2 mean?

Exercise 8.2

1 Match each phrase with an algebraic expression.

A | 7 more than n i | $n - 7$

B | Double n ii | $5n$

C | Half of n iii | $2n$

D | 7 less than n iv | $7 - n$

E | 5 times n v | $\dfrac{n}{2}$

F | n less than 7   vi | $n + 7$

2 Claire has y pets. Write down an expression, in terms of y, for the number of pets each of these people have.

  a Nick has 2 fewer pets than Claire.

  b Stevie has 3 times as many pets as Claire.

  c Rob has 4 more pets than Claire.

  d Simon has half as many pets as Claire.

3 Solve

  a $3x = 24$

  b $2x + 1 = 15$

  c $45 = 9x$

  d $7x - 3 = 46$

4 The formula to work out the number of diagonals, D, in a polygon of n sides is $D = \dfrac{n(n - 3)}{2}$

  a How many diagonals does a pentagon have?

  b How many diagonals does an octagon have?

Q4 hint

Substitute the number of sides, n, into the formula.

Warm up

Worked example

The cost of hiring a bike is £10 plus £5 an hour.

a Construct a formula for working out the cost, C, of hiring a bike for h hours.

b What is the cost of hiring a bike for 8 hours?

c Mike spends £40 on hiring a bike. How many hours did he pay for?

a $C = 10 + 5h$

> There is a one-off charge of £10, and then £5 for every hour, h.

> You are working out a formula for the cost, so write $C = \ldots$

b $C = 10 + 5 \times 8$
$= £50$

> Substitute $h = 8$ into the formula.

c $\quad 40 = 10 + 5h$
$40 - 10 = 5h$
$\quad\quad 30 = 5h$
$\quad\quad\quad h = 6$

> Substitute $C = 40$ into the formula and solve the resulting equation.

He hired the bike for 6 hours.

5 The cost of hiring a hall for a party is £80 plus £10 per person.

a Construct a formula for working out the cost, C, of hiring the hall for p people.

b How much will it cost for a party with 50 people?

c A sports club has a party at the hall and pays £230.
How many people came to the party?

6 A theme park charges $10 for entry plus $5 for each ride.

a Construct a formula to work out the total cost, C, for entering the theme park and going on r rides.

b Suzie goes to the theme park and goes on 8 rides. How much does this cost?

c Ahmed spends all day at the theme park and spends $85.
How many rides did he go on?

7 It costs £8 per adult and £5 per child to visit a museum.

a Construct a formula to work out the total cost, T, for a adults and c children.

b Work out the cost for 4 adults and 6 children to visit the museum.

Discussion A family spent £31 visiting the museum. How many children and how many adults went? Compare your answers with your classmates.

8 Copy and complete this table of values for each value of n.

> **Q8 hint**
> Substitute the value of n into each expression in the 1st column.

n	−2	−1	0	1	2	3
$3n$	$3 \times -2 =$					
$n + 5$	$-2 + 5 =$					
$2n - 2$	$2 \times -2 - 2 =$					
$2n + 3$	$2 \times -2 + 3 =$					

Topic links: Area, Perimeter, Angle properties, Metric units, Solving equations

Subject links: Science (Q13)

9 Use substitution to work out the value of each expression.
   a xy when $x = 6$ and $y = -6$
   b $\dfrac{p}{q}$ when $p = 48$ and $q = -8$
   c $(a - b)^2$ when $a = 5$ and $b = 10$
   d $m - n$ when $m = -4$ and $n = -9$
   e $(3d \times 2e) - 100$ when $d = -5$ and $e = -3$

Q9e hint

Be careful when multiplying negative numbers.

10 **Problem-solving** Pythagoras' theorem is $a^2 + b^2 = c^2$.

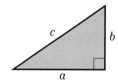

Q10 Strategy hint

Substitute a and b into the formula. Take the square root to work out the value of c.

   a Work out the length of side c when $a = 9\,$cm and $b = 12\,$cm.
   b Work out the length of side c when $a = 15\,$cm and $b = 20\,$cm.

11 **Problem-solving** The diagram shows a triangle.

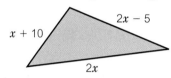

   a Copy and complete this formula for the perimeter, P, of the triangle
   $P = (x + 10) +$ _____ $+$ _____
   b The perimeter of the triangle is 65 cm. Solve the equation to work out x.
   c What is the length of each side?

12 **Problem-solving** Work out the size of each angle in this triangle.

Q12 hint

Write an equation using what you know about the sum of the angles in a triangle.

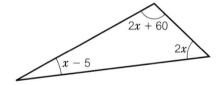

13 **STEM** The formula $F = ma$ shows the relationship between force, F, mass, m and acceleration, a.
   a Work out F when $m = 7$ and $a = 11$
   b Work out m when $F = 70$ and $a = 3.5$
   c Work out F when $m = 2.8$ and $a = 4.9$
   d Work out F when $m = 22.6$ and $a = 15.9$
   e Work out m when $F = 40$ and $a = 8$
   f Work out a when $F = 193.44$ and $m = 12.4$

Q13b hint

Substitute into the formula and rearrange to make m the subject.

14 **Explore** What does the formula =(B1)^2–5*B2 mean?
   Use a computer spreadsheet and choose some sensible numbers to help you answer the question.

15 **Reflect** What is different and what is the same about formulae and equations?

Explore

Reflect

8.3 Formulae in geometry

You will learn to:
- Use inverse operations in formulae
- Know and use the formula for the area of a triangle.

Why learn this?
Architects, designers and engineers need to work out the area of triangles so they can create interesting and functional designs.

Fluency
A square has sides of length 7 cm.
- What is its perimeter?
- What is its area?

Explore
What is the ratio of the area of a triangle to the area of a rectangle?

CONFIDENCE

Exercise 8.3

Warm up

1 Work out
a 8^2
b 11^2
c $\sqrt{100}$
d $\sqrt{144}$
e $9^2 - 6^2$

2 Work out
a 4×2.5
b 3.6×4
c $12.8 \div 4$
d $2.8 \div 4$
e $2 \times (12.6 + 9.8)$
f 3.2×4.5

3 Which diagram shows perpendicular lines?

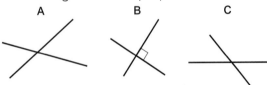

4 Work out the perimeter of each quadrilateral.

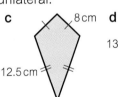

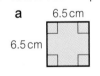

a 6.5 cm, 6.5 cm **b** 14.8 cm, 12.6 cm **c** 8 cm, 12.5 cm **d** 15.9 cm, 13.4 cm

5 a The area of a square is 81 cm². What is the length of one of its sides?
  b The perimeter of a square is 28 cm. What is the length of one side?
  c The perimeter of a square is 48 cm. What is its area?
  d The perimeter of a square is 24.8 cm. What is the length of one of its sides?
  e The perimeter of a rectangle is 31 cm. One side measures 7 cm. What is the length of the other side?
  f The perimeter of a rectangle is 25 cm. One side measures 8.4 cm. What is the length of the other side?
  g The perimeter of an equilateral triangle is 45 cm. What is the length of one of its sides?

Q5a hint

Use the inverse operation.

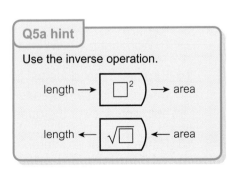

185

Topic links: Properties of triangles, Area, Perimeter, Properties of squares and rectangles

6 Work out the area of each triangle using the grid.

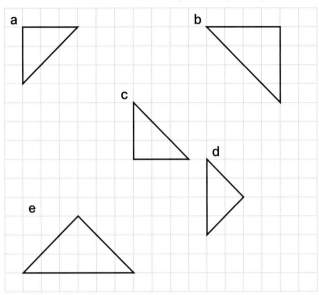

Q6 hint

Count up the whole squares. Now count up the half squares – how many half squares make a whole square?

7 Estimate the area of each triangle.

a

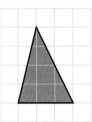

b

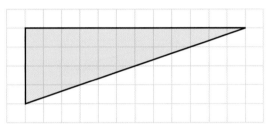

c

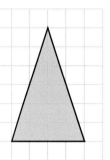

Investigation   **Reasoning**

1 Draw a rectangle on squared paper

2 Work out its area.

3 Draw a diagonal line to split the rectangle into two triangles.

4 Count the squares to work out the area of each triangle.

5 What fraction of the rectangle is taken up by the triangle?

6 Draw another rectangle on squared paper. This time draw two lines from the top edge to the bottom corners.

7 What is the area of the rectangle?

8 What is the area of the biggest triangle?

9 What are the areas of the two smaller triangles?

10 What do you notice?

11 Draw some more triangles inside rectangles to investigate further.

Part 7 hint

Put partial squares together to make a whole square. $\frac{3}{4} + \frac{1}{4} = 1$

8 Work out the area of each triangle.

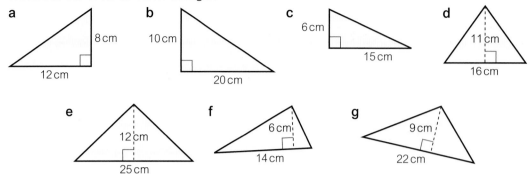

a 8 cm, 12 cm

b 10 cm, 20 cm

c 6 cm, 15 cm

d 11 cm, 16 cm

e 12 cm, 25 cm

f 6 cm, 14 cm

g 9 cm, 22 cm

9 **Reasoning** a Write down the length of the base and the perpendicular height of this triangle.

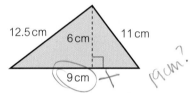

12.5 cm   6 cm   11 cm

9 cm   19 cm?

b Work out the area of the triangle.

10 Work out the area of each triangle.

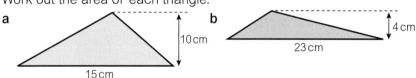

a 10 cm, 15 cm

b 4 cm, 23 cm

11 **Problem-solving** Marc has designed a flowerbed in the shape of a right-angled triangle. The sides which meet at the right angle have lengths 4 m and 2.5 m. What is the area of the flowerbed?

12 **Problem-solving** a Write an expression for the area of this triangle.

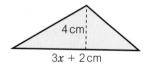

4 cm

3x + 2 cm

b The area of the triangle is 16 cm². Write an equation and solve it to work out the value of x.

13 **Explore** What is the ratio of the area of a triangle to the area of a rectangle?
Look back at the maths you have learned in this lesson. How can you use it to answer this question?

14 **Reflect** In this lesson, you have met and used different formulae used in geometry.
Who else uses formulae?
Why do you think formulae are useful?

Explore

Reflect

8.4 Compound shapes

You will learn to:

- Work out the area and perimeter of shapes made from rectangles and triangles.

Why learn this?
Builders, decorators and landscape designers need to know how to work out areas and perimeters of awkward shapes.

Fluency
Name each quadrilateral.

Explore
In how many ways can you split this shape to work out its area?

Exercise 8.4

1 Work out

a $(12.6 + 7.9) \times 2$

b $10^2 - 5^2 + 3^2$

2 Work out the area and perimeter of each rectangle.

a
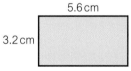
5.6 cm
3.2 cm

b
8.4 cm
2.5 cm

3 a Copy and complete the workings to find the area of this **compound** shape.
Area A = $3 \times 2 = \square$ cm^2
Area B = $\square \times \square = \square$ cm^2
Total area = $\square + \square = \square$ cm^2

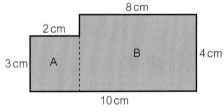

8 cm
2 cm
3 cm | A | B | 4 cm
10 cm

Key point
You can split a **compound** shape up into other shapes to work out its area.

b Work out the perimeter of the whole shape.

4 For this shape, work out
a the area
b the perimeter.

9 cm
8 cm
3 cm
3 cm
12 cm

Q3 Literacy hint
A compound shape is a shape made from other shapes.

5 This compound shape can be split in two different ways.
Work out the area of
a A + B
b C + D

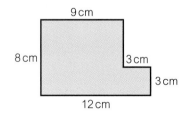

9 cm
8 cm
5 cm
20 cm

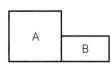

A | B

C
D

6 Problem-solving For this compound shape, work out
   a the area
   b the perimeter.

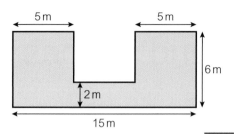

7 Problem-solving This design is made from square tiles. The length of the large tile is double the length of the small tile.
The perimeter of the whole shape is 140 cm.
Work out the side length of a small tile and a large tile.

Q7 Strategy hint

Draw a diagram and label the side of the small tile 'x'. Label the side of the large tile $\square x$.

Worked example

Work out the area of this shape.

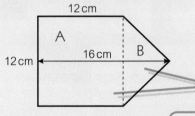

Split the shape into a square A and a triangle B.

Area A = 12 × 12 = 144 cm²   Work out the area of each shape separately.

Height of triangle = 16 − 12 = 4 cm.

Area B = $\frac{1}{2}$ × 12 × 4
       = 24 cm²

Area A + B = 144 + 24   Add the areas together to work out the total area of the shape.
           = 168 cm²

8 This compound shape is made from two **congruent** triangles and a rectangle. What is the total area of the shape?

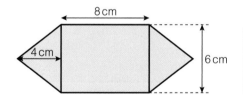

Q8 Literacy hint

Congruent shapes are exactly the same shape and size.

9 Work out the area of this trapezium.

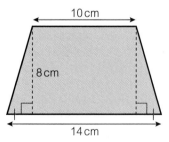

Q9 Literacy hint

The red dashes on the base line show the marked lines are of equal length.

10 Problem-solving The perimeter of this shape is 32 cm. Form an equation to work out the value of x.

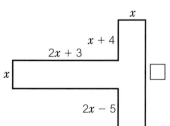

Topic links: 2D shapes

Problem-solving / Reasoning

1 Draw a parallelogram on squared paper. Count the squares to work out the area.

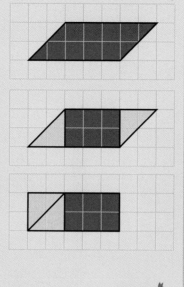

2 Split the parallelogram into a compound shape made of one rectangle and two congruent triangles.

3 The two triangles can be brought together to make a rectangle (in this case, a square).

4 What is the total base length of the new rectangle?

5 What is the height of the new rectangle?

6 Write a formula for working out the length of a parallelogram with height h and base b.

7 Test your formula works for four more parallelograms.

11 Work out the area of each parallelogram.

a

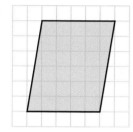

b

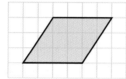

c

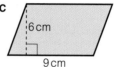

6 cm

9 cm

d

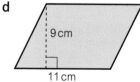

9 cm

11 cm

12 **Problem-solving** The area of this parallelogram is 100 cm². Write an equation and solve it to work out the value of y.

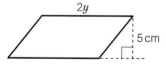

$2y$

5 cm

> **Key point**
>
>
> The area of a parallelogram is given by:
> Area = base × vertical height
> $A = bh$

13 **Explore** In how many ways can you split this shape to work out its area?
Look back at the maths you have learned in this lesson. How can you use it to answer this question?

14 **Reflect** Asif says, 'Working out problems in maths almost always involves knowing some algebra.'
Do you think Asif is right?
For which questions in this lesson did you need to use your algebra skills? Describe some other mathematical problems where you have used algebra.

Explore

Reflect

8.5 Circles

You will learn to:
- Work out the circumference of a circle
- Work out the area of a circle.

Why learn this?
You can use the circumference of a circle to work out how many seats can fit around a circus tent.

Fluency
Substitute $r = 6$ to find the value of
- r^2
- $3r$
- $(r + 4)^2$

Explore
How many different ways can you describe a circle?

CONFIDENCE

Exercise 8.5

Warm up

1 Work out the area and perimeter of this shape.

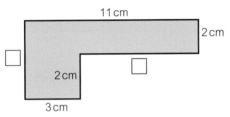

2 Round each number to 2 decimal places.
   a 6.726   **b** 25.0927   **c** 17.456
   d 22.222   **e** 77.77777   **f** 104.8621

3 Copy and complete the sentences about this diagram of a circle.
   a The letter ___ shows the **centre** of the circle.
   b Line AC is the _____ of the circle.
   c Line OB is the _____ of the circle.
   Discussion The radius is the same length wherever you place point B. What can you say about the diameter?

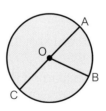

4 Reasoning
   a The radius of a circle is 7.5 cm. What is the diameter of the circle?
   b The diameter of a circle is 11 cm. What is the radius of the circle?

5 Use a pair of compasses to draw a circle with the radius given.
   a 4 cm
   b 7 cm
   c 3.5 cm

Key point

The perimeter of a circle is called the **circumference**.
The **centre** of a circle is usually marked with a dot.
The distance from the centre to the circle edge is called the **radius**.
The distance from edge to edge through the centre is called the **diameter**.

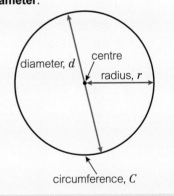

Topic links: Rounding decimals, Calculator skills

Worked example

Work out the circumference and the area of this circle.
Give your answer to 1 decimal place.

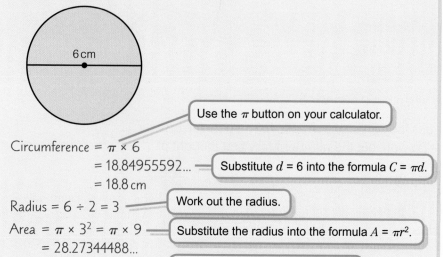

Circumference = $\pi \times 6$

Use the π button on your calculator.

= 18.84955592...

Substitute $d = 6$ into the formula $C = \pi d$.

= 18.8 cm

Radius = 6 ÷ 2 = 3

Work out the radius.

Area = $\pi \times 3^2 = \pi \times 9$

Substitute the radius into the formula $A = \pi r^2$.

= 28.27344488...

= 28.3 cm²

Area is measured in square units.

6 For each circle, work out
     i the circumference   ii the area.

a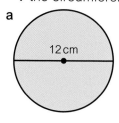
12 cm

b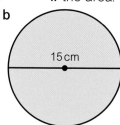
15 cm

c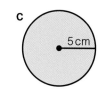
5 cm

d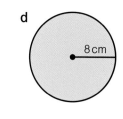
8 cm

7 A circular pond has a diameter of 4 m. What is
   a the area of the pond   **b** the circumference of the pond?
   Give your answers to 1 decimal place.

8 **Problem-solving** This shape is made
   from two squares and a semicircle.
   a Find the perimeter of the shape.
   b Find the area of the shape.

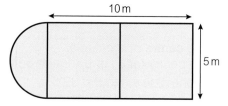
10 m

5 m

9 **Explore** How many different ways can you describe a circle?
   Is it easier to explore this question now you have completed the
   lesson? What further information do you need to be able to
   answer this?

10 **Reflect** Mina sometimes gets confused when answering questions
   like Q8.
   Her friend says that she should always start by writing down the
   formulae she will need to use, such as *Diameter* = 2 × *r*,
   Area of a circle = πr^2.
   Choose one other question from this lesson, and write down two or
   three hints to help a friend who is struggling with it.

Master
P179

CHECK

Strengthen
P195

Extend
P199

Test
P203

8 Check up

Log how you did on your
Student Progression Chart.

Algebra

1. Work out the value of $2x - 3y$ when $x = 9$ and $y = 5$.

2. Mary thinks of a number, divides it by 5 then subtracts 4. She gets the answer 1.
   Write an equation and solve it, to work out the number Mary first thought of.

3. What is the value of $a^2 - b^2$ when $a = 8$ and $b = 4$?

4. Find the value of each expression.

   a $(5x - y) \times 3$ when $x = 5$ and $y = 2$

   b $\dfrac{3g - 4}{2}$ when $g = 10$

   c $\dfrac{(p + q)^2}{(p - q)^2}$ when $p = 6$ and $q = 4$

   d $2x + 3z$ when $x = 6$ and $z = -2$

5. Write a formula to convert millilitres to litres.

6. Amber buys posters online for £5, with a flat fee of £3 for postage.
   a Write a formula to work out the cost, C, of buying p posters, including postage.
   b Work out the cost of buying 8 posters.
   c Rhys spends £28. How many posters does he buy?

7. Hooke's law, $F = kx$, shows the relationship between the force F needed to
   extend a spring by a distance x. k is a constant.
   a What is the force, F, when $k = 10$ and $x = 2.5$?
   b What is the value of x when $F = 16$ and $k = 8$?

Formulae in geometry

8. The perimeter of a square is 22 cm. What is the length of one of its sides?

9. A rectangle is 7 cm wide and has an area of 35 cm². How long is the rectangle?

10. a Write a formula for the perimeter, P, of a regular octagon with sides of length s.
    b What is the length of one side when $P = 32$?
    c What is the value of P when $s = 5$?

11. Match each expression and description to make a formula.

    A πr^2 i | Perimeter of rectangle |

    B $\dfrac{bh}{2}$ ii | Area of a parallelogram |

    C bh iii | Circumference of a circle |

    D $2(l + w)$ iv | Area of a circle |

    E πd v | Area of a triangle |

193

12 The perimeter of this rectangle is 44 cm.

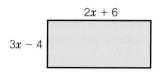

2x + 6

3x − 4

   a Write an equation for the perimeter in terms of x.

   b Solve the equation to work out the value of x.

   c What is the length of each side?

Area and perimeter

13 Estimate the area of this triangle.

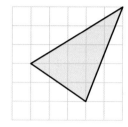

14 Use the formula $A = \dfrac{bh}{2}$ to work out the area of each triangle.

a

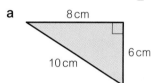

8 cm

6 cm

10 cm

b

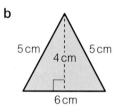

5 cm   5 cm

4 cm

6 cm

15 Use the formula $A = bh$ to work out the area of this parallelogram.

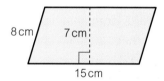

8 cm   7 cm

15 cm

16 a Work out the area of this shape.

    b Work out the perimeter of this shape.

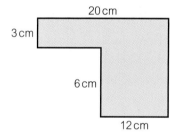

20 cm

3 cm

6 cm

12 cm

17 a Draw a circle.

    b Label the centre O.

    c Draw a diameter on your circle and label it 'Diameter'.

    d Mark a point P anywhere on the circumference.

    e Draw a radius from the point P and label it 'Radius'.

 18 For this circle, work out

    a the area   **b** the circumference.

    Round your answers to 1 decimal place.

14 cm

19 How sure are you of your answers? Were you mostly

    😟 **Just guessing**   😐 **Feeling doubtful**   🙂 **Confident**

    What next? Use your results to decide whether to strengthen or extend your learning.

Challenge

20 a Write the letters of your full name on squared paper using only whole and half squares.

    b Work out the total area of your name.

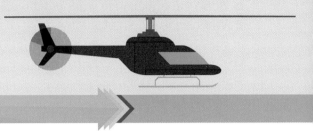

8 Strengthen

You will:

- Strengthen your understanding with practice.

Algebra

1 Copy and complete
  a Addition is the inverse of _____
  b _____ is the inverse of division.
  c Dividing by 2 is the inverse of _____ by 2.
  d Doubling is the inverse of _____
  e Multiplying by 3 is the inverse of _____ by ___
  f Subtracting 10 is the inverse of _____ ___

Q1 Literacy hint

The inverse operation is the reverse operation.

2 Write an expression for the unknown number n.
  a Double n plus 6
  b Subtract 10 from n then multiply by 3
  c Add 6 to n then double
  d Multiply n by 3 then subtract 10

3 Substitute $d = 5$ into each expression.
  a $d + 6$ b $2d$ c d^2

Q3b hint

$2d$ means $2 \times d$.
When $d = 5$, $2d = 2 \times 5$.

4 Substitute $x = 10$ and $y = 6$ into each expression.
  a $x + y$ b $x - y$
  c $3x + 2y$ d $5x - 4y$

Q4 hint

Everywhere you see x, replace it with 10. Everywhere you see y, replace it with 6.

5 Work out the value of $r^2 + t^2$ when
  a $r = 10$ and $t = 2$ b $r = 5$ and $t = 1$
  c $r = 1$ and $t = 9$ d $r = 6$ and $t = 0$

6 Substitute $x = 4$ and $y = 5$ into each expression.
  a $(3x + 2y) \div 2$ b $(4x - 3y) \times 2$
  c $\dfrac{4y}{2}$ d $\dfrac{3xy}{2}$

7 Substitute $n = -4$ into each expression and calculate the value.
  a $n + 6$ $-4 + 6 =$
  b $2n$ $2 \times -4 =$
  c n^2 $-4 \times -4 =$
  d $3n + 2$ $3 \times -4 + 2 =$

8 Ruben is y years old. His brother Max is 2 years older and his cousin Olive is 5 times Ruben's age.
  a Write an expression for each of these people's ages in terms of y.
    i Max
    ii Olive
    iii Finn, who is Ruben's twin
  b Ruben is 2. How old are Max and Olive?

9 Modelling Laura is paid £9 an hour with a daily bonus of £5.
  a Write a formula that connects the total Laura is paid, T, for h hours.
  b One day Laura works for 5 hours. How much does she get paid?

10 STEM The formula for converting between temperatures in Fahrenheit (°F) and Celsius (°C) is $F = \dfrac{9C}{5} + 32$.
  a Work out each temperature in Fahrenheit.
    i 20°C   **ii** 100°C   **iii** 0°C
  b Work out each temperature in Celsius.
    i 59°F   **ii** 212°F   **iii** 32°F

> **Q9a hint**
> How much is she paid per hour?
> $T = \square h + \square$
> What is the daily bonus?

> **Q10b hint**
> Rearrange the formula to make C the subject.

Formulae in geometry

1 The perimeter of this square is 100 cm.
  What is the value of d?

d cm

2 The diagrams show the dimensions of a shape and its perimeter, P.
  For each shape
    i write an equation involving x
    ii solve the equation to work out the value of x.

  a

  x cm $P = 50$ cm
  $\longleftarrow x$ cm $\longrightarrow$

  b
  x cm $P = 60$ cm
  $\longleftarrow 2x$ cm $\longrightarrow$

3 a Write the formula for the area, A, of this rectangle.
  b What is the area when $x = 3$ and $y = 10$?
  c What is the value of x when $A = 30$ and $y = 5$?

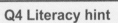
x
y

4 a Show that the perimeter of this trapezium is $9x + 3$.

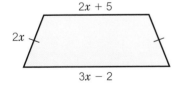
  $2x + 5$
  $2x$
  $3x - 2$

  b What is the length of each side when the perimeter is 30 cm?

> **Q4 Literacy hint**
>
> When a question says 'Show that...',
> you need to show each step of your working out.

5 a Show that the perimeter of this kite is $6x - 4$.

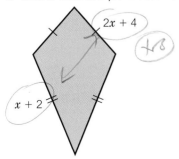
  $2x + 4$
  $x + 2$

  b What is the length of each side when $P = 20$ cm?

Area and perimeter

1 Estimate the area of this triangle.

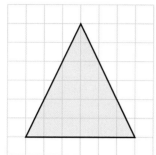

Q1 hint

First count all the whole squares. Then match up parts of squares that make a whole.

2 Look at the triangle in Q1.
   a What is the perpendicular height, h, of the triangle?
   b What is the width of the base, b, of the triangle?
   c Use the formula $A = \dfrac{bh}{2}$ to work out the area of the triangle.

Q2a hint

The perpendicular height is the distance straight up to the top point from the base.

3 Work out the area of each triangle.

a
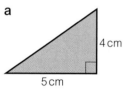
  4 cm
  5 cm

b

  3 m
  6 m

c
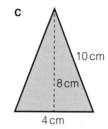
  10 cm
  8 cm
  4 cm

Q3c hint

Which measurement shows the perpendicular height?

4 Use the formula $A = bh$ to work out the area of each parallelogram.

a
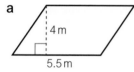
  4 m
  5.5 m

b
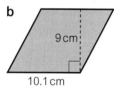
  9 cm
  10.1 cm

c
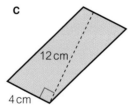
  12 cm
  4 cm

5 a Copy this shape and draw a line to split it into two rectangles.
     Mark the bottom length x and right-hand length y.

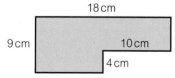
18 cm
9 cm
10 cm
4 cm

  b Work out the area of each rectangle.
  c What is the area of the whole shape?
  d Work out the length of sides x and y.
  e Work out the perimeter of the shape.

6 Haresh puts a triangle and a rectangle together
  to make this shape.
  a What is the perpendicular height of the triangle?
  b What is the area of the triangle?
  c What is the area of the rectangle?
  d What is the total area of Haresh's shape?

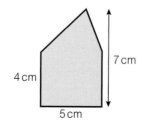
7 cm
4 cm
5 cm

7 What is the area of this shape?

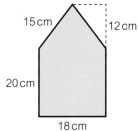

15 cm 12 cm 20 cm 18 cm

8 Use your calculator to find the values. Round each answer to 1 decimal place.

a π **b** $2 \times \pi$ **c** $5 \times \pi$

d $\pi \times 3^2$ **e** 20π **f** $3 \times \pi \times 4^2$

9 The formula for the circumference of a circle with diameter d is $C = \pi d$.

20 cm

a Write down the value of d in this circle.

b Substitute your value of d into the formula to work out the circumference, C. Round your answer to 1 decimal place.

10 The formula for the area of a circle with radius r is $A = \pi r^2$.

a What is r in the circle in Q9 part **a**?

b Substitute your value of r into the formula to work out the area, A. Round your answer to 1 decimal place.

> **Q10a hint**
> The radius is half of the diameter.

11 a Draw these circles on squared paper.

   i radius 3 cm

   ii radius 4 cm

   iii radius 5 cm

b Work out the area of each circle.

c Work out the circumference of each circle.

Enrichment

1 Problem-solving Sasha wants to display a picture on mounting paper to give a border of 2 cm around the edge of the picture. She then puts a frame around the edge of the mounting paper.

a Write an expression for the width of the mounting paper.

b Write a formula for the area A of the mounting paper.

c Sasha's picture is 15 cm wide and 20 cm high. What is the area of mounting paper she needs?

h

w

2 Reflect Ask a classmate to show you a question they got wrong in this section or in the check up. Try and work out what mistake they made. Write a hint that would help any student with this question in future.

Master
P179

Check
P193

Strengthen
P195

EXTEND

Test
P203

8 Extend

You will:

• Extend your understanding with problem-solving.

1 A skate hire company uses the formula $C = 3h + 10$ to work out the cost, C, of hiring skates for h hours.
What is the cost of hiring skates for
   a 1 hour   **b** 2 hours   **c** 4 hours?

2 Substitute $x = 8$, $y = 2.5$ and $z = -2$ into each expression.
   a $2x + 4y - z$ **b** $3z + x^2$ **c** $(x + y) \times z$ **d** $z^2 - xy$

3 Write a formula for working out the mean, M, of a, b and c.

4 **Problem-solving** Use this diagram to write a formula connecting p and q in two different ways.

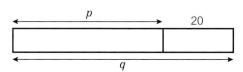

Q4 hint

$p =$
$q =$

5 **a** Write an expression for the area of this rectangle.
   b Multiply out the brackets in your expression.
   c Work out the area when $x = 4$.

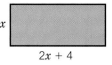

6 For this shape, work out
   a the area   **b** the perimeter.

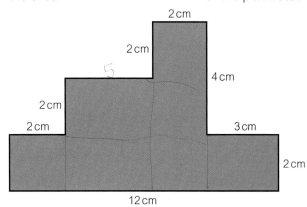

7 Work out the value of r when $s = 6$ and $t = 4$.

   a $r + 7 = s$ **b** $s = \dfrac{r}{2}$ **c** $t = r - 10$

   d $t = rs$ **e** $s = \dfrac{r}{t}$ **f** $s = rt$

Q7 hint

Substitute the values given into the formula. Solve the equation.

8 Write the fact families for each formula.
   a $F = ma$ $m = \square \div \square$ $a = \square$
   b $A = B - C$ $B = \square$ $C = \square$
   c $D \div E = F$ $D = \square$ $E = \square$
   d $P + Q = R$ $P = \square$ $Q = \square$

9 Rearrange each formula to make each letter the subject. The first one has been started for you.

a $D = ST$ $T = \dfrac{D}{S}$ $S = \dfrac{\square}{\square}$

b $a^2 + b^2 = c^2$

c $v = u + at$

Q9 hint

To make a letter the subject, it must be on its own, followed by '='.

10 **STEM** $v = u + at$, where v = final velocity, u = initial velocity, a = acceleration and t = time. Work out

a v when $u = 10$, $a = 40$ and $t = 5$

b u when $v = 100$, $a = 30$ and $t = 2$

c t when $v = 85$, $u = 10$ and $a = 15$.

11 The formula for converting kilometres to miles is, $km = \frac{8}{5} \times miles$.
Use the formula to convert

a 15 miles to km   b 40 miles to km

c 16 km to miles   d 40 km to miles.

12 a Copy and complete the table showing formulae to convert metric to imperial measures.

Metric	Imperial	Formula
28 grams (g)	1 ounce (z)	$28g = z$
1 litre (l)	1.75 pints (p)	
1 kilogram (k)	2.2 pounds (b)	
30 cm (c)	1 foot (f)	
4.5 litres (l)	1 gallon (n)	

b Use your formulae to convert

  i 5 ounces to grams   ii 5 kg to pounds

  iii 3 feet to cm   iv 224 g to ounces

  v 8.75 pints to litres   vi 165 cm to feet

  vii 49.5 litres to gallons

13 Use Pythagoras' theorem, $a^2 + b^2 = c^2$, to work out

a c when $a = 8$ and $b = 6$

b a when $b = 12$ and $c = 15$

c b when $c = 25$ and $a = 15$

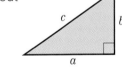

Q13b hint

Use inverse operations to make a the subject.

14 a Work out the area of this trapezium by splitting it into two triangles and a rectangle.

The formula for the area of a trapezium is $A = \dfrac{h}{2}(a + b)$, where a and b are the two parallel sides, and h is the perpendicular height.

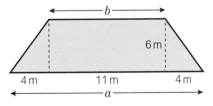

b What are the values of a and b in this trapezium?

c Use the formula to work out the area.

15 **Problem-solving** A circle has a circumference of 62.83 cm.
Work out its diameter to 1 decimal place.

Q15 hint

Rearrange $C = \pi d$ to make d the subject.

16 **Problem-solving** A circle has an area of 50.28 mm².
What is its radius to 1 decimal place?

Q16 hint

Rearrange $A = \pi r^2$ to make r the subject.

17 Problem-solving A dog is tied by a 2.3 m rope to a post in the middle of a garden. What area of the garden can he reach?

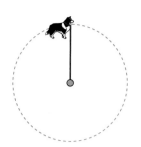

18 Problem-solving The wheels on Moses' bike have a diameter of 54.7 cm. What is the distance he travels with one whole turn of a wheel?

19 Problem-solving Work out the area of the shaded shape when the radius of the circle is 5 cm.

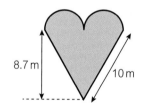

Q19 hint

What fraction of the shape is shaded?

20 On a netball court, the Centre (C) position can move everywhere on the court, except the shooting circles. What area of this court can a Centre player cover?

Q20 hint

The shooting circles are semicircles.

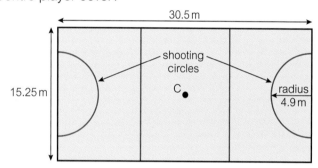

30.5 m

shooting circles

15.25 m

C

radius 4.9 m

21 Problem-solving This heart is made from an equilateral triangle with side length 10 cm and two semicircles.
Calculate its area. Give your answer to 1 decimal place.

8.7 m

10 m

22 Problem-solving Kylie starts with a square with area 25 cm². She puts semicircles around the edge to make this new shape.
What is the perimeter of Kylie's new shape? Give your answer to 2 decimal places.

23 Reasoning / Problem-solving Shmoel makes this net of a cone by cutting a right-angled **sector** out of a circle.
What is the area of the net?

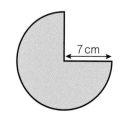

7 cm

Q23 Literacy hint

A **sector** is a part of a circle enclosed by two radii and the part of the circumference between them. Radii is the plural of radius.

24 The formula for the volume, V, of a square-based pyramid is $V = \frac{1}{3}l^2h$ where l is the length of one side of the base, and h is the height of the pyramid.

a Work out the volume of each square-based pyramid.

i

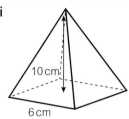

10 cm

6 cm

ii

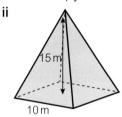

15 m

10 m

b Work out the volume of a square-based pyramid with a base of length 12 cm and a height of 8 cm.

c A square-based pyramid, with base length 5 cm, has a volume of 50 cm³. What is its height?

Q24c hint

Use the inverse: $\dfrac{3V}{l^2} = h$

25 Problem-solving This running track is made from two semicircles and a rectangle. The distance between the outside lane and the inside lane is 30 m.

a Work out the outside perimeter of the outside lane.

b Work out the inside perimeter of the inside lane.

c What is the difference between the two distances?

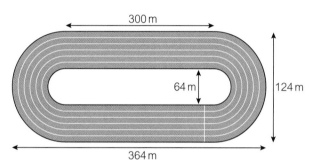

300 m

64 m

124 m

364 m

Investigation   Reasoning / Problem-solving

Here is a section of a spreadsheet.

	A	B	C
1	10	4	6
2	8	12	20

1 Work out

  a =A1+C2   **b** =A2*C1   **c** =B2/B1

  d =(A1+C1+C2)/B2   **e** =(B1+C1)*(C2–B2)   **f** =3.14*C2^2

2 Type the formulae into a spreadsheet to check your answers.

3 Write a geometry question involving finding areas or perimeters for each of the calculations.

Literacy hint

When you use a spreadsheet to work out formulae:

* means ×

/ means ÷

^ means 'to the power of'

C2 means the number in column C, row 2.

26 Reflect Look back at the questions you answered in this extend lesson. Find a question that you could not answer straightaway, or that you really had to think about.

Why couldn't you immediately see what to do?

How did this make you feel?

Did you keep trying or did you give up?

Did you think you would get the answer correct or incorrect?

Write down any strategies you could use when answering tricky questions. Compare your strategies with others.

Reflect

Master
P179

Check
P193

Strengthen
P195

Extend
P199

TEST

Log how you did on your
Student Progression Chart.

8 Unit test

1 The perimeter of a square is 30 cm. What is the length of one of its sides?

2 The area of a rectangle is 45 cm². Its length is 15 cm. What is its width?

3 Work out the value of $5x + 3y$ when $x = 11$ and $y = 6$.

4 Work out the value of $a^2 - b^2$ when $a = 10$ and $b = 5$.

5 Work out the value of each expression.
  a $5(6x + 2y)$ when $x = 2$ and $y = 3$
  b $\dfrac{5r}{4}$ when $r = 8$
  c $\dfrac{(p + q)^2}{(p - q)^2}$ when $p = 6$ and $q = -4$
  d $\sqrt{xy}$ when $x = 2$ and $y = 8$

6 a A packet of stickers cost 25p. Write a formula to work out the cost, C, of n packets.
  b Use your formula to work out the cost of 10 packets of stickers.

7 a Show that the perimeter of this rhombus is $8x + 16$.
  b The perimeter is 48 cm. What is the length of one side?

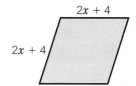

2x + 4

2x + 4

8 Work out the area of each triangle.

  a
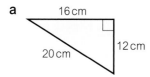
16 cm

20 cm

12 cm

  b
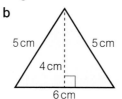
5 cm   5 cm

4 cm

6 cm

9 Work out
  a the area
  b the perimeter of this shape.

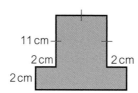
11 cm

2 cm   2 cm

2 cm

10 Rearrange the formula $C = \pi d$ to make d the subject.

11 Substitute $n = -5$ to work out the value of each expression.
  a $n^2 - 1$ b $3n + 1$

12 Work out the area of this parallelogram.

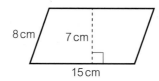
8 cm   7 cm

15 cm

13 Work out the area of this shape, made from two congruent triangles and a square.

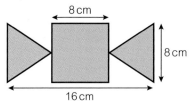

14 a Draw a circle with radius 4 cm.
  b Label the centre O.
  c Draw and label the diameter and the radius.

15 The formula for the area of a trapezium is $\frac{h}{2}(a + b)$ where h is the perpendicular height and a and b are the parallel sides. Work out the area of this trapezium.

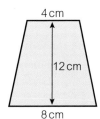

16 For this circle work out
  a the circumference
  b the area.
  Give your answer to 1 decimal place.

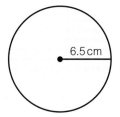

17 The volume of a square-based pyramid is $\frac{1}{3}l^2h$ where l is the base length and h is the height. What is the volume of this pyramid?

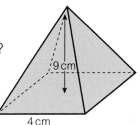

Challenge

18 Troy wants to draw a circle and a square with exactly the same area.
  a Can you do this using only integer lengths?
  b Can you do this using decimal numbers?
  Compare your answers with others in your class.

19 Reflect This may be the first time you have used algebraic and geometric formulae.
  Choose **A**, **B** or **C** to complete each statement.
  In this unit, I did _____   **A** well, **B** ok, **C** not very well.
  I think using formulae is _____   **A** easy, **B** ok, **C** difficult.
  When I think about using formulae, I feel _____   **A** confident, **B** ok, **C**, unsure.
  If you answered mostly **A**s and **B**s, are you surprised? Why?
  If you answered mostly **C**s, look back at the questions in the lessons that you found most tricky. Ask a friend or your teacher to explain them to you. Then complete the statements above again.

9.1 Probability experiments

You will learn to:
- Work out the expected results when an experiment is repeated
- Compare experimental and theoretical probabilities.

Why learn this?
Doctors use the results from probability experiments to test how effective new medicines are.

Fluency
Linda flips a coin.
What is
- P(heads)
- P(tails)?

Explore
How many times do you have to roll a dice to be confident it is fair?

CONFIDENCE

Exercise 9.1

Warm up

1 Erica spins a 3-coloured spinner. She records the colour it lands on in this frequency table.

Colour	Frequency
White	49
Black	27
Red	24
Total frequency	

  a How many times did Erica spin the spinner?

  b Write down the experimental probability of landing on
    i white   **ii** black   **iii** red.

Q1b hint

$$\text{Experimental probability} = \frac{\text{frequency of event}}{\text{total frequency}}$$

2 Modelling Carrie drops a bottle top lots of times. It lands either flat side up or flat side down. She records her results in a frequency table.

Position	Frequency
Flat side up	12
Flat side down	38

  a How many times did Carrie drop the bottle top?

  b Work out the experimental probability of the bottle top landing
    i flat side up   **ii** flat side down.

  c Carrie is going to drop the bottle top 200 times. How many times do you expect it to land flat side up?

3 Modelling Jamie records the results of spinning a spinner with 4 colours.

Colour	Frequency
Red	23
Blue	21
Yellow	26
Green	30

  a How many times did Jamie spin the spinner?

  b Next Jamie spins the spinner 500 times. How many times do you expect it to land on blue?

  c Kesh spins the same spinner and it lands on green 120 times. How many times do you think Kesh spun the spinner?

4 Reasoning Eluned records the results of rolling an ordinary 6-sided dice 100 times.

Score	Frequency
1	18
2	15
3	17
4	18
5	15
6	17

a What is the experimental probability of rolling a
   i 2   **ii** 6?
b What is the **theoretical probability** of rolling a
   i 2   **ii** 6?

Discussion Is the dice biased?

Key point

The **theoretical probability** of an event is the probability of an event happening based on the number of outcomes.

5 Reasoning Angus rolls a 4-sided dice 50 times and records his results in this table.

Score	Frequency
1	9
2	14
3	15
4	12

Is the dice biased? Explain.

Q5 hint

Compare the experimental probability with the theoretical probability.

6 Reasoning / Problem-solving Jessica spins a fair 3-coloured spinner 80 times. Her results are shown in the table.

Sketch a possible spinner.

Colour	Frequency
Blue	18
Red	41
Green	21

Investigation   **Reasoning**

Tom and Sara do 120 trials in all their probability experiments.

1 Tom picks a domino from a bag, records the total number of spots and then replaces the domino in the bag. He does four different experiments, each with one of these bags of dominoes.
For each bag of dominoes, draw a table with the expected frequencies for each number.

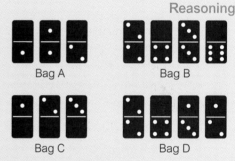
Bag A   Bag B

Bag C   Bag D

2 Sara spins a spinner and records the colour that the spinner lands on. She does four experiments, each with one of these spinners.

Spinner P   Spinner Q   Spinner R   Spinner S

For each spinner, draw a table with the expected frequencies for each colour.

3 Match the expected probabilities of each of Tom's experiments to the expected probabilities for one of Sara's spinners.

4 Make up your own bag of dominoes and a spinner that you would expect to give similar results.

7 Explore How many times do you have to roll a dice to be confident it is fair?
Look back at the maths you have learned in this lesson.
How can you use it to answer this question?

8 Reflect Sam and Misha are playing a game with a fair 6-sided dice.
Sam needs a 6 to win, but he rolls a 2.
Sam says, 'It's not fair. It's harder to roll a 6 than a 2.'
Use what you have learned about probability to decide whether Sam is correct. Explain.

Explore

Reflect

9.2 Sample space diagrams

You will learn to:
- List all the possible outcomes of two events in sample space diagrams
- Work out the theoretical probability of an outcome from two events
- Decide whether a game is fair.

Why learn this?
Calculating probabilities can help you decide whether a game is fair.

Fluency
When picking a card from a pack, what is the probability of picking
- a heart
- a King
- the 7 of spades?

Explore
In which games for two players do both players have an equal chance of winning?

CONFIDENCE

Exercise 9.2

Warm up

1 Ann spins this spinner and records the score.

a Write down all the possible outcomes.

b Which outcome is most likely?

c Which outcomes are least likely?

d Is she more likely to spin an odd number or an even number?

2 These two spinners are spun at the same time.

Spinner A   Spinner B

a Copy and complete this list of possible outcomes.

> Green on spinner A and blue on spinner B
> Green on spinner A and _____

b Work out the probability of getting black on spinner A and red on spinner B.

3 **Reasoning** Helen flips a coin and rolls a 6-sided dice. List all the possible outcomes.

Discussion How many possible outcomes will there be if the dice is a 4-sided dice? What if the dice is an 8-sided dice?

Q3 hint

Each outcome is a pair of events, e.g. (heads, 1).

4 Rory spins these two spinners. Copy and complete this **sample space diagram** for all the possible outcomes.

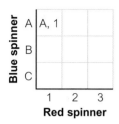

Discussion Are all these outcomes equally likely?

5 Reasoning These dominoes are placed face down. Danielle picks one red and one blue domino.

She writes down the sum of the number of spots of each domino.
a Copy and complete this sample space diagram to show the total for each outcome.

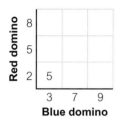

b What score appears more than once in the sample space diagram?
Discussion Is the score in your answer to part **b** more likely to occur than any other score?

Worked example

Sally spins these two spinners and adds the scores.

What is the probability of getting a total score of 8?

Green spinner			
4	8	9	10
3	7	8	9
2	6	7	8
	4	5	6
	Yellow spinner		

Draw a sample space diagram and fill in the total score for each outcome.

There are 3 outcomes which give a total score of 8.

Probability of 8 = $\dfrac{\text{number of outcomes with a score of 8}}{\text{total number of possible outcomes}} = \dfrac{3}{9} = \dfrac{1}{3}$

All of the outcomes are equally likely.

6 These dominoes are placed face down. Alice picks one black and one white domino.
She multiplies the total number of spots on the white domino by the total number of spots on the black domino.
   a Draw a sample space diagram to show all the possible outcomes.
   b What is

   b What is
      i P(5)
      ii P(10)
      iii P(more than 15)
      iv P(even)?

> **Q6b hint**
>
> P(5) means the probability of getting a score of 5.

7 **Reasoning** Seema and Gavin play a game where they roll two dice and work out the difference between the scores.
Seema gets a point if the difference is even and Gavin gets a point if the difference is odd. Neither gets a point if the difference is zero.
   a Copy and complete this sample space diagram.
   b What is the probability of
      i Seema getting a point
      ii Gavin getting a point?
   c Is the game fair? Explain.
   Discussion Gavin and Seema play a similar game where they work out the sum of the scores. Is this game fair?

> **Q7a hint**
>
> The difference between the two scores is always positive.

> **Q7b hint**
>
> Do not simplify the fractions. It is easier to compare fractions with the same denominator.

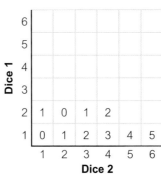

Investigation   **Problem-solving / Reasoning**

Work with a partner.
Design a game using two spinners or dice.
1 Choose whether to find the sum, difference or product of the two numbers.
2 Decide when each player will get a point, for example, using
   • odd numbers
   • even numbers
   • prime numbers
   • square numbers
   • numbers less than 10
   • numbers between 10 and 20.
3 Play the game for 20 rounds. Record your scores. Does the game seem fair?
4 Draw a sample space diagram and work out the theoretical probabilities of getting a point. Is the game fair?
5 Choose different conditions for scoring a point and repeat parts **3** and **4**.

8 **Explore** In which games for two players do both players have an equal chance of winning?
Look back at the maths you have learned in this lesson. How can you use it to answer this question?

9 **Reflect** Suzi has a fair 6-sided dice and a fair spinner with 3 sections numbered 1, 2 and 3.
She rolls the dice and spins the spinner.
Suzi wants to find the probability of the total score being 6. She could make a list of all the possible outcomes, or she could make a sample space diagram. Which method would you choose and why?

*Active*Learn Pi 3, Section 9.2

9.3 MODELLING: Two-way tables

You will learn to:

- Calculate estimates of probability from experiments or survey results
- Use experimental probabilities to predict outcomes.

Why learn this?
You can use two-way tables to record the outcomes from two experiments.

Fluency
Chris can choose 3 different sandwich fillings and 3 different types of bread. How many combinations are there?

Explore
What would a table showing data sorted in three ways look like?

Exercise 9.3: Representing outcomes

1 The table shows the numbers of students attending a youth club on two evenings.

	Friday	Saturday
Boys	12	17
Girls	16	15

a How many boys went to the youth club on Friday?

b How many people went to the youth club on Saturday?

2 A smartphone manufacturer tested 5000 smartphones at a factory.
They found that 200 were faulty.
Estimate the probability that a smartphone from that factory is faulty.

3 Modelling Zach flips a gold coin and a silver coin at the same time.
He records his results in a **two-way table**.

		Silver coin		
		Heads	Tails	Total
Gold coin	Heads	23	30	
	Tails	26	21	
	Total			

a Copy and complete the table.

b How many times did Zach flip the coins?

c Work out the experimental probability of getting

  i heads with the gold coin and tails with the silver coin

  ii tails with the gold coin.

Discussion Do you think both coins are fair?

Key point

When the outcomes of an experiment are pairs of results, the frequencies can be shown in a **two-way table**.

Q3c i hint

What fraction of the total is gold heads and silver tails?

Warm up

4 Modelling Alice spins these two spinners at the same time.

Spinner A   Spinner B

This two-way table shows her results.

		Spinner B		
		Blue	Red	Green
Spinner A	Blue	7	6	11
	Red	5	9	12
	Green	8	4	10

Work out the experimental probability of getting
a red with both spinners
b blue with spinner A and green with spinner B
c green with spinner A
d green with one spinner and blue with the other.

> **Q4d hint**
>
> Spinner A could be green and spinner B blue, or the other way round.
> Add the probabilities of each outcome.

 5 Real / Modelling Approximately 1000 babies are born each month at a hospital. Researchers recorded the day of the week and the time of birth over a month.

	0001–0600	0601–1200	1201–1800	1801–0000
Weekday	250	168	176	273
Weekend	42	28	30	33

a Copy the table and add an extra column and row for totals. Work out the totals.
b Are babies more likely to be born at the weekend or on a weekday? Explain.
c Estimate the probability that a baby is born between 0601 and 1200 on any day. Give your answer to 2 decimal places.
d Over a year, how many babies would you expect to be born
  i on a weekday
  ii between 0601 and 1800?

6 Explore What would a table showing data sorted in three ways look like?
Look back at the maths you have learned in this lesson. How can you use it to answer this question?

7 Reflect Several questions in this lesson are about experimental probability. How is experimental probability different to theoretical probability?
Choose one of the questions and suggest what the theoretical probabilities would be for that question.

9.4 Tree diagrams

You will learn to:
- Use tree diagrams
- Work out probabilities from tree diagrams.

Why learn this?
Biologists use probability models to help predict the characteristics of different animals.

Fluency
For this spinner, work out
- P(green)
- P(blue)
- P(red).

Explore
When flipping a coin, what is the probability of getting four tails in a row?

Exercise 9.4

1 Here are three spinners. The probability of them landing on blue is shown on the probability scale. Match each spinner to the probability of it landing on blue.

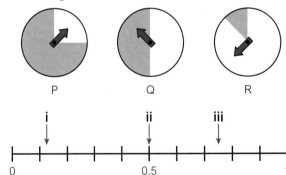

P   Q   R

i   ii   iii

0   0.5   1

2 Work out

a $\frac{1}{2} \times \frac{1}{2}$

b $\frac{1}{2} \times \frac{1}{4}$

c $\frac{1}{3} \times \frac{1}{2}$

d $\frac{3}{5} \times \frac{1}{4}$

e $\frac{1}{6} \times \frac{2}{3}$

f $\frac{1}{5} \times \frac{1}{2}$

3 The probability it will rain tomorrow is $\frac{1}{3}$
What is the probability that it will not rain tomorrow?

> **Q3 hint**
> P(no rain) = 1 – P(rain)

4 **Reasoning** In a bag of counters there are 4 green counters and 3 blue counters.

a What is the probability of picking a green counter?

Mick takes out a green counter and doesn't put it back.

b What is the probability that the next counter is green?

Discussion Are the two events, picking a green counter the first time and picking a green counter the second time, **independent**?

> **Key point**
> Two events are **independent** if one happening does not affect the probability of the other.

Warm up

5 Reasoning For each pair of events, say whether they are dependent or independent.

a Event A: flipping a coin
   Event B: spinning a 3-coloured spinner

b Event C: picking a blue sock from a drawer and putting it on
   Event D: picking another sock

c Event E: taking a card from a pack of cards, returning it and shuffling the pack
   Event F: taking another card from the pack

Investigation | Problem-solving

1 What is the probability of a coin landing on tails?

2 What is the probability of picking a spade from an ordinary pack of cards?

3 A coin is flipped and a card is picked from an ordinary pack.

   a Copy and complete the sample space diagram to show the possible outcomes.

   b What is the probability of flipping tails and picking a spade?

4 Multiply your answers to parts **1** and **2** together. What do you notice?

5 Repeat parts **1–3** for rolling a dice and flipping a coin. Find the probability of scoring 3 on the dice and flipping heads on the coin.

---

6 Caroline rolls a fair 6-sided dice and spins this spinner. Work out

   a P(5 and orange)

   b P(an even number and blue)

   c P(a number less than 6 and orange).

> **Key point**
>
> To find the probability of two independent events, multiply their probabilities.
> P(A and B) = P(A) × P(B)

Worked example

Margie flips a coin and spins this spinner.

a Draw a **tree diagram** to show all the possible outcomes.

> **Key point**
>
> A **tree diagram** shows two or more events and their probabilities.

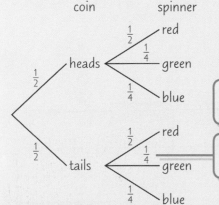

> There are two possible outcomes for flipping the coin and three for the spinner.

> Write the probability of each event on the branch of the tree.

b Work out the probability of flipping heads and spinning green.

P(heads, green) = P(heads) × P(green)

$= \frac{1}{2} \times \frac{1}{4} = \frac{1}{8}$

> Read along the branches for heads, then green. Multiply the probabilities.

7 Ben flips a coin and picks a coloured card.

   a Draw a tree diagram to show all the possible outcomes.
   b How many outcomes are there altogether?
   c What is the probability of
      i heads and red
      ii tails and blue?

8 This sample space diagram shows the possible outcomes when a £1 coin and a 50p coin are flipped.

	H	T
H	HH	TH
T	HT	TT

£1 coin / 50p coin

   a Copy and complete the tree diagram to show the same information.

£1 coin

      H
      T

   b What is the probability that both coins land on tails?
   c What is the probability that one coin lands on heads and the other lands on tails?

9 **Real / Modelling** A factory makes cups and saucers. The factory owners have found that the probability that a cup is damaged during production is 0.04. The probability that a saucer is damaged is 0.06.
   a What is the probability that a cup is not damaged?
   b Copy and complete this tree diagram to show the possible outcomes of picking a cup and a saucer.

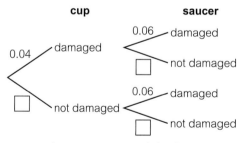

   c A cup and a saucer are picked.
      i What is the probability that they are both damaged?
      ii What is the probability that neither is damaged?

10 **Explore** When flipping a coin, what is the probability of getting four tails in a row?
Look back at the maths you have learned in this lesson. How can you use it to answer this question?

11 **Reflect** Write a probability question for two independent events, where the answer is 0.06.
Check your question by drawing a tree diagram. Swap questions with a classmate.

> **Q8c hint**
> The £1 coin could show heads and the 50p coin tails, or the other way round. Add the probabilities of each outcome.

> **Q9 hint**
> Probabilities can be shown as fractions, decimals or percentages.

> **Q11 hint**
> Independent events could be:
> - flipping a coin and rolling a dice
> - the school bus is on time and you have forgotten your lunch
> - it is raining today and you have a guitar lesson today.

Explore

Reflect

9 Check up

Log how you did on your Student Progression Chart.

Probability experiments

1 Jason records the results of spinning this spinner.

Colour	Frequency
Red	19
Blue	23
Green	18

   a How many times did Jason spin the spinner?

   b Work out the experimental probability of the spinner landing on
      i red   **ii** blue   **iii** green.

   c Jason then spins the spinner 180 times. How many times do you expect it to land on blue?

2 Kieran records the results of flipping a coin and rolling a 4-sided dice.

		Dice result			
		1	**2**	**3**	**4**
Coin result	Heads	11	13	12	11
	Tails	14	15	13	11

   a Estimate the probability of rolling a 4 and getting tails at the same time.

   b Estimate the probability of getting a 3.

   c Do you think that the coin is fair? Explain.

3 Sonya surveys all the students in her year to find out which month their birthday is in.

	Jan–Mar	Apr–Jun	Jul–Sep	Oct–Dec	Total
Girl	13	16	18	11	58
Boy	10	21	21	10	62
Total	23	37	39	21	120

   a Estimate the probability of a randomly picked student in Sonya's year
      i being a boy with a birthday in the months April to June
      ii being a girl with a birthday in the months July to September
      iii having a birthday in the months January to March.

   b There are 715 students in the whole school. Approximately how many students are likely to have their birthday in the months October to December?

Theoretical probability

4 These dominoes are placed face down. Beatrice picks one green and one yellow domino.

   She multiplies the number of spots on the green domino by the number of spots on the yellow domino.

   a Draw a sample space diagram to show the possible outcomes.

   b What is the probability that the product will be
      i 10   **ii** 12   **iii** less than 10?

5 In a game for two players, each player takes it in turn to spin these two spinners and add the scores together.

- If the sum is odd, Player A gets a point.
- If the sum is even, Player B gets a point.

Is the game fair? Explain.

6 Sandy picks one of these dominoes and one of these playing cards. He records the value of the card and the total number of spots on the domino.

a Copy and complete the tree diagram to show the possible outcomes.

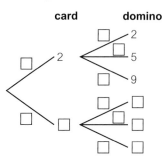

b What is the probability that the card value and number of spots are both 5?

c What is the probability that one result is 2 and the other is 5?

7 **How sure are you of your answers? Were you mostly**

☹ **Just guessing**   😐 **Feeling doubtful**   🙂 **Confident**

What next? Use your results to decide whether to strengthen or extend your learning.

Challenge

8 Draw several copies of a spinner with three equal sections and another spinner with two equal sections.

The spinners are spun together. The two scores are added. Player A wins if the total score is even. Player B wins if the total score is odd.

a Write a number in each section to make a fair game.

b Write a number in each section to make an unfair game.

c Is it possible to make a fair game (using the same rules) with these spinners?

9 Strengthen

You will:

- Strengthen your understanding with practice.

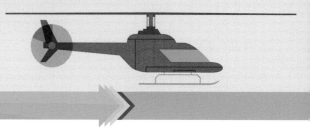

Probability experiments

1 Modelling Alex records the results of flipping a coin.

Outcome	Frequency
Heads	48
Tails	52

a How many times did he flip the coin in total?

b Copy and complete the working to find the experimental probability of heads.

$$P(\text{heads}) = \frac{\text{frequency of heads}}{\text{number of trials}} = \frac{48}{\square} = \frac{\square}{\square}$$

c Work out the experimental probability of tails.

d Alex is going to flip the coin 200 times. Using your answer to part **b**, how many times would you expect the coin to land heads?

Q1a hint

Add the number of heads and the number of tails.

2 Modelling Anna takes a counter from a bag, records the colour and replaces the counter.

Outcome	Frequency
Green	59
Yellow	19
Blue	22

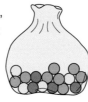

a How many trials did she do?

b Work out the experimental probability of picking

   i green   ii yellow   iii blue.

c Anna is going to do 300 trials. How many times would you expect her to pick yellow?

3 Modelling Habiba rolls a 4-sided dice 100 times and records the results in a table.

Outcome	Frequency
1	20
2	19
3	23
4	38

a Habiba is going to roll the dice 200 times. How many times would you expect the score to be

   i 1   ii 4?

b In another experiment, Habiba scores three 138 times. How many times do you think she rolled the dice?

217

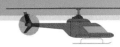

4 **Modelling** Ivan rolls a 4-sided dice and a 6-sided dice. He records whether the score showing on each dice is odd or even.

		6-sided dice		
		Odd	Even	Total
	Odd	8	11	
4-sided dice	**Even**	9	12	
	Total			

a Copy the table and work out the totals for each row and column.
b How many trials did Ivan do?
c What is the frequency of getting odd on the 4-sided dice and even on the 6-sided dice?
d Copy and complete the working to find the experimental probability of getting odd on both dice.

$$P(\text{both odd}) = \frac{\text{frequency of both odd}}{\text{number of trials}} = \frac{8}{\square}$$

e Work out the experimental probability of getting
  i even on the 4-sided dice and odd on the 6-sided dice
  ii even on the 6-sided dice
  iii both odd or both even.

5 **Modelling** These bags contain red and blue tiles numbered 1 to 3. Rajiv picks a red tile and a blue tile. He records the numbers and then replaces both tiles.

		Number on blue tile			
		1	2	3	Total
Number on red tile	**1**	5	4	3	
	2	6	5	4	
	3	3	4	2	
	Total				

12
15
9
30

a Copy and complete the two-way table. How many trials did Rajiv do?
b Work out the experimental probability of getting
  i 1 on the red tile and 3 on the blue tile
  ii 2 on the blue tile
  iii the same number on both tiles.

Theoretical probability

1 Angela spins these fair spinners.
  a Copy and complete this sample space diagram for all the possible pairs of outcomes.

Spinner 1   Spinner 2

Spinner 1		
Yellow	Y, B	
Green		
	Blue	Orange

Spinner 2

b Work out the probability of getting green on spinner 1 and orange on spinner 2.

2 These tiles are placed face down. David picks one black tile and one white tile and adds the numbers.

a Copy and complete the sample space diagram to show all the possible equally likely outcomes.

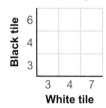

b What is the probability that the **sum** will be

i 10   **ii** 8   **iii** less than 9?

Q2 Literacy hint

The **sum** is the result of adding numbers.

3 **Reasoning** In a game, Joe and Lisa roll two dice and multiply the numbers together.
- If the product is odd, Joe scores a point.
- If the product is even, Lisa scores a point.

a Copy and complete the sample space diagram.

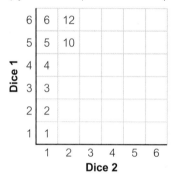

b Work out the probability that the product is

i odd   **ii** even.

c Is the game fair?

Q3c hint

For the game to be fair,
P(odd) = P(even)

4 Tony spins both of these spinners. The sample space diagram shows the possible outcomes.

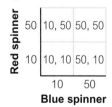

a Copy and complete the tree diagram to show the same information as the table. Put the probability of each outcome on the branches of the tree.

b Work out the probability of
i both spinners landing on 50
ii the spinners landing on different numbers.

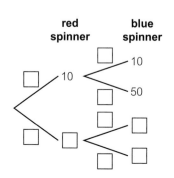

5 The tree diagram shows the probabilities of picking yellow and purple counters from a bag when the first counter is replaced before the second is picked.

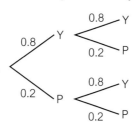

1st pick   2nd pick

a Work out probability of picking two yellows.
b Work out the probability of picking
   i purple then yellow (P, Y)
   ii yellow then purple (Y, P)
   iii yellow and purple in any order.

Q5a hint

Move your finger along the branches for yellow, then yellow.
P(Y, Y) = P(Y) × P(Y)

6 The tree diagram shows the probabilities of picking coloured counters from two bags.

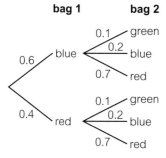

Work out the probability of picking
a red then green
b blue then red
c two colours the same.

Q6c hint

There are two possible outcomes.

Enrichment

1 **Reasoning / Modelling** Katrin has these two bags. One contains purple and yellow counters, the other contains green and white counters.

Katrin takes one counter from each bag, records the colour in this two-way table and puts the counters back.

Bag 1   Bag 2

		Bag 2	
		Green	White
Bag 1	Purple		
	Yellow		

She does this 40 times.
Copy the two-way table and write down likely frequencies for each event.
Compare your answers with a partner.

Q1 hint

How many times would you expect her to pick a purple counter?

2 **Reflect** Naringa is playing a game with a fair 6-sided dice. She needs to roll two 4s to win. She rolls one 4 and says, 'Oh, I don't think I'll be able to get a 4 on *both* dice!'
Use what you have learned in this lesson to decide if Naringa is less likely to roll a 4 on the second dice, given that she has already rolled a 4.

Reflect

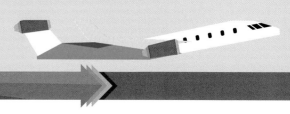

9 Extend

You will:
• Extend your understanding with problem-solving.

1 **Reasoning / Problem-solving** Three students do an experiment with a spinner coloured blue, red and green.
The table shows the results from all three experiments.

Colour	Student A	Student B	Student C
Blue	33	25	19
Red	35	46	22
Green	32	29	19

Did they all use the same spinner? Explain.

2 **Reasoning / Problem-solving** Jessica spins a fair 3-coloured spinner 90 times. Her results are shown in the table.
Sketch a possible arrangement of the colours of the spinner.

Colour	Frequency
Orange	29
Purple	31
Green	30

3 **Problem-solving** A bag contains €1 and £1 coins.
Li takes out a coin, looks at it and replaces it.
He records his results after 25, 50, 75 and 100 trials.

Number of trials	Number of €1 coins
25	13
50	21
75	33
100	45

a What is the most accurate experimental probability of picking a €1 coin?

b Li weighs the bag and works out that there are 40 coins in it.
How many are likely to be €1 coins?

4 **Problem-solving** Pip spins two spinners.
This table shows her results.

		Spinner B		
		Blue	Red	Green
Spinner A	Blue	14	16	28
	Red	4	6	12

a Work out the experimental probability of getting
  i blue with spinner A
  ii blue with spinner B
  iii green with spinner B.

b Sketch a possible arrangement of the colours for each spinner.

5 **Modelling / Problem-solving** A school recorded photocopier use over the autumn term.

	Black and white	Colour	Total
A3	981	1724	2705
A4	13776	2379	16155
Total	14757	4103	18860

   a Giving your answers to 2 decimal places, estimate the probability of the next copy being

      i black and white, A4   **ii** colour.

   The autumn term was 16 weeks. The spring term is 12 weeks.

   b The school needs to order photocopy paper for the spring term. Paper comes in packs of 500 sheets. How many packs does the school need to order of

      i A3 paper   **ii** A4 paper?

6 **Problem-solving** Katya divides two spinners into three equal parts. She writes a number on each part.
Katya spins both spinners.
She works out 'silver number – gold number'.

   a Copy and complete this sample space diagram to show all possible results, and the values of a, b, c, p and q.

   b Is each score equally likely?

Gold spinner

1		
2	4	
3	5	7

7

Silver spinner

7 **Reasoning / Problem-solving** Katya uses the same spinners as in Q6. She writes different numbers on them and works out 'silver number – gold number'.

   • The probability of getting a difference of 5 is $\frac{2}{9}$

   • The probability of getting a difference of 7 is $\frac{1}{9}$

   a Copy and complete this sample space diagram for each outcome.

   b What is the probability of getting a difference that is less than 9?

Gold spinner

4	1	2	
	3		
			8

Silver spinner

8 **Reasoning** Nala and Greg use all the diamonds from a pack of cards in a game. Ace counts as 1, Jack as 11, Queen as 12 and King as 13.

   They shuffle the cards and lay them face down. One player turns over a card.

   Nala keeps the card if the sum of the digits is 3 or less.

   Greg keeps the card if the sum of the digits is greater than 3.

   a What is the probability that

      i Nala keeps the card   **ii** Greg keeps the card?

   b Explain why the game is unfair.

   c One of 7 cards can be removed to make the game fair. List the 7 cards.

9 **Reasoning / Modelling** In a game, two players take turns to throw a piece of string onto this board.

- Player A wins if the red end lands in a blue square.
- Player B wins if the red end lands in a green square.

a What is the probability that
  i Player A wins
  ii Player B wins?

b Explain why the game is unfair.

c How many squares must change colour for the game to become fair? Should they change from green to blue or from blue to green?

d Draw a board for a fair game.

Discussion What assumptions have you made to calculate the probabilities?

10 Cassie has four red dominoes and four blue dominoes. She picks one red domino and one blue domino and records the number of spots on each. This tree diagram shows the possible outcomes and some of the probabilities.

a Copy the tree diagram, and fill in the five missing probabilities on the branches.

b What is the probability that
  i the blue domino has 2 spots
  ii the red domino has 4 spots
  iii both dominoes have 6 spots?

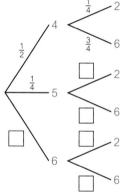

> **Q10a hint**
>
> The probabilities of all the **mutually exclusive** outcomes of an event should add to 1.

> **Q10 Literacy hint**
>
> Two events are **mutually exclusive** if they cannot happen at the same time.

11 **Problem-solving** The tree diagram shows the possible outcomes when a fair 10-sided dice, numbered from 1 to 10, is rolled three times.

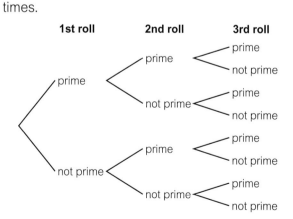

What is the probability of rolling a prime number
a every time
b in none of the rolls
c once?

> **Q11a hint**
>
> First work out the probability of rolling a prime number with a 10-sided dice once. How many numbers between 1 and 10 are prime?

12 James picks a counter from this bag, replaces it and picks another counter.

   a Draw a tree diagram to show the possible outcomes and probabilities.

   b Work out the probability of James picking

     i two green counters

     ii at least one green counter.

Q12b ii hint

One or both counters must be green.

13 John picks one playing card from each of these groups.

 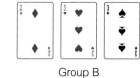

            Group A   Group B

Q13 Literacy hint

A playing card is described by giving its value and suit, such as '3 of diamonds'.

   a Draw a tree diagram showing all possible outcomes and their probabilities.

   b What is the probability that

     i both cards are 2s

     ii both cards are diamonds

     iii the cards are different numbers

     iv one card is red and the other is black?

Investigation   **Reasoning**

1 Roll two 6-sided dice and record the sum of their scores. Do this 75 times and record the results in a frequency table.

2 Draw a bar chart for the results.

3 Which is the most likely total?

4 Work out the theoretical probability of getting a total of 8.

5 Compare your experimental probability of an 8 with the theoretical probability.

6 Do you think your dice are fair? Explain.

Part 4 hint

Draw a sample space diagram for the possible outcomes.

---

14 Reflect In these extend lessons you have answered probability questions that use

  • sample space diagrams

  • two-way tables

  • tree diagrams.

Which types of question were easiest? Why?

Which types of question were hardest? Why?

Write down one probability topic you think you need more practice on.

Reflect

9 Unit test

Log how you did on your Student Progression Chart.

1 Sandra buys scratch cards. There is always a red square, a blue square and a green square, with a smiley face in one of the squares. You win a prize if the smiley face is green.

  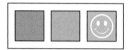

Sandra records the colour of the smiley face in this table.

a How many cards did she buy?

b Work out the experimental probability of getting a green smiley face.

c Sandra buys 20 more cards. How many more prizes is she likely to win?

Colour of square with smiley face	Frequency
Red	47
Blue	43
Green	10

 2 Sam spins this spinner 100 times.

Score	Frequency
Red	35
Blue	36
Green	29

In his next set of trials, the spinner lands on blue 72 times. How many trials do you think Sam did?

3 Bernard records the results of spinning two spinners.

		Spinner A		
		Orange	Green	Yellow
Spinner B	Green	7	12	11
	Orange	23	19	18

a Estimate the probability of getting orange with both spinners.

b Estimate the probability of getting green with spinner A.

c Do you think spinner A is divided into thirds? Explain.

4 Laila does a survey of the cars in a local car park.

	Saloon	Hatchback	Estate	Total
Petrol	5	18	15	38
Diesel	10	36	6	52
Total	15	54	21	90

a Estimate the probability of a car being

i a petrol saloon car

ii diesel

iii a saloon or hatchback.

b The car park holds 450 cars. When it is full, how many are likely to be diesel estate cars?

5 These dominoes are placed face down. Ricky picks one green and one blue domino. He subtracts the number of spots on the green domino from the number on the blue domino.

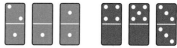

  a Draw a sample space diagram to show the possible outcomes.
  b What is the probability that the outcome will be
    i 5   **ii** 3   **iii** more than 2?

6 In a game for two players, these dominoes are placed face down. Players take turns to turn over a red domino and a blue domino.

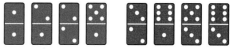

  • If the sum is 10 or less, Player A gets a point.
  • If the sum more than 10, Player B gets a point.
  Is the game fair? Explain.

7 Tom flips a coin and rolls an ordinary 6-sided dice.

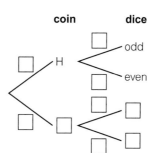

  a Copy and complete the tree diagram to show the possible outcomes.
  b What is the probability that the coin lands on heads and the dice score is even?
  c What is the probability that the dice score is odd?

8 Sally colours in thirds on these spinners, and then spins them both.

Spinner 1   Spinner 2

  a Draw a tree diagram to show the possible outcomes.
  b What is the probability that both spinners land on red?
  c What is the probability that only one spinner lands on red?

Challenge

9 A word game set has 100 letter tiles.
  42 are vowels, 56 are consonants and 2 are blanks.

1st pick

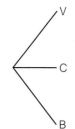

  a Amanda takes one tile, and then another from a complete set of tiles. Copy and complete the tree diagram to show all the possible outcomes. The first set of branches have been done for you.
  b Work out the probability that the tiles are the same type.
  c Work out the probability that the tiles are different types.
  d Look at your answers to parts **b** and **c**. What do you notice?
  e Amanda now takes a third tile. Work out the probability of all three tiles being the same type.

> **Q9 Strategy hint**
> Amanda doesn't put the tile back before picking the second tile. How does this affect the probabilities?

10 Reflect Look back at the questions you answered in this test.
  • Which are you most confident that you have answered correctly? What makes you feel confident?
  • Which are you least confident that you have answered correctly? What makes you least confident?
  • Discuss the question you feel least confident about with a classmate. How does discussing it make you feel?

> **Q10 hint**
> Comment on your understanding of the question and your confidence.

Reflect

10.1 Quadrilaterals

CONFIDENCE

You will learn to:
• Identify the properties of quadrilaterals.

Why learn this?
Architects and engineers use properties of quadrilaterals when designing buildings.

Fluency
What are the coordinates of these points?

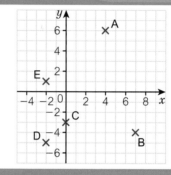

Explore
Does a quadrilateral with a right angle have to have a pair of parallel sides?

Exercise 10.1

Warm up

1 How many lines of symmetry do these shapes have?
   a square
   b rectangle
   c rhombus
   d parallelogram
   e kite
   f trapezium

Key point

The **properties** of a shape are facts about its sides, angles, diagonals and symmetry.
Here are some of the properties of some well-known quadrilaterals.

Square	• all sides are equal in length • opposite sides are parallel • all angles are 90° • diagonals bisect each other at 90°	Rectangle	• opposite sides are equal in length • opposite sides are parallel • all angles are 90° • diagonals bisect each other
Rhombus	• all sides are equal in length • opposite sides are parallel • opposite angles are equal • diagonals bisect each other at 90°	Parallelogram	• opposite sides are equal in length • opposite sides are parallel • opposite angles are equal • diagonals bisect each other
Kite	• 2 pairs of sides are equal in length • no parallel sides • 1 pair of equal angles • diagonals cross each other at 90°	Trapezium	• 1 pair of parallel sides
		Isosceles trapezium	• 2 sides are equal in length • 1 pair of parallel sides • 2 pairs of equal angles

Topic links: Coordinates, Symmetry

2 Write down which quadrilaterals
- **a** have all sides equal
- **b** have 4 right angles
- **c** have 2 pairs of equal sides
- **d** have exactly one pair of parallel sides
- **e** have bisecting diagonals
- **f** can have 4 different sized angles.

3 Draw a coordinate grid on squared paper with x and y axes from –10 to 10.
For each set of coordinates
- **a** plot the points on your coordinate grid
- **b** join A to B, B to C, C to D and D to A
- **c** name the quadrilateral.
  - **i** A(2, 4), B(–1, 4), C(–1, –1), D(2, –1)
  - **ii** A(–2, 2), B(–3, 4), C(–2, 7), D(–1, 4)
  - **iii** A(–4, –4), B(–2, 2), C(3, 2), D(1, –4)
  - **iv** A(2, 7), B(4, –3), C(–7, –3), D(–1, 7)

Investigation   **Problem-solving**

A square with sides of length 4 units has one vertex at
the point (2, 1).
1 Give the coordinates of the other three vertices.
2 How many different solutions can you find?

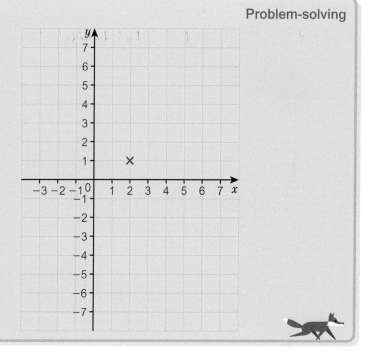

Worked example

An isosceles trapezium has vertices at coordinates (2, 3), (3, 5) and (5, 5).
What are the coordinates of the fourth vertex?

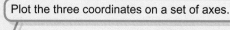
Plot the three coordinates on a set of axes.

An isosceles trapezium has one pair of parallel
sides so the fourth vertex must have y-coordinate 3.

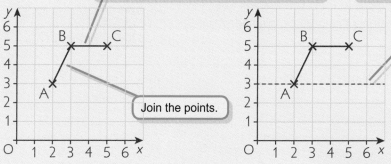

Join the points.

An isosceles trapezium also has 2 sides of equal length.

The fourth vertex must have coordinates (6, 3).

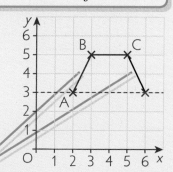

4 **Problem-solving** Find the coordinates of the fourth vertex of
   a a rectangle with vertices (4, 5), (6, 5), (6, 6)
   b a parallelogram with vertices (1, −2), (2, −6), (7, −6)
   c a square with vertices (2, 1), (2, −5), (−4, −5)

Q4 Strategy hint

Draw a coordinate grid and plot the points to help you.

5 Three vertices of a quadrilateral are plotted.

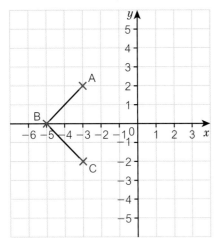

   a What is the coordinate of the missing vertex if the shape is a square?
   b Give two different possible coordinates for the missing vertex if the shape is a kite.
   Discussion Are there more than two different possible solutions to part **b**?

6 **Problem-solving** A quadrilateral contains four right angles.
   Write down all the shapes it could be.

7 **Problem-solving** A quadrilateral contains four angles measuring 120°, 60°, 90° and 90°.
   What is the name of the shape?

8 **Explore** Does a quadrilateral with a right angle have to have a pair of parallel sides?
   Is it easier to explore this question now you have completed the lesson? What further information do you need to be able to answer this?

9 **Reflect** Did you use the worked example to help you answer Q4 and 5? How did it help you to understand this type of question?

10.2 Triangles

You will learn to:
- Calculate missing angles in triangles
- Find the length of missing sides in triangles.

Why learn this?
Calculating angles helps sailors to navigate.

Fluency
Name each triangle.

  A B

  C D

Explore
How many different shapes can you make using 6 equilateral triangles?

Exercise 10.2

1 Work out the size of the angles marked with letters.

a
132° *a*

b
49° *b*

c
24° *c*

d
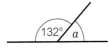
62° 35° *d*

e
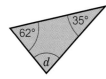
68° *e*

f
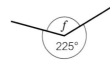
f 225°

2 Work out the size of the angles marked with letters.

a

3 cm 3 cm *p* 3 cm

b

72° *n*

c
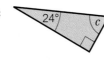
m

d
12 mm *q* 34° 8 mm 12 mm

Q2 hint
In an equilateral triangle all the angles are equal. In an isosceles triangle two of the angles are equal.

3 Write down the lengths of sides *x* and *y*.

a

60° 5 cm 60° 60° *x*

b
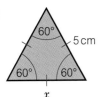 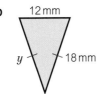
12 mm *y* 18 mm

4 Problem-solving The length of one side of an equilateral triangle is 5 cm.
What is the perimeter of the triangle?

Q4 hint
What are the lengths of the other two sides?

Worked example

Work out the size of angle a. Give reasons for your answer.

> The two small lines indicate that the sides have equal length, so the triangle is isosceles.

$b = 68°$ (The base angles of an isosceles triangle are equal)

$a = 180° - (2 \times 68°)$ (The angles in a triangle sum to 180°.)

$\quad = 180° - 136°$

$\quad = 44°$

5 **Reasoning** Work out the size of the angles marked with letters. Give reasons for your answer.

a

b
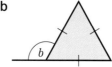

c
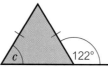

d
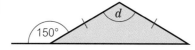

e
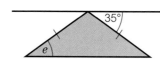

6 **Problem-solving** Work out the perimeter of this triangle.

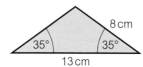

7 **Problem-solving** Work out the size of the angles marked with letters.

a
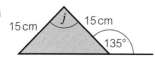

b
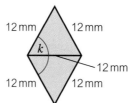

8 **Problem-solving / Reasoning** One angle of an isosceles triangle is 124°. What are the other two angles? Explain your reasoning.

9 **Problem-solving** Rusal draws this isosceles triangle.

Not drawn to scale.

a Write down a possible value of x and y.

b Write down another possible value of x and y.

Topic links: Symmetry, Properties of triangles

10 **STEM / Real** The angle between a roof beam and the
ceiling is 75°. What is the size of the angle a between
the two roof beams at the top?

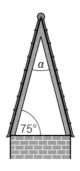

11 Work out the size of the angles marked with letters.

a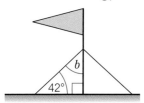

b

c

12 **Reasoning** Can an isosceles right-angled triangle contain an
angle of 35°?
Explain.

Q12 hint

Try and draw the triangle.

13 **STEM / Real** A flagpole is held up by a wire on either side.

The angle between one wire and the ground is 42°.
What is the angle, b, between the wire and the flagpole?

14 **Explore** How many different shapes can you make using 6
equilateral triangles?
Look back at the maths you have learned in this lesson.
How can you use it to answer the question?

15 **Reflect** Choose one of the problem-solving questions in this lesson.
Imagine you had to write a hint to help a classmate answer the
question. What would you write and how would it help?

Explore

Reflect

10.3 Transformations

You will learn to:
- Transform shapes on the coordinate axis
- Use combinations of transformations.

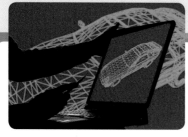

Why learn this?
Computers use transformations to move pictures around a screen.

Fluency
What angle has shape A been rotated through to give shapes B, C and D?

Explore
What transformations could take shape A to shape B?

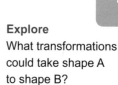

Exercise 10.3

1 Copy this diagram onto squared paper.
Reflect the arrow in
a the green line
b the blue line.

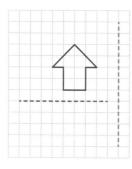

2 Copy this diagram onto squared paper.
 a Rotate the rectangle
  i 180° about the green cross
  ii 90° clockwise about the red cross
  iii 270° anticlockwise about the blue cross.
 b Translate the rectangle 3 squares right and 2 squares down.

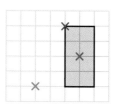

Q2a hint

Use tracing paper to help you draw the rotations.

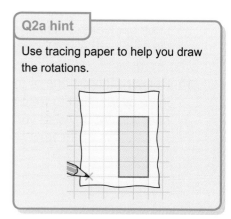

3 a Copy the shape and coordinate grid onto squared paper.
 b Plot the point (2, 1).
 c Rotate triangle A 180° about this point. Label this triangle B.
 d Plot the point (−2, 4).
 e Rotate triangle A 90° anticlockwise about this point. Label this triangle C.

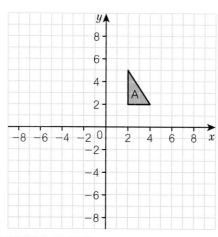

Topic links: Coordinates, Equations of graphs

4 a Copy the diagram onto squared paper.

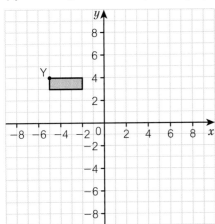

b Translate the rectangle
  i 5 right
  ii 4 down
  iii 2 left, 1 down
  iv 3 right, 8 down.
c Write down the coordinates of point y after each translation.

5 a Draw a coordinate grid with x and y axes from –10 to 10.
b Plot the point (3, 5).
c Write down the translation that would move this point to
  i (4, 5)
  ii (3, –2)
  iii (5, 7)
  iv (–4, –7).

6 a Copy the diagram.

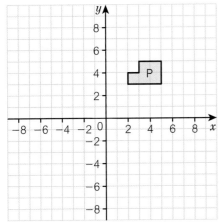

b Reflect shape P in
  i the x-axis
  ii the y-axis.
c Draw the graph of $x = -2$.
d Reflect shape P in the line $x = -2$.
e Draw the graph of $y = 3$.
f Reflect shape P in the line $y = 3$.

Q6c hint

Every point on the line $x = -2$ has an x-coordinate of –2.

Worked example

Transform this shape by translating it 5 left and 2 up followed by a reflection in the x-axis.

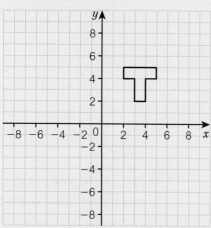

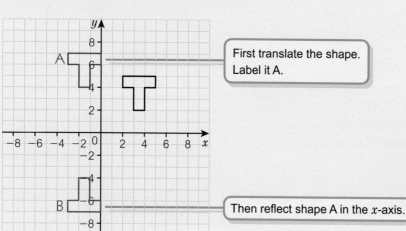

First translate the shape. Label it A.

Then reflect shape A in the x-axis.

7 Copy the diagram.
On separate copies, transform the shape using these transformations.

a Reflection in the x-axis followed by a reflection in the y-axis.

b Translation 3 left and 4 down followed by a translation 1 left and 2 down.

c 180° rotation about the point (0, 0) followed by a reflection in the y-axis.

d 90° rotation clockwise about the point (0, 0) followed by a 180° rotation about the point (0, 0).

e Reflection in the line y = 2, followed by a reflection in the x-axis.

Discussion Can you describe each of these as a single transformation?

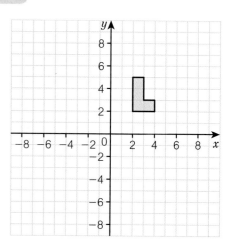

8 Explore What transformations could take shape A to shape B? Look back at the maths you have learned in this lesson. How can you use it to answer this question?

9 Reflect June says, 'You have to be good at art to enjoy lessons about transformations.' Do you agree with this statement? Explain why or why not.

ActiveLearn Pi 3, Section 10.3

10.4 Enlargement

You will learn to:
- Enlarge 2D shapes.

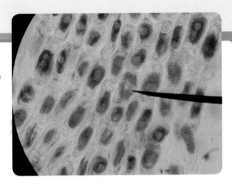

Why learn this?
Microscopes enlarge microscopic objects so scientists can study them.

Fluency
Work out
- 3 × 4
- 9 × 2
- 4 × 3
- 6 × 5

Explore
How much can you enlarge a photograph by on a computer?

Exercise 10.4

1 Copy and complete
- **a** $3 \times \square = 90$
- **b** $\square \times 2 = 7$
- **c** $9 \div \square = 1$
- **d** $20 \div \square = 4$

2 Copy these shapes onto squared paper.
Now **enlarge** each shape by
  - **i** scale factor 2
  - **ii** scale factor 4.

a **b** **c** **d**

> **Key point**
> An **enlargement** is a type of transformation. The **scale factor** tells you how much to enlarge the shape by.
> For example, to enlarge a shape by scale factor 2, multiply the lengths of each side by 2.

3 Real A photograph measuring 15 cm by 10 cm is enlarged by scale factor 3. What is the new length and width?

> **Worked example**
> Enlarge this triangle by scale factor 3 and the marked centre of enlargement.
>
>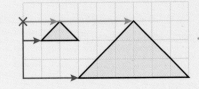
>
> Multiply all the distances from the centre by the scale factor. Count the squares from the centre of enlargement:
> - The top vertex of the triangle changes from 2 right to 6 right.
> - The bottom left vertex changes from 1 down and 1 right to 3 down and 3 right.

4 a Copy this diagram.

b Enlarge the shape by scale factor 2 with centre of enlargement (8, 7).

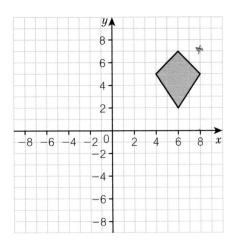

5 Copy these shapes and the centres of enlargement onto squared paper. Enlarge them by the scale factors given.

a Scale factor 2

b Scale factor 4

c Scale factor 3

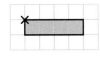

Q5c hint

When the centre of enlargement lies on the edge of the shape, the point is in the same place on the enlarged shape.

d Scale factor 2

e Scale factor 3

f Scale factor 4

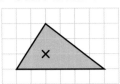

6 a Draw a coordinate axis from −10 to 10.

b Plot the points (−4, 2), (−6, 2) and (−5, 4) and join them to form a triangle.

c Enlarge the triangle by scale factor 3 about the point (−5, 4).

7 Reasoning For each shape, decide whether it is
- congruent to shape A
- **similar** to shape A
- neither of these
Explain how you know.

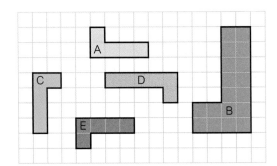

Key point

Enlargement produces **similar** shapes. The angles and proportions are the same.

8 Explore How much can you enlarge a photograph by on a computer? Is it easier to explore this question now you have completed the lesson? What further information do you need to be able to answer this?

9 Reflect Scientists and graphic designers use enlargement techniques in their work. Suggest some other careers where these skills would be useful.

Topic links: Coordinates **Subject links:** Design and technology (Q3) *Active* Learn Pi 3, Section 10.4

10.5 Congruent shapes

You will learn to:
- Solve problems using congruent shapes
- Recognise when triangles are congruent.

Why learn this?
Congruent shapes are used in wallpaper designs.

Fluency
Which shapes are congruent?

A   B   C   D

Explore
How many congruent shapes are there in the Union Jack flag?

Exercise 10.5

1 Copy this shape onto a coordinate grid.

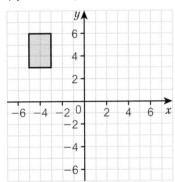

a Translate the shape 4 right, 3 down. Label the **image** A.
b Rotate the shape 180° about the origin. Label the image B.
c Reflect the shape in the y-axis. Label the image C.
d Enlarge the shape by scale factor 2 about the point (−3, 6). Label the image D.

Q1 Literacy hint
The **image** is the new shape after a transformation.

2 Work out the size of the angles marked with letters.

a

b

c

3 Which two of these triangles are **congruent**?

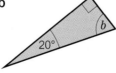

A 4 cm 3 cm 5 cm

B 8 cm 10 cm 6 cm

C 3 cm 5 cm 4 cm

Q3 Literacy hint
Congruent shapes are exactly the same.

Warm up

Stevie is constructing a triangle with three angles measuring 35°, 65° and 80°.

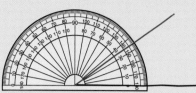 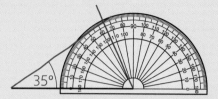

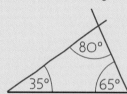

She starts by drawing a horizontal line with a ruler.

Then she uses a protractor to measure an angle of 35° at one end and draws a long line.

Finally she measures an angle of 65° at the other end and draws a long line.

The result is this triangle.

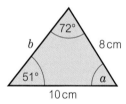

1 Draw your own triangle using Stevie's method, starting with a 10 cm line.
2 Is your triangle congruent to everyone else's in the class?
3 Is your triangle congruent to Stevie's?
4 Is your triangle similar to Stevie's?
5 Draw a right-angled isosceles triangle.
   Compare with a partner.
   Are they congruent? Are they similar? Explain.

4 These triangles are congruent. Work out the missing sides and angles.

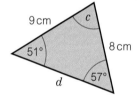

5 Copy the diagram onto squared paper.

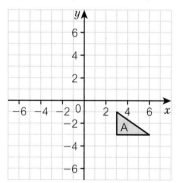

   a On separate copies carry out these transformations.
      i Translate shape A 6 left, 2 up.
      ii Rotate shape A 90° clockwise about the point (1, 2).
      iii Reflect shape A in the line $y = 2$.
      iv Enlarge shape A by scale factor 3 with centre of enlargement (6, –3).
   b Which of the four transformations result in a congruent triangle?
   Discussion Which transformation will always result in congruent shapes?

Topic links: Coordinates, Straight-line graphs, Constructing triangles, Measuring angles

6 Decide if these statements are true or false.

   a An enlargement will always result in a congruent image.

   b A reflection will always result in a congruent image.

   c Two shapes are congruent if the angles are equal.

   d Two shapes are congruent if one is a rotation of the other.

   e If you translate a shape the image is not congruent.

7 a On a coordinate grid plot the points (3, 2), (5, 2) and (4, 4) and join them to form a triangle.

   b Enlarge the triangle

      i by scale factor 2 with centre of enlargement (4, 4)

     ii by scale factor 3 with centre of enlargement (4, 4).

   Discussion What scale factor would result in a congruent image?

8 Decide which of these transformations will result in a congruent image.

   a A 180° rotation followed by reflection in the x-axis.

   b A translation 3 right, 4 down, followed by an enlargement by scale factor 2.

   c An enlargement by scale factor 1, centre of enlargement (3, −2), followed by a reflection in the y-axis.

9 Explore How many congruent shapes are there in the Union Jack flag?

   Is it easier to explore this question now you have completed the lesson? What further information do you need to be able to answer this?

10 Reflect In your own words, explain the difference between congruent and similar shapes.

10 Check up

Properties of shapes

1 Work out the length of the missing sides and angles in these triangles.

a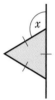

b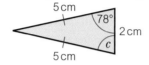

2 Work out the size of angles x and y. Give reasons for your answers.

a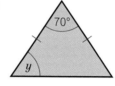

b

3 a Plot the points (1, 1), (5, 1), (2, 2), (6, 2) on a copy of this coordinate grid.
What is the name of this shape?

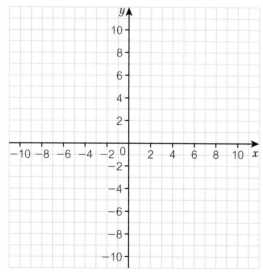

b Three vertices of a rectangle have coordinates (0, 5), (0, −1) and (−3, 5). What are the coordinates of the fourth vertex?

4 Niamh draws a diagonal line through the middle of this square.
Work out the size of angle a.
Show each step of your working.

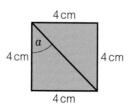

5 A quadrilateral has two sides of equal length, one pair of parallel sides and two pairs of equal angles. Name the quadrilateral.

Transformations and congruence

6 Copy this diagram onto squared paper.

   a Translate triangle X 3 right and
6 down. Label the new triangle A.

   b Reflect triangle X in the *x*-axis.
Label the triangle B.

   c Rotate triangle X 90° clockwise
about the point (1, 1).
Label the triangle C.

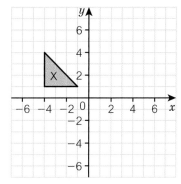

7 These triangles are congruent. Work out the sides and angles marked with letters.

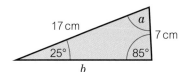 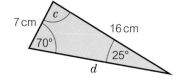

8 a Draw a coordinate grid with *x*- and *y*-axes from −10 to 10.

   b Plot the points (2, 1), (5, 1), (2, 3) and (5, 3). Join them to form a rectangle.

   c Rotate the rectangle 90° clockwise about the origin and then reflect it in the *y*-axis.

9 Mia reflects a hexagon in a mirror line. Is the image congruent?

10 Copy this diagram onto squared paper.

   a Plot the point (−4, 4).

   b Use this point as the centre of
enlargement and enlarge the shape
by scale factor 3.

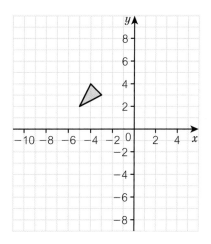

11 How sure are you of your answers? Were you mostly

   😣 **Just guessing**   😐 **Feeling doubtful**   🙂 **Confident**

   **What next? Use your results to decide whether to strengthen or extend
your learning.**

Challenge

12 a Draw a rectangle on squared paper and enlarge it by scale factor 2.

   b How many of the smaller rectangles can you fit into the larger rectangle?

   c Repeat for other rectangles and right-angled triangles. What happens?

   d Choose some other polygons to explore this further.

Master
P227

Check
P241

STRENGTHEN

Extend
P247

Test
P251

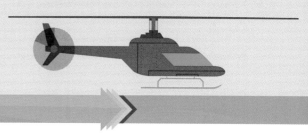

10 Strengthen

You will:
* Strengthen your understanding with practice.

Properties of shapes

1 a Which of these triangles are
  i equilateral   **ii** isosceles   **iii** right angled?

 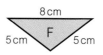

  b Work out the missing angles in triangles A and C.

2 The diagram shows a triangle.
  a What do the two small lines mean?
  b What does this tell you about the angles?
  c What type of triangle is this?
  d Work out the length of side m.
  e Work out the size of angle x.

> **Q2e hint**
>
> $180 - \square = \square$
> $\square \div 2 = \square°$

3 a Work out the size of angle x.
  b Copy and complete the calculation
     to work out the size of angle y.
     $y = 90° - \square = \square°$

> **Q3a Strategy hint**
>
> Use your knowledge of equilateral triangles.

4 Reasoning Choose words and angles
  from the cloud to complete the
  calculations and explanation
  for each triangle.

  a

Cloud: 180° 120° 35° isosceles equal equilateral 145° 60° right angle

> **Q4 hint**
>
> You may use the words and values more than once.

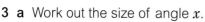

The angles in the triangle are all _____ because it is an
_____ triangle.

$f = \square° - \square° = \square°$ because angles on a straight line sum to ____°

  b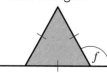

$g = \square°$ because the triangle is _____ and the two angles in
an _____ triangle are equal.

$h = \square° - \square° = \square°$ because angles on a straight line sum to ____°

5 Work out the size of
  a angle a
  b angle b
  c angle c.

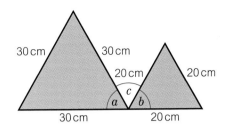

30 cm   30 cm
20 cm   20 cm
c
a b
30 cm   20 cm

Q5a, b hint

What type of triangle are these?

6 **Problem-solving** Three vertices of a kite are plotted.
  a Copy the diagram onto squared paper and mark on the position of the fourth vertex.
  b What is the coordinate of the fourth vertex?

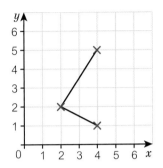

Q6b hint

Plot the point and check your answer by joining it to form a kite.

7 On each diagram three vertices of a quadrilateral are drawn.
  Write down the coordinates of the fourth vertex for each shape.

a

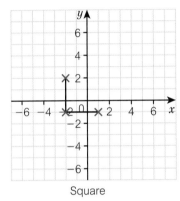

Square

b

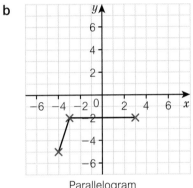

Parallelogram

8 Copy the table below and match the properties to the shapes.
  Some have been done for you.

  A   All sides are equal
  B   Opposite sides are equal
  C   Two pairs of sides are equal
  D   Two sides are equal
  E   Opposite sides are parallel
  F   One pair of parallel sides
  G   No parallel sides
  H   All angles are 90°
  I   Opposite angles are equal
  J   One pair of equal angles
  K   2 pairs of equal angles
  L   Diagonals bisect each other at 90°
  M   Diagonals bisect each other

Quadrilateral	Properties
Square	
Rhombus	A, E, I, L
Kite	
Rectangle	B
Parallelogram	
Trapezium	
Isosceles trapezium	D

Q8 hint

Draw each of the shapes.

Transformations and congruence

1 Reasoning Which shows a correct reflection of rectangle A in the y-axis?

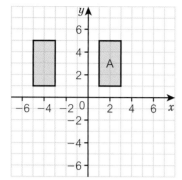

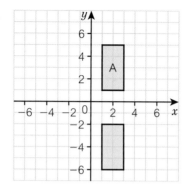

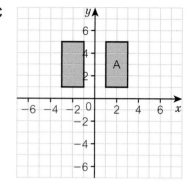

2 Copy the diagram onto squared paper.

  a Translate triangle A 3 left and 2 down. Label the image B.

  b Translate triangle A 1 right and 5 down. Label the image C.

  c Translate triangle A 8 left and 10 down. Label the image D.

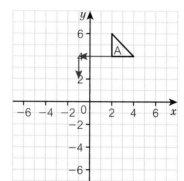

> **Q2 Literacy hint**
>
> The image is the new shape after a transformation.

3 Copy this diagram.

  a Rotate square S 90° clockwise about the origin.

  b Reflect square S in the y-axis then rotate 90° clockwise about the origin.

  c Reflect square S in the y-axis then translate 4 right and 6 down.

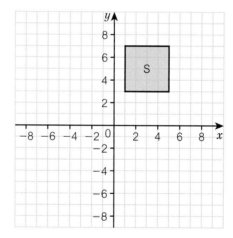

4 Copy and complete the enlargements.

a

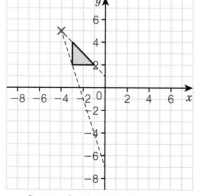

Centre of enlargement (1, 2)
Scale factor 2

b

Centre of enlargement (−4, 5)
Scale factor 4

5 Using the diagrams below, decide which of the four transformations result in congruent images.

A Reflection

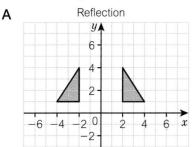

B Rotation

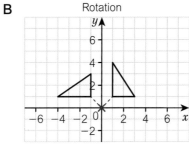

C Translation

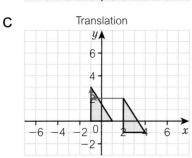

D Enlargement

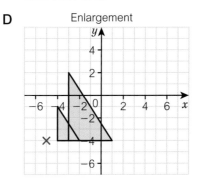

Q5 hint

Congruent shapes have the same angles and lengths.

Enrichment

1 In a video game, the aim is to build a wall using different shaped pieces without leaving any gaps.

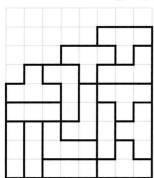

   a Copy the diagram onto squared paper and shade all congruent shapes using the same colour.

   b Which transformations have been used in this game?

   c Can you fill an 8 × 20 rectangle with these pieces?

2 Reflect Explain how you checked your answers in this lesson. Did the checks help you spot any mistakes or did they confirm your answers were correct?

Reflect

Master
P227

Check
P241

Strengthen
P243

EXTEND

Test
P251

10 Extend

You will:

• Extend your understanding with problem-solving.

1 a Copy the diagram onto squared paper.
  i Rotate shape A 90° clockwise about the point (0, 5). Label the image B.
  ii Reflect B in the line $y = 5$. Label the image C.
  iii Translate A through 10 units left.
  b Muriel uses the steps above to create a logo. How many lines of symmetry does the logo have?

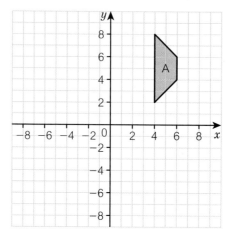

2 Work out the size of the angles marked with letters.

a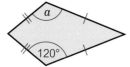

b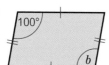

c

d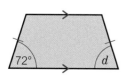

3 Work out the perimeter of each quadrilateral.

a
5 cm / 2 cm

b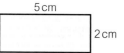
2.6 cm

c
5.8 cm

d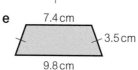
9.1 cm / 3.6 cm

e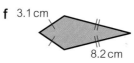
7.4 cm / 3.5 cm / 9.8 cm

f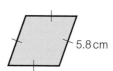
3.1 cm / 8.2 cm

4 This triangle is enlarged by scale factor 3.
  a Work out the
    i perimeter of the enlarged triangle
    ii area of the enlarged triangle.
  b Convert the area of the enlarged triangle into cm^2.

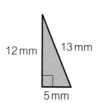
12 mm / 13 mm / 5 mm

Topic links: Properties of angles, Algebraic equations, Symmetry, Area and perimeter, Exterior angles

5 a Work out the area of this parallelogram.

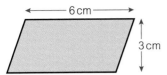

b Work out the area of the image when the shape is enlarged by
  i scale factor 2
  ii scale factor 3
  iii scale factor 5.

Q5b hint

Work out the length and height of the enlarged parallelogram.

6 Real This is a scale diagram of the cross-section of a barn. It is one ninth of the actual size.
  a Work out the height of the wall in real life.
  b Work out the angle between the two roof beams.

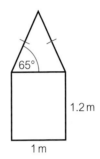

7 Work out the size of angle *a*. Give reasons for your answer.

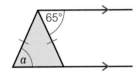

Q7 hint

Look for alternate angles.

8 Work out the size of angles *j*, *k* and *m*.
Give reasons for your answers.

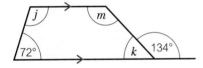

9 a Draw a coordinate grid with *x* and *y* axes from −10 to 10.
  b Plot the graph of $y = x$.
  c Plot the points (4, 2), (6, 2) and (6, 4) and join them to form a triangle.
  d Reflect the triangle in the line $y = x$.

Q9b hint

The *x*- and *y*-coordinates are equal on the line $y = x$.

10 On a copy of this diagram, transform shape A using these transformations.
  a Reflection in the line $x = 2$ followed by a translation 3 left and 1 down
  b 180° rotation about the point (1, 1) followed by a reflection in the line $y = 1$
  c Translation 4 down followed by 90° rotation clockwise about the point (2, −2)

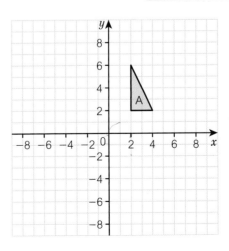

11 a Draw a coordinate grid with x- and y-axes from −10 to 10.

b Plot the points (3, 2), (5, 2), (3, 5) and (5, 5) and join them to form a rectangle. Label it A.

c Translate rectangle A 3 right and 1 up, then reflect it in the y-axis. Label the image B.

d What single translation maps shape A to shape B?

Discussion Does this work with any shape?

Investigation   Reasoning

Copy the diagram onto squared paper.

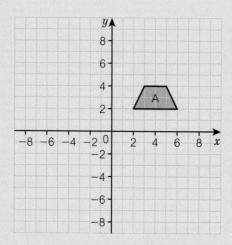

1 Transform shape A by
  a a 180° rotation about the point (0, 0) followed by a reflection in the x-axis. Label the image B.
  b a reflection in the x-axis followed by a 180° rotation about the point (0, 0). Label the image C.
2 Does the order in which you carry out two transformations matter?
  Check your answer by trying other combinations of transformations.

---

12 Mariana transforms this shape in four different ways.
What is the area of the image in each case?

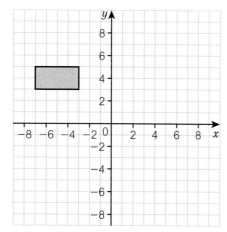

> **Q12 hint**
>
> Since no units of length are given the perimeter will be measured in 'units' and the area square units.

a Reflection in the line $x = 2$
b Translation 4 units left and 5 units down
c 90° clockwise rotation about the point (−1, 1)
d Enlargement by scale factor 2 with centre of enlargement (−7, 5)

13 Problem-solving A 4 cm by 5 cm rectangle is enlarged by scale factor 4.
Work out the area of the enlarged shape
  a in cm² 　　　　　　　　　　　**b** in mm².

14 Problem-solving Work out the size of the angles marked with letters.

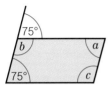

15 Problem-solving The angles in a kite are given in terms of x.

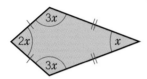

a Write down and simplify an algebraic expression for the sum of the angles in the kite.

b Form an equation and solve it to find the value of x.

c Work out the size of each angle.

Q15b hint

The angles in a quadrilateral sum to ☐°.

16 A hexagon is made using six equilateral triangles.

a What is the size of angle a?

b What is the sum of the exterior angles of the hexagon?

17 Reflect Make a list of five things that you know how to do now that you didn't know before you started this topic.

Your list might begin, 'I know how to recognise congruent shapes'.

10 Unit test

Log how you did on your Student Progression Chart.

1 Work out the value of a and b. a

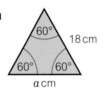

b

2 Copy the diagram.
Carry out these transformations on shape T.
  a Translate 3 right and 7 down.
    Label the image U.
  b Rotate 90° clockwise about the origin.
    Label the image V.
  c Reflect in the line $y = -2$.
    Label the image W.

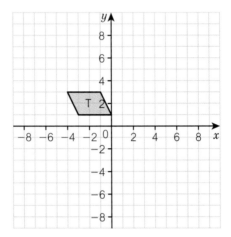

3 What is the length of BD?
  Explain your answer.

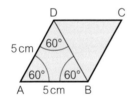

4 These triangles are congruent. Work out the missing sides and angles.

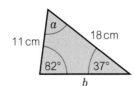 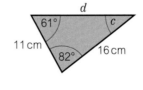

5 The diagram shows three vertices of a quadrilateral.
  a What are the coordinates of the fourth vertex that will create a parallelogram?
  b What is the name of the quadrilateral formed if the fourth vertex is at (0, 1)?

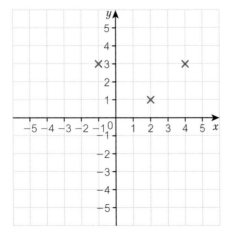

6 An isosceles triangle contains an angle of 126°.
  What are the sizes of the other two angles?

7 Work out the size of angle a.

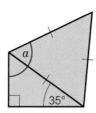

8 A quadrilateral has two pairs of sides of equal length. The diagonals are perpendicular bisectors. There are no right angles in the shape. What is the name of the shape?

9 The triangle shown is rotated 90° clockwise about the point (0, 0).
On the image what is
a the size of angle CAB
b the length of line AB?

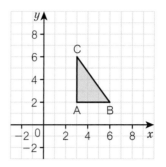

10 Copy the diagram.
Enlarge the triangle by scale factor 3 with centre of enlargement (4, 4).

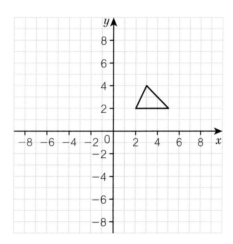

Challenge

11 Shape B is the image of shape A after a transformation.
List as many transformations as you can that could have been used. You may use more than one transformation at a time.

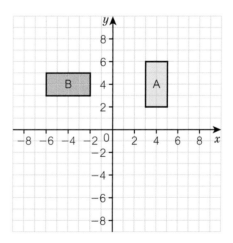

12 **Reflect** In this unit you have studied triangles, quadrilaterals, transformations and congruency. Which topic did you find easiest and which hardest? For the one you found hardest, make up some hints or practice questions to help you.